Introduction to the World's Major Religions

BUDDHISM

Volume 3

John M. Thompson

Lee W. Bailey, General Editor

GREENWOOD PRESS
Westport, Connecticut • London

Library of Congress Cataloging-in-Publication Data
available on request from the Library of Congress.

British Library Cataloguing in Publication Data is available.

ISBN 0–313–33634–2 (set)
  0–313–33327–0 (vol. 1)
  0–313–32724–6 (vol. 2)
  0–313–33251–7 (vol. 3)
  0–313–32683–5 (vol. 4)
  0–313–32846–3 (vol. 5)
  0–313–33590–7 (vol. 6)

First published in 2006

Greenwood Press, 88 Post Road West, Westport, CT 06881
An imprint of Greenwood Publishing Group, Inc.
www.greenwood.com

Printed in the United States of America

∞™

The paper used in this book complies with the
Permanent Paper Standard issued by the National
Information Standards Organization (Z39.48–1984).

10 9 8 7 6 5 4 3 2 1

INTRODUCTION TO THE WORLD'S MAJOR RELIGIONS

Introduction to the World's Major Religions
Lee W. Bailey, General Editor

Judaism, Volume 1
Emily Taitz

Confucianism and Taoism, Volume 2
Randall L. Nadeau

Buddhism, Volume 3
John M. Thompson

Christianity, Volume 4
Lee W. Bailey

Islam, Volume 5
Zayn R. Kassam

Hinduism, Volume 6
Steven J. Rosen

CONTENTS

SET FOREWORD

This set, *Introduction to the World's Major Religions,* was developed to fill a niche between sophisticated texts for adults and the less in-depth references for middle schoolers. It includes six volumes on religions from both Eastern and Western traditions: Judaism, Christianity, Islam, Hinduism, Confucianism and Taoism, and Buddhism. Each volume gives a balanced, accessible introduction to the religion.

Each volume follows a set format so readers can easily find parallel information in each religion. After a Timeline and Introduction, narrative chapters are as follows: the "History of Foundation" chapter describes the founding people, the major events, and the most important decisions made in the faith's early history. The "Texts and Major Tenets" chapter explains the central canon, or sacred texts, and the core beliefs, doctrines, or tenets, such as the nature of deities, the meaning of life, and the theories of the afterlife. The chapter on "Branches" outlines the major divisions of the religion, their reasons for being, their distinctive doctrines, their historical background, and structures today. The chapter on "Practice Worldwide" describes the weekly worship practices, the demographic statistics indicating the sizes of various branches of religions, the global locations, and historical turning points. The chapter on "Rituals and Holidays" describes the ritual practices of the religions in all their varieties and the holidays worldwide, such as the Birth of the Buddha, as they have developed historically. The chapter on "Major Figures" covers selected notable people in the history of each religion and their important influence. A glossary provides definitions for major special terms, and the index gives an alphabetic locator for major themes. A set index is included in volume 6 (to facilitate comparison).

In a world of about 6 billion people, today the religion with the greatest number of adherents is Christianity, with about 2 billion members, comprising 33 percent of the globe's population. Next largest is Islam, with about 1.3 billion members, (about 22 percent). Hindus number about 900 million (about 15 percent). Those who follow traditional Chinese religions number about 225 million (4 percent). Although China has the world's largest population, it is officially Communist, and Buddhism has been blended with traditional Confucianism and Taoism, so numbers in China are difficult to verify. Buddhism claims about 360 million members (about 6 percent of the world's population). Judaism, although historically influential, has a small number of adherents—about 14 million (0.2 percent of the world's population). These numbers are constantly shifting, because religions are always changing and various surveys define groups differently.[1]

Religions are important elements of the worldview of a culture. They express, for example, the cultural beliefs about cosmology, or picture of the universe (e.g., created by God or spontaneous), and the origin of humanity (e.g., purposeful or random), its social norms (e.g., monogamy or polygamy), its ways of relating to ultimate reality (e.g., sacrifice or obedience to law), the historical destiny (e.g., linear or cyclical), life after death (e.g., none or judgment), and ethics (e.g., tribal or universal).

As the world gets smaller with modern communications and global travel, people come in contact with those of other religions far more frequently than in the past. This can cause conflicts or lead to cooperation, but the potential for hostile misunderstanding is so great that it is important to foster knowledge and understanding. Noting parallels in world religions can help readers understand each religion better. Religions can provide ethical guidance that can help solve serious cultural problems. During war the political question "why do they hate us?" may have serious religious aspects in the answer. New answers to the question of how science and religion in one culture can be reconciled may come from another religion's approach. Scientists are increasingly analyzing the ecological crisis, but the solutions will require more than new technologies. They will also require ethical restraint, the motivation to change the destructive ecological habits of industrial societies, and some radical revisioning of worldviews. Other contemporary issues, such as women's rights, will also require patriarchal religions to undertake self-examination. Personal faith is regularly called into consideration with daily news of human destructiveness or in times of crisis, when the very meaning of life comes into question. Is life basically good? Will goodness in the big picture overcome immediate evil? Should horrendous behavior be forgiven? Are people alone in a huge, indifferent universe, or is the ultimate reality a caring, just power behind the scenes of human and cosmic history? Religions offer various approaches, ethics, and motivations to deal with such issues. Readers can use the books in this set to rethink their own beliefs and practices.

NOTE

1. United Nations, "Worldwide Adherents of All Religions by Six Continental Areas, Mid-2002," *World Population Prospects: The 1998 Revision* (New York: United Nations, 1999).

ACKNOWLEDGMENTS

There are a number of people I need to thank for helping me complete this book. First, let me thank Lee Bailey, the series editor, for approaching me to do the project in the first place. It has proven to be a valuable learning experience and I am grateful for being granted the opportunity. Second, I need to thank Wendi Schnaufer, my primary editor at Greenwood Press, for her help and patience through what has proven to be a far more involved and time-consuming task than I think any of us anticipated. I would also like to thank the staff at Apex Publishing for their hard work in the often thankless task of copyediting. Of course I must also thank my own teachers who introduced me to the teachings of Buddhism. I begin with William Cobb, my undergraduate philosophy mentor at William and Mary, who first alerted me to the fact that Buddhism warranted serious philosophical investigation from even the most hard-headed rationalist. I would add John Berthrong of Boston University, who really encouraged me to go on to doctoral study in Asian and Buddhist traditions. However, I would especially like to thank Rev. Ron Y. Nakasone, my dissertation advisor and himself a priest of True Pure Land (Jodoshin shu) Buddhism, whose guidance continues to play an important role in my professional life. I owe thanks as well to my many students at Hood College and Christopher Newport University for sitting through the lectures from which much of the material in this book derives. May the Buddhas of all the worlds shower you with merit! Most of all I wish to thank my wife Cathy and my two daughters, Julia and Sophia, without whose constant support and encouragement (and occasional prodding) I never would have finished the book. You girls are the best.

INTRODUCTION

Buddhism has exerted a powerful influence on world civilization. Like Christianity and Islam, it can be found on every continent and remains one of the great world religions.[1] Moreover, few religious traditions enjoy the popular cachet that Buddhism currently has in the West, particularly the United States. In large part this popularity is due to the influence of "celebrity Buddhists" such as Richard Gere or international figures such as the Dalai Lama, but such notable adherents aside, Buddhism is making great inroads into Western culture. In fact, although the number of its adherents is relatively small when compared with those of Christianity, Buddhism is one of the fastest-growing religions in North America.[2] Although the reasons for such demographic growth are varied, the very fact that such a distinctly non-Western religion is gaining followers in the heart of the West calls for serious attention.

In recent decades there has been a veritable explosion of books on Buddhism, both popular and academic, and many of these are excellent sources for anyone interested in exploring such a vital tradition. However, as the field of Buddhist studies continues to grow, standard textbooks have become ever more complicated, proving too challenging for all but the most disciplined university student. There is thus an increasing need for works aimed at secondary, community college, and undergraduate levels and the general public, such as this one. This book is meant to be a factual overview of Buddhist tradition, broad yet not so detailed that it will overwhelm the beginner. Moreover, I have endeavored to draw parallels between Buddhism and other religions (notably Christianity) on the understanding that analogies to more familiar subjects will help readers better understand what can often seem an entirely alien tradition.

This book follows the format of other books in the Greenwood set, Introduction to the World's Major Religions. Chapter 1 relates the basic history of Buddhism, including its founding and initial spread throughout India and beyond. Chapter 2 focuses on Buddhism's sacred texts and provides a basic explanation of core Buddhist teachings. Chapter 3 describes the major branches of Buddhism, outlining their distinctive features and the manner in which some of these differences have evolved over time. Chapters 4 and 5 present an overview of common Buddhist practices (along with basic demographic information) and detail some of the more popular Buddhist festivals and rituals. Chapter 6 comprises short biographies of important Buddhist figures throughout history.

In addition to the basic text, I have also included in the front matter a chronology of important events in Buddhist history. The book concludes with an annotated bibliography of sources (including electronic and Internet resources) as well as a set index. It is hoped that such reference material will be of special use to students and those wishing to explore in greater depth many of the subjects touched on here.

NOTES

1. The expression *world religion* is used here to refer to a religious tradition that has spread beyond its original place of origin to other regions and cultures versus those traditions that remain confined to a specific geographical area. World religions include Christianity, Judaism, Islam, Hinduism, Buddhism, Bahai, and the Chinese traditions of Confucianism and Daoism.

2. See http://www.adherents.com and John H. Berthrong, *The Divine Deli: Religious Identity in the North American Cultural Mosaic* (Maryknoll, NY: Orbis Books, 1999), 8–9.

NOTE ON LANGUAGE

Unlike other religious traditions, Buddhism does not have a specific sacred language like Hebrew (regarded as sacred in Judaism) or Arabic (held to be the sacred language by Muslims). According to traditional accounts, the Buddha (563–483 B.C.E.) himself enjoined his followers to preach Buddhist teaching or doctrine (the *Dharma*) in the language of whatever country they entered. This fact greatly facilitated the spread of Buddhism into various societies around the world, but it poses certain challenges for scholars. Among other things it means that in giving an overview of Buddhist tradition as a whole, one must make use of a bewildering array of technical terms from a number of different languages: Sanskrit, Pali, Chinese, Japanese, Tibetan, and so forth.

Rendering Buddhist terms into English entails two distinct but interrelated processes: *transliteration* (rendering terms from one language into another, usually so as to approximate the sound of the original terms) and *translation* (finding more or less equivalent terms in one language for terms in another, generally as a way to convey the original terms' meanings). In Buddhist parlance, we can view both transliteration and translation as "skillful means," expedient devices for helping convey the Dharma to those who wish to understand. The Buddha and his followers used "skillful means" to pitch their message(s) to their audience, putting basic teachings in terms that could be readily understood. Naturally, there were differences in the audience in terms of their ability to grasp the Dharma, but the overriding concern was to make it accessible to the widest possible audience.

Throughout this book I use a number of such "skillful means" (although I would never claim to be a "wisdom being," or *bodhisattva,* an advanced follower of Buddhism dedicated to the welfare of sentient beings). I make a point of italicizing all technical Buddhist terms, even many such as *nirvana* that have been accepted into English and appear in standard dictionaries, because such terms often have a special sense in Buddhism and are prone to being misunderstood. In addition, I define all such terms repeatedly in each chapter in which they appear as well as in the glossary. My repeated definitions are not always identical, but the subtle differences between them will help convey some of the nuances of meaning.

Transliteration is a way of transcribing into English terms from languages that do not use the Latin alphabet. There are various officially recognized systems of transliteration, depending on the original language. My selection has been guided by a sense of what is phonetically "most sensible" for an English speaker, but this is by no means always apparent. Indeed, major difficulties arise here when it comes to Sanskrit, Pali, and Tibetan. I have, for instance, omitted the diacritical marks that are commonly used by specialists in transliterating Sanskrit, Pali, and Tibetan terms for an academic audience. Instead, I opt for phonetic transcription, which in many cases is a practical (if not theoretical) impossibility. Much of the time this comes down to including an h after an s in certain words or names (e.g., Ashoka) to mimic the Sanskrit or Pali pronunciation.

Chinese and Japanese are a different matter. There have been various officially recognized systems of transliterating these languages, particularly the former. I have opted to use Pinyin for Chinese, as it is used in widely read newspapers such as the *New York Times* and has become the standard in scholarly circles over the past decade or so. For Japanese terms I use Hepburn, which is intentionally phonetic, commonly used by scholars, and generally is easy for Westerners to pronounce.

Despite such precautions, the plethora of foreign terms in Buddhism can be daunting for those new to the subject. Buddha always maintained that life was suffering, and that suffering could not be avoided but could be overcome. I ask, then, that my readers learn to develop both acceptance and understanding—two virtues that will serve them well no matter where their studies take them.

TIMELINE

Dates for ancient events and persons are approximate.

563–483 B.C.E.   Commonly accepted dates of Siddhartha Gautama, aka Shakyamuni Buddha, the historical founder of Buddhism.

483   Passing of Shakyamuni Buddha and First Great Council, at which time major portions of the canon were recited.

395   Great Council of Vaishali and beginning of first major schisms.

300   Beginning of composition of Abhidharma (Further Teachings) texts.

274   King Ashoka ascends the throne of the Mauryan Empire and eventually converts to Buddhism. Under his patronage, Buddhism spreads throughout most of India and into areas of Central and Western Asia.

250   Third Council at Pataliputra under Ashoka.

225   Mahinda, son of Ashoka, takes Theravada Buddhism to Sri Lanka.

200   Beginning of memorial mound *(stupa)* cults in which laity take increasingly large roles.

150   Buddhist canon written down.

100	Various branches of "scholastic" Buddhism firmly established.
50	Earliest Perfection of Wisdom texts *(sutras)* composed; beginnings of Mahayana Buddhism.
25	Introduction of Buddhism to China.
100 C.E.	Emergence of Mahayana as a recognizable movement in India, including Pure Land forms. Continued composition of early Mahayana texts.
150–250	Life of Nagarjuna, "founder" of Madhyamika (Middle Way) school of philosophy, often regarded as the most original thinker in Buddhism after the historical Buddha.
200	Great monastic university of Nalanda founded. It becomes a flourishing center of Buddhist study for 1,000 years.
220	Collapse of Han dynasty in China and beginning of the "period of disunity." Confucianism falls into disrepute, thus opening the way for Buddhism to take hold of the Chinese populace.
344–414	Life of Kumarajiva, Central Asian translator of Buddhist texts into Chinese.
350	Beginning of Yogachara (Practice of Yoga) as a distinct school of philosophy in India.
372	Introduction of Buddhism into Korea from China.
399	Faxian, a Chinese monk, becomes the first Chinese pilgrim to journey to India.
500	Emergence of Tantra (a pan-Indian esoteric movement focusing on ritual and occult powers) in India.
526	Legendary Bodhidharma, legendary "First Patriarch," brings Chan/Zen teachings to southern China.
538–597	Life of Zhiyi, founder of Tiantai (Heavenly Terrace) school.
550	Early development of Pure Land and Chan schools in China.
574–622	Life of Prince Shotoku, "founder" of Japanese Buddhism and author of Japan's first "constitution." A concerted ef-

	fort is made to import Buddhism to Japan from Korea as part of Chinese culture.
589	China reunited under Sui and Tang dynasties. Beginning of Buddhism's "golden age."
596–664	Life of Xuanzang, Chinese Buddhist pilgrim who travels throughout Asia to India in search of the original scriptures. He brings back thousands of texts to be translated and becomes one of the great heroes in Chinese culture. His travels are later immortalized in the famous novel *Journey to the West* (1592).
641–650	Construction of first Buddhist temples in Tibet to house images of Buddha.
700–800	Nyingma school, oldest order of Tibetan Buddhism, established.
710–794	Nara period. Buddhism becomes established as Japan's official religion, although it remains mainly confined to the nobility. The Great Eastern Temple, the largest wooden structure in the world, is built as a symbol of Japanese unity under Buddhism. It houses the *Great Buddha*, the world's largest bronze statue.
749	Sam-ye monastery founded in Tibet.
750	Spread of Buddhism to Indonesia and Java; construction of Borobudur, monumental pyramid temple outside of present-day Jakarta.
775	Padmasambhava, Tantric (esoteric and magical) adept, transmits Vajrayana Buddhism to Tibet. This event is sometimes known as the "First Propagation of Buddhism."
766–822	Life of Saicho, founder of Tendai (Japanese Tiantai), who establishes Buddhist center on Mount Hiei.
774–835	Life of Kukai, founder of Shingon (Japanese Tantra).
800–900	Biography of the Buddha translated into Greek in Christian guise as the tale of Balaam and Josaphat by John of Damascus.
845	Great suppression of Buddhism in China during latter Tang dynasty.

868	Oldest existing printed book in the world, a Chinese translation of the Diamond Sutra.
983	First complete printing of the Chinese Buddhist canon.
1000	Spread of Theravada Buddhism throughout Southeast Asia, "Second Propagation of Buddhism" in Tibet under the scholar-monk Atisha.
1100	Construction of Angkor Wat, a major temple complex, in Cambodia.
1173–1263	Life of Shinran, disciple of Pure Land priest Honen (1133–1212) and founder of True Pure Land school.
1200	Decline of Buddhism in India as a result of the growth of popular Hinduism and Muslim invasions; introduction of Chan/Zen to Japan.
1222–82	Life of Nichiren, founder of the Lotus sect and major force for Buddhism as a part of Japanese nationalism.
1279	Last evidence of Theravada nunnery in Burma.
1357–1419	Life of Tsongkhapa, Tibetan monk who systematized Buddhist teachings and founded the Gelugpa school, Tibet's dominant monastic order.
1360	Buddhism becomes state religion of Thailand.
1600–1867	Tokugawa era. Japanese government exercises increasing control over Buddhism and begins promoting Shinto as the "true religion" of Japan.
1617	Dalai Lamas become rulers of Tibet.
1800	European intellectuals "discover" Buddhism and begin to appropriate Buddhist ideas.
1852	First Western translation (German) of the Lotus Sutra, the most popular Buddhist scripture in East Asia.
1853	First Chinese temple founded in the United States (San Francisco).
1862	First Western translation (German) of the Dhammapada, a well-known collection of Buddhist teaching.
1868	Fifth Council, held in Burma. Pali canon (the collection of texts held as sacred by Buddhists of Southeast Asia) inscribed on 729 marble steles (memorial plaques).

1893	World's Parliament of Religions held in Chicago. Buddhism (in the form of Theravada and Rinzai Zen) is introduced to a large American audience.
1900	Beginning of Buddhist missionary activity in the West.
1916	Founding of Won, a major form of contemporary Korean Buddhism.
1932	Buddhadasa, prominent Thai monk, founds a private forest retreat that eventually grows to be his base of operations.
1940	Five-year-old Tenzin Gyatso is enthroned as 14th Dalai Lama in Lhasa, Tibet.
1945–50	European colonies in Asia (India, Sri Lanka, Burma, Vietnam, etc.) officially become independent nations.
1949	Mao Dzedong leads Communist Party takeover of China. Aspects of traditional Chinese culture (including Buddhism) are systematically destroyed.
1956	B. R. Ambedkar, Indian prime minister, converts to Buddhism along with some 500,000 other "untouchables" (lowest caste).
1959	Chinese takeover of Tibet and beginning of systematic suppression of Tibetan Buddhism. Fourteenth Dalai Lama flees to India.
1960	Buddhist centers begin to be established in the West.
1966	Founding of Buddhist Compassionate Relief Love and Mercy Foundation (Ciji) in Taiwan; Buddhist Churches of America (official association of True Pure Land Buddhism in America) establishes Institute of Buddhist Studies, first Buddhist seminary in the United States, in Berkeley, California.
1975	Vietnam War ends with Communist takeover. Buddhism is officially suppressed.
1977	Buddhist Peace Fellowship (BPF) founded in Berkeley, CA.
1980s	Sri Lankan government sponsors updating of the Great Commentary, the most authoritative explanation of Buddhist scriptures for Southeast Asians.

1981	United Buddhist Church of Vietnam (UBCV) banned by Vietnamese government.
1984	Chinese government opens Tibet to tourists.
1989	Dalai Lama awarded Nobel Peace Prize.
1991	Burmese lay activist Aung San Suu Kyi awarded Nobel Peace Prize.
1999	Chinese government instigates major crackdown on Falun Gong, a popular religious movement that draws heavily on Buddhist teachings and practices.
2000	Minor scandal arises concerning alleged monetary contributions received by Democratic presidential candidate Al Gore from Hsi Lai Buddhist temple located just outside of Los Angeles.
2001	Taliban destroys colossal Buddhist statues at Bamiyan, Afghanistan.
2004	*For the Lady,* tribute CD dedicated to Burmese 1991 Nobel Peace Prize winner Aung San Suu Kyi, is recorded by various rock and pop stars. Proceeds go to help liberate the people of Burma (Myanmar).

1

HISTORY OF FOUNDATION

The history of Buddhism is a complex mixture of fact, myth, and legend. Of course, the same could be said of other religions, but it is especially true of Buddhism, which, like Hinduism, places far less emphasis on historicity than Western traditions such as Christianity. Nonetheless, Buddhist history cannot be ignored. For more than 2,500 years Buddhism has been a major influence on world civilization. Although it began as a relatively small protest movement, Buddhism grew to become a truly world religion claiming followers from all over mainland Asia, the island nations of Japan and Indonesia, and most recently Europe and North America. The following account traces the origins of Buddhism, the legendary life of its historical founder Siddhartha Gautama (Buddha), the spread of Buddhist teachings in India, and the manner in which Buddhism expanded beyond the Indian cultural region.

BUDDHISM'S HISTORICAL CONTEXT

Scholars agree that Buddhism began in approximately the sixth century B.C.E. in the Ganges River region of northeastern India and southern Nepal. Pious Buddhists maintain that the Buddha merely rediscovered the eternal truths of reality but even if this is so, we cannot get around the fact that the social and cultural context of his era substantially shaped how he taught and how his audience received his teachings. Thus, a brief overview of social, political, and religious currents of pre-Buddhist India is needed here.

In the centuries before the rise of Buddhism, India was under the domination of people who called themselves *Aryans* (nobles). The Aryans were nomadic invaders who entered northwest India sometime around 1600 B.C.E. and conquered the indigenous Indian peoples. The Aryans were an aristocratic warrior society much like that depicted in Homer's *Iliad* and *Odyssey*. They spoke Sanskrit, a language related to ancient Greek and Latin, and the main vehicle of their culture were religious hymns (the Vedas) lauding the exploits of their gods and detailing elaborate sacrifices in their honor. These hymns were memorized by the hereditary priestly class known as *brahmins,* who were the custodians of Vedic knowledge and who were adept at performing sacrifices to tap into the cosmic powers and use them to grant the wishes of their clients.

The brahmins viewed the world as a constant flow in which all things participated. The world process was powered by "action" *(karma)*, a force that propelled all beings through countless lives; all living things were continuously being born, living, dying, and being reborn. This infinite cycle of life, death, and rebirth was later known as *samsara.* As time went on, the

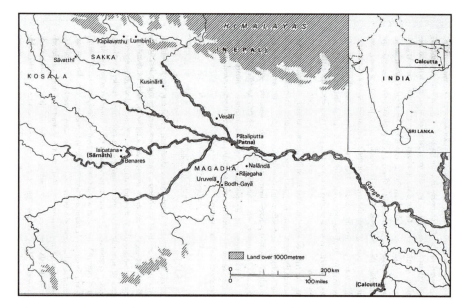

The region where Buddha lived and taught. From Peter Harvey, *An Introduction to Buddhism Teachings, History and Practices.* Cambridge: Cambridge University Press, 1990, 12. Reprinted with the permission of Cambridge University Press.

brahmins also developed a body of philosophical speculation on the nature of the sacrifices and their relationship to the cosmic processes. Most often, these speculative theories tied the underlying cosmic power (sometimes known as *Brahman* and personified as the creator god Brahma) to the sacrificial procedures known only to the brahmins. One Vedic theory held that the world was created from the primordial self-sacrifice of the "cosmic person," which, among other things, led to the establishment of a society in which the brahmins (descendents of the mouth of the "cosmic person") reigned over the other castes (warriors, producers, laborers). The brahmins were the highest and most pure caste, and they held a monopoly on ritual knowledge and ultimate truth. This system of thought, known as *Brahmanism,* became the dominant religious and philosophical scheme of Indian culture during the first millennium B.C.E.

The Brahmanical system, however, did not go unchallenged. As the Aryans spread throughout India, their nomadic warrior society changed to a more settled, agricultural one. The pre-Aryan populations of India were gradually assimilated into Aryan society, but some of their earlier beliefs began to assert themselves, giving rise to movements that were critical of Vedic assumptions. The transition to a more settled way of life brought other castes to power. Some of these new elites had little or no access to Vedic truths and found themselves drawn to religious and philosophical teachings that were open to people of any caste through reason or meditative training. Such views were spread by groups of wandering ascetics *(shramanas),* people who abandoned traditional family life to live in pursuit of spiritual truth. These *shramanas* formed fluid communities around masters (often non-brahmins) who propounded a variety of teachings ranging from extreme asceticism to radical hedonism, skepticism, and even fatalism. Despite their differences, though, the *shramanas* were united in their commitment to the existential quest for spiritual truth and had profound effect on Indian society.

Critical questioning of Vedic ways was especially acute in the Ganges region. The area had long been a stronghold of indigenous Indian, pre-Vedic beliefs, and the overall Aryan influence was relatively shallow. By the sixth century B.C.E. major social changes in the area furthered anti-Brahmanical criticism. Rulers were establishing urban centers of political and economic power, spawning a monetary economy driven by a new class of wealthy merchants and property owners. This overturning of older social norms encouraged many to rethink the basis of their society and opened them to the possibility that human life and the cosmos itself might be very different than previously supposed. Such a situation encouraged the growth of *shramana* movements, and many people gave up their settled lives and joined these wanderers in their quest for spiritual enlightenment. One such person was Siddhartha Gautama (c. 563–483 B.C.E.), the man who became the historical Buddha.

THE LEGEND OF SIDDHARTHA GAUTAMA

The story of Siddhartha Gautama as it has come down to us is a complex tangle of embellished fact and pious fiction. Many of the details of the Buddha's life are the products of later tradition, although there is substantial agreement between these various "biographies."[1] Traditional accounts of his life begin not with his birth but with his previous lives stretching back thousands of eons. These past life stories relate how in numerous previous existences (animal, human, and god) he demonstrated unparalleled virtue and wisdom, building up the moral and spiritual perfections necessary to become a Buddha. It is his last life, however, that is the most significant for it is during that time that he became enlightened.

The future Buddha's last birth was in the republic of the Shakyas, an area straddling the border of northeastern India and southern Nepal. It is from his birth among these people that he is sometimes called Shakyamuni (Sage of the Shakyas). His father, Suddhodana, was chief (later accounts consider him a king), making Siddhartha a member of the warrior caste and thus destined to rule over his subjects as his father did.

According to traditional accounts, Siddhartha was conceived one night when his mother, Mahamaya, dreamed that a white elephant entered her womb. Suddhodana called on 64 brahmins to interpret the dream, and they predicted she would give birth to a son who would become either a universal monarch or a universal teacher, a Buddha. Ten months later, Mahamaya was returning to her ancestral home to give birth (as was the custom) when she was passing through a park called Lumbini. There she went into labor while standing under a tree and gave birth to a son. Some accounts tell of a mysterious light illuminating the world while gods attended to the birth and a miraculous stream of water descended from the sky to wash the child. The baby immediately stood, walked seven paces, surveyed all directions, and declared this would be his final rebirth. The miraculous events continued during Siddhartha's infancy. Tradition says that a sage named Atisha recognized the auspicious marks on his body and confirmed the brahmins' prediction that the boy would either be a universal monarch or a Buddha. Five days after his birth during his name-giving ceremony, several other priests made a similar proclamation.

On the seventh day following his birth, Mahamaya died and so his father's second wife, his mother's sister, brought up Siddhartha. Most texts say little about his childhood other than it was a life of supreme luxury. Siddhartha seems to have been an unusually intelligent and compassionate youth and one event, in particular, foreshadowed his career. One day while attending a local festival, Siddhartha's attendants left the young prince while they went to get a look at a performance. When they returned to where they had left him (some texts say under a tree) they found him sitting cross-legged in the posture of a yogi (a spiritual seeker and practitioner of yoga), absorbed in a meditative trance.

When Siddhartha came of age, he married a beautiful cousin named Yasodhara. Their marriage was a happy one, eventually producing a son they named Rahula when Siddhartha turned 29. King Suddhodana, pleased at having such a noble son, wanted to insure that Siddhartha remained at home and became a king. He thus took great pains to shield him from the sufferings of the world, fearing they would awaken a religious impulse. However, his plan failed and at the age of 29, his son was confronted with the true nature of life.

Legend holds that Siddhartha was out riding in his chariot beyond the confines of the palace when he experienced four sights that precipitated an existential crisis. The first of these was an old man, decrepit and grizzled, leaning on a staff as he walked. The second was a man who was deathly ill, groaning in pain and soiled by his own filth. The third was a human corpse being loaded on to a funeral pyre. The fourth and final sight was a shaven-headed monk, calm and quiet in his simple yellow robe. Together these four sights forced the realization upon Siddhartha that suffering marked human existence. Shaken to the core, Siddhartha understood that he could no longer live the way he was raised; he had to solve the riddle of suffering. Returning to his palace, he gazed at his sleeping wife and son one last time before renouncing all his possessions and his noble status. Discarding his princely robes and cutting off his hair, Siddhartha fled into the forest to become a *shramana*.

Siddhartha spent the next six years wandering the Ganges plain, seeking to understand the mysteries of existence and human misery. He studied with various yogis and gurus (spiritual teachers), including two sages who taught him meditative techniques to reach the "state of nothingness" and the "state of neither perception nor nonperception." However, Siddhartha knew that even these rarefied mystical states did not lead to final awakening. At this point he vowed to follow a path of severe austerity in hopes of achieving enlightenment. Journeying to a village near Uruvela (modern-day Gaya), he joined five other ascetics and engaged in severe ascetic practices. According to traditional accounts, Siddhartha sat on beds of thorns, let filth accumulate on his body, exposed himself to the elements, and starved himself near the point of death. Yet even such extremes brought no great realization. Siddhartha understood that he needed to find a "middle way" between luxury and asceticism to awaken and so broke his fast. His five companions, disgusted with what they considered this surrender to self-indulgence, abandoned him.

Determined to find the true way, Siddhartha set off by himself until he came to a pipal tree (now called a *bodhi* tree, "the tree of enlightenment"). There he sat down, crossed his legs, and vowed not to arise until he penetrated the depths of existence and became enlightened. Sitting in great concentration, Siddhartha confronted the very limits of human existence. The traditional texts personify these forces as Mara, the tempter, who aimed to prevent Siddhartha's search. Mara tempted Siddhartha three times, but each time he was unsuccessful. First, Mara tried to convince him that enemies had revolted back home, taking his wife and imprisoning his father. Siddhartha, though, continued sitting. Second, Mara sent his three beautiful daughters with an entire retinue of dancers to seduce Siddhartha by any means at their disposal. Yet again, the Buddha-to-be remained unmoved. Finally, out of desperation Mara assaulted Siddhartha with a host of demons, challenging his very right to his quest for enlightenment. In response Siddhartha touched the ground with his right hand and the earth goddess herself quaked, thundering out her testimony to his virtue. Mara and his army fled in terror.

With the defeat of Mara, Siddhartha entered a deep meditative trance. Passing through progressively deeper and deeper states of consciousness, he surveyed all of his former lives, gaining a thorough knowledge of existence in all forms. From such knowledge he realized the cause of the cycle of rebirth and suffering as well as the way to eliminate suffering. Finally, just as dawn was breaking, Siddhartha emerged from the darkness of ignorance to full enlightenment. Thus, at age 35 he awoke to the truth of reality, attaining *nirvana,* a state beyond suffering. No longer was he Siddhartha Gautama; he was Buddha.

Buddhist texts speak of various cosmic events that marked his awakening: the sky shone brightly, thunder pealed, fruit and blossoms rained upon the earth, the heavens were filled with the rejoicing of myriad gods and goddesses. Buddha remained in meditation for several weeks, deepening his understanding of the truth he had realized and debating whether he should try to communicate it to others. Just as he was resolving not to attempt to teach his wisdom, the great god Brahma appeared and pleaded with him, arguing that although the Buddha's truth was subtle and difficult to comprehend, and that most beings were unable to grasp it, there were some who could. Reflecting on Brahma's words, the Buddha cast his divine gaze across the cosmos and saw that although beings did indeed differ in their capacity to comprehend truth, some were capable of understanding his discovery. Out of his compassion, the Buddha vowed, he would teach these beings and so lead them out of *samsara.*

All accounts agree that the Buddha's Awakening was a transformative experience that visibly changed him. Whenever he met people they immediately knew he was more than human. One story relates that a passing ascetic, noticing his aura of holiness, asked him whether he was a god. The Buddha answered he was neither man nor god but something entirely different, a being beyond the reach of suffering. He referred to himself as "the thus come one" *(tathagata)* to indicate that ordinary words could not adequately describe what he now was.

After ascertaining with his divine powers that his earlier yogic teachers were dead, the Buddha began his preaching career by seeking out the five ascetics with whom he had formerly practiced harsh austerities. He found them in a deer park at Sarnath, just outside the city of Benares (modern-day Varanasi). At first the ascetics ignored this backslider, but his charisma overcame their resolve. The Buddha then informed them of his awakening and that he would share his discovery with them. His companions protested that one who abandons the path of striving could never attain enlightenment, but the Buddha responded that he had never given up striving. He then challenged them as to whether they had ever heard him speak as he did now and they confessed they had not. At that point the Buddha delivered his first sermon, in which he laid out his realization and the path toward enlightenment.[2] The five ascetics received his teaching openly and, upon hearing his words, one of them was partially enlightened, and asked to be taken as his first disciple. Over the next few days, the other four devoted themselves to begging alms for the group and listening to the Buddha's teachings. Soon, all five were awakened and so became the founding members of the Buddhist community *(sangha)*.

From this point on, the Buddha devoted himself to proclaiming his teaching. In rapid succession he converted his father, stepmother, former wife, and son. Many other people followed suit. Although a number of these early followers were from lower castes (caste rankings, so prevalent in Indian society, were not recognized among the Buddha's disciples) several brahmins also joined the *sangha*'s ranks. Vast numbers of lay supporters were also attracted to the new movement.

Within short order the Buddha had some 60 monastic disciples *(arhats)* who had attained liberation by following his teachings. He sent them forth to spread the teachings for the welfare of all beings throughout greater India and beyond, and so lead the whole world to peace. The Buddha himself remained in India, dedicated to converting various ascetics, rulers, and ordinary people. As the movement grew, wealthy patrons donated land and built monasteries for the Buddha and his monks in most major cities.

One of the most notable features of the early *sangha* was its inclusion of women, a rarity in ancient India. Although Buddhism was male dominated, women were welcomed as lay followers from the very beginning. Some five years after his Enlightenment, however, the Buddha was approached by a large group of women led by his foster mother who asked to be ordained into the monastic community. At first the Buddha hesitated, but then Ananda, his chief attendant and cousin, pleaded with him on their behalf and he relented. From that day onward, the *sangha* included both monks and nuns.

In all, the Buddha's mission lasted 45 years, during which time he traveled throughout the Ganges region preaching to all who came, displaying marvelous powers, and aiding his followers along the path toward enlightenment. Over the course of his life he amassed a large group of devout monastic and lay followers. His career ended at the age of 80 when he succumbed to illness as a result of eating tainted food (a dish of pork or perhaps mushrooms). Unable to continue his wandering life, the Buddha settled down outside the village of Kusinara (now Kasia, in Uttar Pradesh) lying down on his right side between two trees with his head to the north and one foot on top of the other. The trees burst into bloom and showered his body with blossoms. Gods from throughout the universe, knowing that his end was near, assembled to witness the Buddha's passing. Even in the midst of great physical pain and discomfort, he remained calm. He reassured his disciples that he had held nothing back from them and told them to test out his teachings rather than accepting them on his authority. After urging his followers to be "lamps unto themselves," the Buddha asked them one last time whether they had any questions. None did. Finally, the Buddha spoke his last words: "Now, monks, I declare to you: all conditioned things are of a nature to decay—strive on untiringly."[3] He then methodically entered a meditative trance, moving through various levels of consciousness before passing on.[4] The texts state that earthquakes and peals of thunder marked the moment of his death, and that his followers who had yet to attain *nirvana* burst into loud lamentations.

After the Buddha's earthly death, the people of Kusingara mourned for six days and then cremated his body in accordance with Indian custom. It is said that messengers came from various clans asking for relics. Following the Buddha's instructions, his relics were divided among eight different groups, who took them home and built memorial mounds *(stupas)* for them. Such relic mounds were common across India and served as shrines for popular veneration. Eventually they became major holy sites of the Buddhist faith.

The Buddha's life story is one of the greatest in human history. It tells how a wise and compassionate man sought a way to solve the perennial riddles of human existence to end suffering and then devoted himself to sharing his discovery. His teachings offered the sort of rational, systematic view of the world and human life that many people in sixth-century India were looking for. Perhaps most of all, he founded an ideal society (the *sangha*) that provided the social support necessary for following his teachings and living out a life of peace and freedom.

MYTHIC FEATURES OF SIDDHARTHA'S LIFE

Even after more than two thousand years, Siddhartha's life continues to inspire people. However, filled as it is with all manner of fantastic and supernatural detail, it is difficult for most contemporary Westerners to believe. Quite obviously, many of the incidents are the product of later embellishing, but this does not mean they should be dismissed. Rather, these wondrous aspects of the Buddha's story can help us to understand Buddhism and Indian thought in general. They provide a window on ancient Indian worldviews and present a critical response to many of the prevailing beliefs and practices of ancient times. Moreover, scholars have shown that the traditional accounts of the Buddha's life follow the basic structure of hero myths the world over.[5]

The stories concerning the Buddha's various previous lives, so beloved by Buddhists throughout the ages, vividly depict the traditional Indian cosmology in which all beings move through numerous existences based on their earlier actions. They thus reinforce basic Buddhist teachings concerning *karma* and rebirth. These stories also provide proper models of behavior to guide those on the Buddhist path. In addition, the stories of the Buddha's earlier lives testify to the eternal nature of Buddhist teachings and Buddhahood itself.

The various miracles attributed to Siddhartha from the moment of his birth mark him as extraordinary from the very beginning. His powers show him to be supreme over gods and demons. The cosmic events that accompany his birth, awakening, and final passing graphically emphasize the wondrous nature of his life and teachings, underscoring that he lived and taught a *universal* truth. His composure and control at the time of his passing are fully in line with traditions concerning yogis and other holy persons in Indian sacred lore. Some scholars have even suggested that the Buddha's Enlightenment has similarities to initiations into ancient mystery cults and the shamanic quest undertaken by the Inuit and other tribal peoples.[6]

The parallels between the life of the Buddha and the life of Jesus are especially noteworthy. Both figures had miraculous births heralded by cosmic and supernatural signs. As infants they also received predictions from holy men (Atisha in the case of Buddha, Simeon in the case of Jesus) that they would lead extraordinary lives, and as children both experienced events foreshadowing their preaching careers. Both Buddha and Jesus also endured a severe fast and were tempted by demonic powers (Mara for the Buddha, Satan for Jesus) before setting out on their missions. In addition, both men were charismatic individuals whose teachings drew large crowds wherever they went, and both sent out their most loyal followers to help spread their message for the benefit of all humankind. Although there are important differences between the Buddha and Jesus, the similarities between their lives provide food for thought and may point to historical connections between the Greco-Roman world and ancient India.[7]

Whatever historical truth there may be to the story of Siddhartha Gautama, the mythic features of his life indicate that his story has more than literal meaning. Many of the events are highly symbolic and may never have actually happened. Such considerations, though, may be beside the point. The story of the Buddha, like all myths, is a sacred tale that binds all

Buddhists together. More importantly, the Buddha's story serves as a blue-print for later Buddhists to follow. By tracing out the path and embodying his teachings, the Buddha is an exemplar of the ultimate goal to which all Buddhists aspire.

THE SPREAD OF BUDDHISM IN INDIA

Like other religious movements in history, Buddhism did not die off with its founder. Indeed, the *sangha* continued to grow, preserving the memory of Siddhartha and his teachings. Although the details of early Buddhist history are sketchy, tradition holds that a great council was called at Rajagraha, India immediately after Siddhartha's passing. This council, attended by five hundred monks, formulated an authoritative canon and a set of rules governing monastic life. It was during this council that Ananda, the Buddha's faithful attendant, recited all the Buddha's discourses.[8] Many scholars, though, view the claim that most of the extant scriptures were recited at this council as pious exaggeration.

Another great council was held approximately a century later (~383 B.C.E.) during which several monks were censured for violating disciplin-ary rules and the seeds were sown for the first major schism in the *sangha*. Historical records also speak of a Third Council in 250 B.C.E. at the city of Pataliputra that resulted in the further divisions. The first schisms were pri-marily over disagreements on rules of monastic discipline and practice, but eventually doctrinal differences also surfaced. According to tradition, the *sangha* eventually split into 18 different sects. The principal split occurred between a group known as the "members of the Great Sangha" *(Maha-sangikas)*, who took a liberal interpretation of the teachings and disciplin-ary rules, and those who claimed to adhere to the "Teachings of the Elders," and thus maintained a more conservative interpretation.[9] Such divisions, however, did not prevent monks from different groups from sharing the same monasteries or studying each other's doctrines. Moreover, it seems likely that the laity was not concerned about the differences between these schools.

Buddhism received its greatest boost during the third century B.C.E. under the reign of the Mauryan Emperor Ashoka (~268–39 B.C.E.). Ashoka converted to Buddhism after a bloody war of conquest in 260 B.C.E. The slaughter on the battlefield so horrified him that he abandoned his policies of "might makes right," vowing to govern and protect his subjects according to Buddhist teachings of peace and harmony. With his support, Buddhism

Inscription of Greek and Aramaic erected
by Emperor Ashoka, Kandahar, Afghanistan. Courtesy of American Institute of
Indian Studies.

reached most of the Indian subcontinent, becoming one of the first "world
religions." Ashoka promoted all moral and religious ways of life (Buddhist
or otherwise), encouraged virtue among his subjects, and inaugurated various public works (wells and rest houses for travelers, hospitals, etc.). He
erected shrines and memorial pillars throughout his empire, which eventually stretched beyond what is now Pakistan and into modern-day Afghanistan. Ashoka's devotion to Buddhism led to his presiding over the Third
Council at Pataliputra and sending Buddhist missionaries to many foreign
lands. Because of his great support and devotion, Buddhism developed into
a major popular religion.

For centuries after Ashoka's reign Buddhism continued to thrive in
India and surrounding regions under various royal patrons, and with their
support numerous Buddhist universities, temples, and monuments were
erected. One of the most important periods of such support was the Kushan
dynasty (50–320 C.E.), which was centered in Kashmir but included much
of central Asia. It was under Kushan rule that Buddhism expanded along
the Silk Road, a network of caravan routes extending from China to Asia
Minor (modern-day Turkey), and many Silk Road cities became major centers of Buddhism. Among the most prominent of these was Bamiyan, a city

in what is now southern Afghanistan that became famous for the colossal Buddha statues carved out of the cliffs on its outskirts. Bamiyan and similar sites in central Asia were home to thriving Buddhist communities, both lay and monastic, for centuries.

However, Buddhism began to decline in both India and central Asia from about the seventh century of the common era. The reasons for this decline are complex, but it was largely the result of the rise of Hinduism and Islam. During the later Middle Ages in India, Hinduism absorbed many of Buddhism's teachings and practices, gradually attracting most of India's lay population. At the same time, Islam began its meteoric rise on the world scene, expanding both westward and eastward beyond Arabia. From the eighth through the eleventh centuries, Islamic control extended throughout central Asia, provoking mass conversions of the populace and making inroads as far as China. By the twelfth century Muslim armies had overrun much of India, destroying many great Buddhist centers and slaying scores of monks. Many of those monks who survived either converted to Islam or fled to Tibet and other Himalayan countries. From then on Buddhism dwindled in its native land until it was all but wiped out.

BUDDHISM'S SPREAD BEYOND INDIA

Although Buddhism arose in India, most of its growth has been beyond its native land. Ashoka sent out missionaries to Southeast and central Asia, Syria, Egypt, and even Macedonia, the heart of the Hellenistic world. Over the centuries much of Asia came under Buddhist influence, and in many of these areas, Buddhism remained quite strong despite its gradual eclipse by Islam. Much of Buddhism's spread has come through missionaries sent out by Ashoka and other Buddhist rulers, but the faith has also spread by merchants and traders.

Southeast Asia (Sri Lanka, Burma, Thailand, Laos, Cambodia, Indonesia)

Southeast Asia has long been a stronghold of Buddhism, where over the centuries it came to define the societies of the region. Buddhism spread along maritime routes from India's east coast, often as part of Indian culture. Local rulers seem to have eagerly embraced Indian cultural and religious ideas and practices, most likely as a means of establishing social order and consolidating political power. The great ruins of the temple complexes

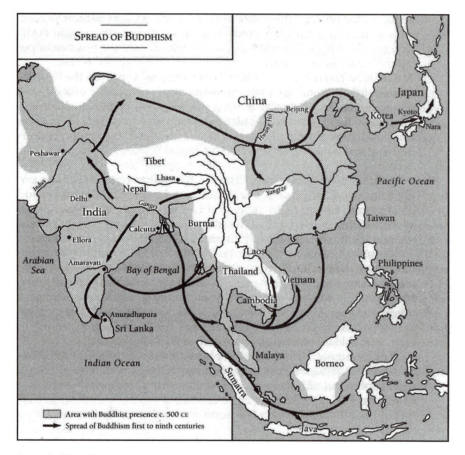

Spread of Buddhism. From S. A. Nigosian, *World Religions: A Historical Approach,* 3rd edition (New York: Bedford/St. Martin's Copyright 2000, 75). Reprinted with permission of Bedford/St. Martin's.

at Angkor in Cambodia, Pagan in Burma (Myanmar), and Borobudur in Java strongly attest to grip of Buddhism on the peoples of Southeast Asia, and rank among the world's great architectural treasures.

According to Buddhist tradition, Buddhism entered Southeast Asia as a result of Ashoka's missionary activities. Most notable among these was a mission to Sri Lanka headed by the monk Mahinda, Ashoka's son. There, he established an indigenous *sangha* and his sister, a nun named Sanghamitta, brought a cutting of the original *bodhi* tree to plant at the capital, Anuradhapura, as well as several relics that were quickly enshrined in the first *stupas* on the island. From that time on, Buddhism was Sri Lanka's major religion. The Sinhalese (native inhabitants of Sri Lanka) have generally felt that monks are essential for civilized life and monks have often served as tutors and advisers to kings, who were required to be Buddhists. Buddhism enjoyed great support until the tenth century, when Hindu Tamils (immigrants from the Tamil region of Southern India) invaded from southern India and began a series of civil wars during which Buddhism declined. The decline continued as Western colonial powers (Portuguese, Dutch, British) lay claim to the island and, in the sixteenth century, persecution by a Hindu king stamped out the ordination line for monks. Buddhism, however, continued to have a hold on many lay people.

Tradition holds that a small Buddhist community was also founded during Ashoka's reign in the area of southern Burma and central Thailand. However, solid archaeological evidence of Buddhism in this region dates back only to a period between the fifth and eighth centuries c.e., when Theravada, the conservative "southern" branch, enjoyed patronage by the ruling classes. Other forms of Buddhism were also introduced into the region from Sri Lanka as well as China and India, often, in the latter case, mixed with Hinduism. From 802 to 1432, much of Southeast Asia was ruled by the Khmers, a people that originated in what is now Cambodia. The Khmer king was often depicted as an incarnation of the Hindu god Shiva as well as a great Buddhist benefactor. He ruled from the great complex at Angkor, whose temples depicts both Hindu and Buddhist themes. Eventually, though, the Khmer empire was destroyed by the armies of neighboring states. Gradually, Theravada Buddhism came to dominate the region, fostered by close connections between Sri Lankan, Thai, and Burmese rulers.

Angkor Wat, Cambodia. © Getty Images/210006816.

When the Thai people migrated from China into the region, they established various small kingdoms in the southern and central areas of what is now Thailand. During the thirteenth and fourteenth centuries, Theravada Buddhism became widespread and provided major religious inspiration for the construction of several large-scale temples. These grand structures indicate not only that Buddhism had major backing by the social and political elites but that it had a central place in Thai society. Most scholars agree that it is from this point on that Buddhism came to define popular religious life throughout the region.

Buddhism was present in what is now Malaysia from about the fourth century. It was through the Buddhist kingdoms of the Malay Peninsula that Buddhism spread to the Indonesian islands of Java and Sumatra. Around 800, a huge *stupa* was built at Borobudur on Java, and this remains the largest monument in the Southern Hemisphere. Various forms of Buddhism (along with Hindu cults) thrived in the region until the fourteenth century, when Islam arrived in Indonesia with merchants. By the fifteenth century Islam had become the dominant religion, although Hindu-Buddhist blending continued to thrive on Bali, and Buddhism remained the dominant religion of Indonesia's immigrant Chinese community.

China

Many of the most significant developments in Buddhist history were the result of its interaction with Chinese culture. Buddhism appeared in China during the first century C.E., by which time it had already reached areas far beyond India. The Himalayas, though, formed a formidable barrier between India and China and effectively barred direct transmission. Instead, Buddhism came to China with foreign merchants and missionaries by way of central Asia.

During this time China was ruled by the Han dynasty (206 B.C.E.–220 C.E.), a great empire that rivaled Rome. The Han dominated much of the eastern half of Asia, stretching from Korea to central Asia and from the Gobi desert to Vietnam. The official state creed of China during the Han dynasty was Confucianism, a tradition promoting order and harmony through a clearly defined social hierarchy and family structure. Confucian teachings stress a moral code based on human virtue and respect for ancient rituals and customs. In addition, various forms of Daoism, a complex amalgamation of beliefs and practices, some of which stem from prehistoric times, was also quite strong.[10]

Legends say that the first Chinese Buddhist monastery, the White Horse Temple, was founded as a result of the Buddha manifesting as a "golden man" in a dream of Emperor Ming (58–76 C.E.). The earliest Chinese references to Buddhism, though, date from 65 C.E., when it was one of many exotic faiths practiced in the capital by foreign traders. This curious faith began to attract Chinese converts from the educated classes, and by the middle of the second century, Buddha was worshipped in the imperial palace alongside other deities.

The Han dynasty fell to invading Turkish and Tibetan armies in 220, and for the next few centuries China was a patchwork of small states. In short order these "barbarian" invaders conquered many of these northern states and came to dominate the native Chinese population. Many educated and elite Chinese fled their homes to exile in the regions south of the Yangtze River. These developments produced a social climate ripe for Buddhism to spread. Not only did the northern invaders embrace Buddhism to consolidate their conquests and insure prosperity, they also liked the supernatural powers that monks often displayed. Chinese adherents, meanwhile, realized that by becoming monks, they could avoid military and labor service as well as taxation. The social disruption and anxiety that came with the fall of the Han and the barbarian conquests provoked an inward turn among the Chinese, some of whom abandoned Confucianism for Daoist speculation and naturalism. Daoist teachings of "nonaction" and "nonbeing" as the source of all things, and Daoism's promotion of "retirement" to a simpler way of life seemed to mirror Buddhist ideals of *nirvana* and monasticism, and a sympathetic dialogue evolved between Daoist intellectuals and Buddhist monks.[11] Such trends enabled Buddhism to gain many converts among the wealthy and educated classes.

During the fourth century many eminent scholar-monks laid the philosophical foundation of Chinese Buddhism, which became a major force among Chinese intellectuals for the next several centuries. It was also during this time that several cave temples were carved out of the rock hills at places such as Yungang and Dunhuang to serve traveling monks and native believers. These cave temples gradually became great pilgrimage centers for the next thousand years and remain repositories of Buddhist art and texts to this day.

The fifth century marked important changes in Buddhism in China. As their knowledge of Buddhism increased, several Chinese monks began to realize how their new faith differed from Confucianism and Daoism. In 399, a monk named Faxian went on a pilgrimage to India (the Buddhist

Cave temples at Dunhuang, China. Courtesy of the author.

"holy land") via central Asia, suffering great hardships along the way. He visited the sacred sites along the Ganges, studied with Indian masters, visited Sri Lanka, and returned to China with many new texts in 414. Before that, however, the Chinese view of Buddhism had deepened considerably under the tutelage of Kumarajiva, a central Asian missionary. In 401 he had been captured by Chinese forces and brought back to the Chinese capital of Chang'an. There he was made head of the Chinese *sangha* and chief of the state translation bureau. Kumarajiva gave the Chinese their first systematic understanding of Buddhist doctrine, and until his death in 413, he oversaw the work of an immense translation team. In all, Kumarajiva and his followers produced Chinese translations of hundreds of important Buddhist texts, thus allowing access to Buddhist teachings by increasing numbers of the Chinese population. Kumarajiva also was among the first figures in Chinese Buddhism to focus on harmonizing various strains of Buddhist teaching. This practice, stimulated by the love of harmony that has so long been a part of Chinese culture, became a major feature of Chinese Buddhism. Later thinkers such as Zhiyi (539–97) and Dushun (557–640) continued this harmonizing trend by founding the Tiantai and Huayan schools of Buddhism, distinctively Chinese schools that ranked the various Buddhist teachings according to the periods of the Buddha's preaching career and the audience he was addressing.

As a result of such activities, Buddhism gained a great hold on the Chinese population. By providing well-thought-out notions of the afterlife and offering a way of transcending the sufferings of the world, Buddhism met the spiritual needs of a wide range of people. Its strong ethical code worked well with ingrained Confucian virtues as well. In particular, Buddhism held great appeal to women, as it generally placed men and women on a more equal spiritual footing than other Chinese traditions. Moreover, by allowing widows the option of becoming nuns, it actually offered them a place in Chinese society.

Over the centuries Buddhism had tremendous impact on China. Great temples and monasteries were built in most cities and in remote areas as well. The great impression made by Buddhist art had lasting effects, and some of the first truly monumental religious art in Chinese history was Buddhist inspired. Many wealthy merchants, nobles, and rulers became great patrons of Buddhism (donating money or otherwise supporting the *sangha* was a way to earn merit). One of the most generous of such royal patrons was Emperor Wudi of Liang (r. 502–49), who banned meat and wine from his court, constructed numerous temples in his realm, sponsored large ceremonies, and even wrote commentaries to several sacred texts *(sutras)*.

During the Sui (581–618) and Tang (618–907) dynasties, when China was once again the center of a united empire, Chinese Buddhism reached its zenith. The capital of Chang'an housed several major monasteries and temples, and was an important center along the Silk Road. Buddhist monks had unparalleled access to the imperial court, and scholar-monks of both the Tiantai and Huayan schools wrote numerous treatises and commentaries elaborating their schools' teachings. Some of the most famous names in Chinese history such as Xuanzang (599–664), a monk who spent 17 years on a pilgrimage throughout central Asia and India, and Fazang (643–712), a Huayan patriarch and a great favorite of the Empress Wu (r. 690–705), lived during this period.

In the Tang dynasty Buddhism was for all intents and purposes an arm of the state, headed by the "superintendent of the *sangha*," a state official appointed by the emperor, and the emperor himself was often portrayed in art as a Buddha. Although such practices were controversial in some quarters, they reflected a general alignment summed up by the phrase "protect the country, protect Buddhism." This motto is perhaps best seen in the person of Amoghavarja, an eighth-century superintendent and leader of an esoteric (Tantric) Buddhist school. He and his followers regularly practiced magical rites and staged huge ceremonies for state protection, all at government expense.

Large Buddhist monasteries were often supported by the government and became major social and economic institutions, just as Christian monasteries did in medieval Europe. Chinese monasteries engaged in such practices as money lending, served as pawnshops, housed grain mills and the like, and employed large numbers of peasant laborers. In addition, they were often charitable centers, serving as hospitals, inns, and local schools. Monasteries also served as the staging areas for many popular festivals, of which the best known was the Festival of the Hungry Ghosts (15th day of the seventh month). This festival, based on Indian Buddhist practices, became quite large in China, where it fused with the indigenous Chinese observance of ancestral rites. The idea behind these rites was to feed not only the ancestors of the local households but all troubled beings in the netherworld.[12]

Other schools of Buddhism also arose during the Sui and Tang dynasties, chief among them Pure Land and Chan. Pure Land taught a doctrine of faith and reliance on the saving power of the Buddha Amitabha (a cosmic deity much like the Judeo-Christian God), who out of compassion established a paradise in the west where his faithful will be reborn after death. Chan (from the Sanskrit word for "meditation," *dhyana*) derived from Indian meditation techniques that were widely popular in some quarters of Chinese society. Unlike Pure Land, though, Chan taught that by stilling the mind, one could see into one's basic Buddha-nature and spontaneously awaken. Both Chan and Pure Land eschewed the complex doctrines of the Tiantai and Huayan scholars, and, by promoting simple practices, helped Buddhism spread among the lower classes of Chinese society.

Despite such community involvement, though, some critics denounced Buddhism as "un-Chinese." To become a monk or nun (officially known as "leaving home") required giving up one's name, shaving one's head, and taking a vow of celibacy—all of which meant stepping outside of traditional Chinese social and familial ties, and even abandoning the ancestral cults. Such controversial practices resulted in prominent Confucians repeatedly accusing Buddhism of encouraging unfilial behavior, a serious charge in China's family-centered culture. Daoists, on the other hand, felt threatened by competition from monks and nuns, and so denounced Buddhism as a "foreign" cult. In addition, monks refused to bow to rulers, did not serve in the army, and did not pay taxes. Critics said that they were parasites who siphoned money from the state for useless projects such as temple building, making lavish Buddha images, and performing large ceremonies. These charges were made repeatedly, and the Buddhists wrote numerous texts in response. For example, when charged with encouraging unfilial behavior, Buddhists countered that they were filial by praying for parents and ancestors, and helping them in the afterlife through various rituals. They also maintained that Buddhism aided the state by its lavish ceremonies and prayers, which warded off evil and protected against various disasters.

Critics of Buddhism, however, were right in pointing out certain problems. Buddhism did pose some economic difficulties for the state—it took land off tax registers (temples and monasteries were exempt), and monks as well as their attendants did not pay taxes. At various times the Chinese government tried to impose state control of Buddhism by regulating monasteries and ensuring that monks and nuns were not just evading taxes. There had been two state suppressions of Buddhism in earlier centuries (446–52 and 574–79) during which the government closed many monasteries and forced their inhabitants back to lay life. Yet Chinese rulers never attempted to stop private belief and practices. Moreover, later rulers made generous amends. However, by the end of the Tang, there was growing opposition to Buddhism in many areas. Such opposition was part of growing opposition to other "foreign religions" as military and social problems arose. At the same time there was a tremendous resurgence of Confucianism, and the old charges that monks were parasites and that their great temples and lavish ceremonies constituted a drain on the populace began to get a greater hearing.

Finally, from 841 to 845 there was a massive suppression of Buddhism that marked the end of Buddhist dominance in China. The government confiscated numerous temples and monasteries as well as works of art, and forced thousands of monks and nuns back to lay life. This suppression coincided with the cut-off from central Asian influence because of the decline of Buddhism there and the rise of Islam. In China only popular sects that relied very little on government support (Chan and Pure Land) survived relatively intact, although Buddhism was never abolished. At the elite level, Buddhism declined during the Song dynasty (960–1270), when a revitalized form of Confucianism (called "Neo-Confucianism") came to dominate Chinese intellectual life. However, Buddhism continued to flourish at the popular level. Under the Mongolian rule of the Yuan dynasty (1280–1368), Buddhism enjoyed a brief resurgence of state patronage, and this situation carried over into the early Ming dynasty (1368–1644) until Neo-Confucianism again rose to the fore. Buddhism, however, thrived at the popular level, and during this time there was a strong move toward religious syncretism, blending Buddhism with Confucianism and Daoism. Many Chinese actively proclaimed the "unity of the Three Teachings," a practice that continued into the Qing dynasty (1644–1911).

Korea

Korea as a united entity did not exist until the early centuries of the common era. Before then the Korean peninsula was divided into the three kingdoms of Koguryo, Paekche, and Silla. Buddhism was introduced by way of China in the fourth century, bringing much of Chinese culture with it, and was instrumental in uniting the region. By the sixth century Buddhism had spread throughout Korean territory, and over time it mixed with the indigenous shamanistic religion—a harmonizing trend that continues to this day. During the sixth and seventh centuries, Korean monks studying in China brought back Buddhist teachings and schools, and Buddhism became the religion of the elite. A common view arose during this time that Korea had been the home of Shakyamuni Buddha in a previous life, so that in fact, the Chinese did not import a new teaching so much as help revive Korea's own heritage. Buddhism gradually grew in influence during the Silla (668–918) and Koryo (918–1392) periods, making greater inroads among the commoners. It enjoyed much influence and patronage among the nobility, with monks succeeding in abolishing the death penalty in 1036 as well as in getting the government to print the entire Chinese canon.[13] By the fourteenth century, Buddhism dominated Korean society.

Much as it did in China, Buddhism enjoyed strong political patronage from Korean rulers, and as a result, monasteries grew in size and influence. Many monasteries became large landowners with large numbers of serfs, and several developed into major commercial and economic centers involved in the production and selling of tea, alcohol, and noodles. Such worldly ventures led to charges of corruption and ushered in a series of attacks, both from within and outside the Buddhist community. As a result, the government instituted various restrictions on monks' involvement in secular matters. However, these attempts at government control never escalated to the level of official suppression that had existed in China.

One of the hallmarks of Korean Buddhism has been a tendency to harmonize various schools and teachings with indigenous traditions—a feature Korea shares with other East Asian societies. The great scholar-monk Chinul (1158–1210), a follower of Son (the Korean form of Chan/Zen), was a major force in shaping this harmonizing trend. He synthesized various teachings and practices from several schools based on a pragmatic approach in which the Dharma should be taught according to the needs of peoples of differing capacities.

During the Yi dynasty (1392–1910), however, Buddhism suffered a stunning reversal of fortune. Chinese Neo-Confucianism was adopted as the state ideology, and as a result, the government confiscated monastery lands and reduced the number of Buddhist schools. By the sixteenth century monks were banned from entering the capital, and the children of aristocrats were forbidden from being ordained. Buddhism, thus, retreated to monasteries deep in the mountains while continuing as a popular religion among the masses.

Japan

Buddhism has also enjoyed great success in Japan. Buddhism arrived in Japan in the sixth century by way of Korea, mainly as a carrier of Chinese culture (Japanese rulers imported Chinese civilization as a way of elevating what to their minds was their primitive indigenous culture). At first, the new religion drew followers mainly from the imperial court and high aristocracy. These early Japanese Buddhists were for the most part ignorant of their faith's intricacies, seeming to view it as a talisman for national protection and prosperity not too different from the native tradition of Shinto, a simple animistic faith that venerated the gods of the Japanese landscape *(kami)*. During the Nara period (710–94), however, Buddhism was proclaimed the state religion and the imperial capital city of Nara evolved into a major cultic center. Various temples were erected there housing Buddhist statues, paintings, artifacts, and texts from all over Asia. A giant statue of Buddha was constructed at state expense along with an enormous temple to house it. Over time Nara attracted visitors and pilgrims from various Asian countries, and the city was the home of several Buddhist schools imported from China. For the most part, however, Buddhism remained confined to the urban elites and those who dwelt in the Nara vicinity. Eventually, the imperial court moved the capital some 30 miles away and this new city, Heian-kyo (Kyoto), became the center of Japanese religious and political power.

With the new capital, Japan entered the Heian period (804–1185), one of the high points in Japanese cultural history. Along with major developments in literature and art, the Heian also saw the rise of two important Japanese Buddhist sects, Tendai and Shingon. Both were Chinese imports like the earlier Nara schools, but they had vastly more influence on Japanese society. Tendai, the Japanese form of Tiantai, was founded by Saicho (767–822), a monk who established a monastery on Mount Hiei just northeast of the capital. Tendai, like its Chinese counterpart, aimed at synthesizing and harmonizing various Buddhist teachings into a single coherent system. Its headquarters on Mount Hiei was a major center of Japanese Buddhism for centuries and was home to more than 30,000 monks in its heyday. Shingon, as an esoteric Tantric sect, differed considerably. Its founder was Kukai (774–835), one of the greatest figures in Japanese history. Drawing on Chinese Huayan as well as Tantric teachings, Shingon relied heavily on elaborate rituals and visualizations as the way to realization. Crucial to such realization was the special training Shingon adepts received in the use of secret chants *(mantras),* ritual hand gestures *(mudras),* and symbolic diagrams of the Buddhist cosmos *(mandalas)* to aid in harmonizing their body, speech, and mind with the universe itself. Kukai's impressive ritual performances featuring colorful costumes, dramatic dances, and magnificent images resonated with the traditional Japanese view in which art and religion were essentially one, and greatly increased Shingon's appeal among the Heian elite. Although Kukai established a center far from Kyoto on Mount Koya, he also set up another center at Toji, just on the outskirts of the capital.

The Tendai and Shingon schools fiercely competed for imperial sponsorship, but the two sects also borrowed heavily from each other over time. Both sects ministered primarily to the imperial court but also worked to spread Buddhism among commoners. The Heian period also saw the beginnings of Pure Land practices (especially among Tendai monks and laity), and the emergence of a mountain sect called *shugendo* that combined Buddhist teachings with indigenous tribal practices and beliefs.

The Heian period gradually collapsed in a period of social, political, and religious chaos. Order was eventually reestablished by a series of powerful military dictators (shoguns) who, along with their troops of samurai warriors, ruled the country from Kamakura, near modern-day Tokyo. The ensuing Kamakura era (1185–1333) was a tremendously creative time for Japanese Buddhism, as it became widespread among the general populace.

During the Kamakura era several new schools of Buddhism arose, often based on Tendai reform movements. One of the most important of these new Japanese schools was Zen, the Japanese form of Chan. The first major figure in Zen history was Eisei (1141–1215), a Tendai monk who traveled to China for intense religious training. Eisei's lineage became the Rinzai school, which quickly developed a strong following among the samurai, who found its strict discipline and stern monastic lifestyle very amenable to their warrior code. Even more influential than Eisei, though, was Dogen

(1200–1253), another Tendai monk who journeyed to China to study. More independent and philosophical in temperament than Eisei, Dogen went on to found the Soto school, which, along with the Rinzai school, has exerted tremendous influence on Japanese culture. Another important figure in Kamakura Buddhism was Honen (1133–1212), a charismatic Tendai monk whose promotion of Pure Land practice and teachings led to the founding of the Japanese Pure Land school (Jodoshu). One of Honen's main disciples, Shinran (1173–1262), carried his master's work even further, eventually founding another sect, the True Pure Land school (Jodoshin shu). Both schools proved very popular among the lower classes. Honen and Shinran, however, were almost eclipsed by Nichiren (1222–82), a figure whose exploits were legendary. Convinced that the true teachings of the Buddha resided in the Lotus Sutra, Nichiren advocated devotion to this scripture as the only way to salvation. He spent his life wandering Japan, preaching the truth of the Lotus Sutra and promoting the practice of chanting the phrase *Namu myoho renge kyo* (Hail the Scripture of the Lotus of the Perfect Truth). Nichiren's powerfully charismatic personality drew numerous followers even as he earned the wrath of many in the shogun's court. The Nichiren sect prospered through the centuries and continues to do so to this day.

With the end of the Kamakura era, Buddhism entered a period of decline. Although Zen monasteries prospered thanks to their close relations with the imperial court, there was very little real innovation in the religion. Instead, there was a marked emphasis on art as a mode of Buddhist expression. It was during this period that Zen monks became especially skilled in such traditional Japanese arts as poetry, calligraphy, and the tea ceremony. This aesthetic emphasis coincided with growing laxity in monastic discipline and increasing charges of corruption among the monks because of involvement in politics. By the fifteenth century Japan was rent by a series of civil wars, during which various Buddhist sects mustered their own armies and engaged in armed conflict. After decades of constant warfare a drive toward reunification was instigated through the combined efforts of three brilliant warlords, Oda Nobunaga (1534–82), Toyotomi Hideoyoshi (1536–98), and Tokugawa Ieyasu (1542–1616). Of the three, the one who had the most effect on Buddhism was Nobunaga, who ruthlessly suppressed Buddhism in his quest to reunite Japan. Nobunaga destroyed the great monastic complex on Mount Hiei and put all monks to the sword, attacked the Shingon headquarters on Mount Koya, and slaughtered various Nichiren and Pure Land armies throughout Japan. After succeeding Nobunaga, Hideoyoshi continued to unite the country, disarming the populace and attacking rebellious monastic communities. Japan was finally united under Ieyasu, who moved the capital to Edo (present-day Tokyo), and so ushered in the Tokugawa era (1603–1867).

The Tokugawa era was a time of sweeping changes in Japanese society, characterized by major drives toward centralization and modernization. Although Buddhism was officially encouraged, the government began to exert direct control over the *sangha* by requiring all families to register as members of Buddhist temples. Moreover, Chinese Neo-Confucianism exercised greater and greater influence on state policy, in large part because of what was perceived as Buddhist-inspired disunity during the previous century. In addition, a new movement began to develop, claiming that Shinto was the "true religion" of the Japanese, not the "foreign creed" of Buddhism. Such trends culminated in a coup in 1868, in which the Tokugawa shogunate was defeated and the Meiji emperor was installed on the throne. During the Meji era (1868–1911), Japan entered the modern world and became a major political and military entity. The government began an active campaign of persecution against Buddhism, severely weakening the faith but not wiping it out altogether. Buddhism remained a major factor in Japanese society, albeit increasingly in the service of Japanese imperialism and nationalism.

Tibet

Because of Tibet's remote and isolated location, Buddhism did not reach there until the seventh century. Before that, Tibetans followed an animistic religion later known as Bon. The first indications of Buddhist influence occurred when a Tibetan king converted through the influence of his Nepalese and Indian wives. However, the religion died out after his reign. Buddhism was reintroduced in the latter half of the eighth century, when, according to legend, Santarakshita (~705–788), a great Indian scholar-monk from Nalanda University, was brought to Tibet to bless the site of a proposed monastery. Noting the Tibetans' great love of the magical and fantastic, he suggested that the king invite the great master of ritual and occult lore Padmasambhava (one of Tibet's national heroes) to exorcise the area's evil influences. Padmasambhava came in 775 and subdued many Bon deities and spirits, converting many of the Tibetan people in the process. In 779 Buddhism was declared the official religion.

Early on the Tibetans gravitated toward Tantric Buddhism, whose magical and esoteric rituals resembled their indigenous rites. Over time, Buddhism and Bon mixed and influenced each other. The first recognized sect of Tibetan Buddhism, the School of the Followers of the Old (Nyingma), traces itself to Padmasambhava, whose magic powers were so instrumental in gaining a following for the new faith. However, hostility from Bon wizards led to sporadic persecution of Buddhism in the ninth century and a period of political turmoil. By the eleventh century there was a religious resurgence, and soon Buddhism was firmly established throughout the country. In 1042 the Indian scholar-monk Atisha toured the region at the request of a king and promoted a more disciplined and orthodox version of Buddhism. His efforts led to a new school being established, the School of Those Bound by Monastic Discipline (Kadmapa). Soon two other schools were established in Tibet as well. The Whispered Tradition (Kagyupa) school is famous for its secret system of yogas (meditation practices) and tantras (magical rites) passed down from legendary adepts such as Marpa (1012–96) and Milarepa (1040–1123). The School of Shakya Monastery (Shakyapa), in contrast, is known for its scholarship. By the fourteenth century the Tibetan canon was completed based on careful translations of northern Indian scriptures.

The great reformer Tsongkhapa (1357–1410) founded the last major school of Tibetan Buddhism, Virtuous School (Gelugpa), drawing on Atisha's systematic arrangement of Buddhist teachings and a purified monastic discipline. Gelugpa monks were distinguished by their yellow ceremonial hats and rigorous training, and soon this school rose to the forefront of Tibetan Buddhism. Several Gelugpa monasteries were founded near the capital of Lhasa and these became great centers for Buddhist scholarship and debate. In the sixteenth century a Mongol ruler gave the head of the Gelugpa order the official Mongolian title *Dalai Lama* (Teacher of Oceanic Wisdom) and proclaimed him to be a manifestation of the Cosmic Bodhisattva Avalokiteshvara (literally, the "Lord who looks down," the most popular and compassionate Buddhist deity). The title of Dalai Lama was passed down to each successive head of the Gelugpa order, with each Dalai Lama understood to be the reincarnation of his predecessor. This method of succession eventually became the norm for all Tibetan monasteries.

The Mongols invaded Tibet in 1641 and established the fifth Dalai Lama as the ruler of the country. From that point on, the Gelugpa school dominated religious and political life. Some monks and lamas of rival schools were unhappy with Gelugpa dominance and so moved to the neighboring territories of Sikkim and Bhutan, bringing Buddhism to those areas. Tibetan influence also spread to Mongolia, where much of the populace converted, thereby ending their legendary warlike ways. Tibet continued to thrive under Gelugpa rule in relative isolation from the rest of the world well into the modern era.

Vietnam

Although Vietnam is part of Southeast Asia, the prominent role of Buddhism in its history warrants separate treatment. The Buddhist presence in Vietnam goes back to the third century, having come into the north from China and the south from India. The northern territory was, in fact, part of the Chinese Empire during the Tang dynasty and Chinese governors promoted Buddhism as a way of pacifying the native population. North Vietnam gained its independence in the late tenth century, during which time Buddhism was proclaimed the national religion. Not surprisingly, Pure Land proved especially popular at the grassroots level throughout the Vietnam region, whereas Chan (in Vietnamese, *Thien*) came to be the dominant school in the monasteries.

Buddhism flourished in both the north and south. In northern areas it continued to enjoy royal patronage for the next few centuries, with particular favor shown to the Chan school. Chan monks were often drawn from the most learned and elite classes. In the south, Buddhism also received royal sponsorship, although there it was heavily mixed with Hinduism.

During the fifteenth century, the north invaded and conquered the southern kingdom, resulting in the increased dominance of Chinese-based forms of Buddhism throughout Vietnam, although Theravada remained strong near the southern border with Cambodia. Over time, the fate of Buddhism in Vietnam followed closely that of Buddhism in China, Korea, and Japan in that it enjoyed official patronage for some time until Neo-Confucianism became more and more influential at court. Buddhism did not disappear, however, and became the main faith of the masses. It continued to have a strong hold over the Vietnamese populace even as it was challenged by Christian missionaries when the region came under European colonial rule.

Buddhism Moves West

It is difficult to determine when Buddhism first reached the Western world, but some early texts say that Ashoka sent missionaries to the Mediterranean region during the third century B.C.E. In addition, there were some sporadic contacts between Greco-Roman civilization and India beginning with the military campaigns of Alexander the Great. Such contacts continued with the opening up of the Silk Road, a series of overlapping and intertwining caravan routes linking east and central Asia with Europe.

There are possible references to Buddhism in the writings of early Christian thinkers, and some scholars speculate that the Egyptian Desert Fathers, the inspiration for Christian monastic orders, evince Buddhist influence. However, clearly attested European contact with Buddhist lands did not occur until the late Middle Ages, when occasional merchants and travelers like Marco Polo ventured into Asia. By the late fifteenth and sixteenth century, Europe had entered the Age of Exploration, and vast areas of the globe were opened up to commercial interests. Often, missionaries, whose primary aim was to convert the "heathens" to Christianity, accompanied European explorers and merchants. The Jesuits were particularly zealous in their efforts in Asian countries, and their writings contained some of the first detailed descriptions of Buddhist belief and practice.

It was in the wake of the discoveries of the fifteenth and sixteenth centuries that European nations began to bring major portions of the globe under colonial rule, heralding the beginning of the modern world. During this era of Western dominance much of Asian civilization (including most traditional forms of Buddhism) came under serious assault and entered a period of major decline. This period of Western dominance continues to this day, although since the middle of the twentieth century, Asian countries have increasingly asserted their independence. Perhaps as a result of such political developments, Buddhists worldwide begun to respond to modernity in various creative ways, often drawing on Western ideas and influences in the process. These reform movements indicate that the Dharma may be enjoying something of a renaissance, although it is perhaps still too early to tell.

NOTES

1. This retelling of the Buddha's life is based on the early sources, especially Ashvaghosha's Buddhacarita (Life of the Buddha), composed during the first century C.E.

2. This sermon, called the Turning of the Wheel of Dharma, presents basic Buddhist teachings on the Middle Way, the Four Noble Truths, and the Eightfold Path. It remains one of the most famous discourses in all of Buddhism.

3.   Quoted in the Mahaparinibbana Sutta, trans. Maurice Walshe, in *Indian Religions: A Historical Reader of Spiritual Expression and Experience*, ed. Peter Heehs (New York: New York University Press, 2002), 115.

4.   Technically speaking, this should not be referred to as the Buddha's "death," since by attaining *nirvana*, he had gone beyond life and death. Buddhists refer to his passing as the Buddha's "final *nirvana*" (*parinirvana*).

5.   See, for instance, Joseph Campbell, *The Hero with a Thousand Faces* (Princeton, NJ: Princeton University Press, 1949).

6.   Richard H. Robinson and Willard L. Johnson, *The Buddhist Religion: A Historical Introduction*, 4th ed. (Belmont, CA: Wadsworth, 1997), 18.

7.   See Stephan Batchelor, *The Awakening of the West: The Encounter of Buddhism and Western Culture* (Berkeley, CA: Parallax Press, 1994), 25–35. Batchelor notes that story of the Indian Christian saints Barlaam and Josaphat is based tales of the Buddha's life that circulated throughout the Middle East and Europe during the Middle Ages.

8.   Buddhist tradition preserves the memory of Ananda's recitation with the formula "Thus have I heard" that prefaces every *sutra*.

9.   These two traditions eventually evolved into the Theravada and Mahayana schools, two of the main branches of Buddhism today. Theravada and Mahayana are discussed in more detail in Chapter 3.

10.   Daoism presents numerous problems for Western study, since it ranges from mystical-philosophical acceptance of the workings of nature to intense meditation practices aimed at transcending the human condition. Often scholars speak of three distinct yet interrelated strands of Daoism: philosophical, esoteric, and liturgical.

11.   Chinese intellectuals used Daoist terms to translate Buddhist texts, Buddhist meditation practices seemed remarkably Daoist, and many even conceived of Buddha as another Daoist immortal. One common story was that Laozi, the legendary author of the Daoist classic the Daode Jing, ventured west after leaving China and eventually reached India where, as the Buddha, he preached a simplified form of Daoism suited to the "barbarians".

12.   The Festival of the Hungry Ghosts spread with Buddhism to Korea and Japan. In Japan it is known as *Obon* and remains a major cultural holiday.

13.   The first Korean version of the Chinese canon, carved on more than 80,000 wooden blocks, was ordered by royal decree to protect the country from barbarian attacks. It did not succeed and was eventually destroyed by the Mongols. A second version was carved in the thirteenth century and still survives. In the early twentieth century this version formed the basis of the Japanese Taisho edition of the Chinese canon, still regarded as the most authoritative version by east Asian Buddhists.

2

TEXTS AND MAJOR TENETS

Buddhist texts and teachings are complicated. This modest overview is designed to provide a basic sense of the most important points. One Buddhist scholar has insightfully noted that "Buddhist teaching is transformation manifesting as information."[1] This is a particularly important point to bear in mind when it comes to texts, language, and their relationship to Buddhist teachings (the Dharma). Buddhists often used the metaphor of the finger pointing to the moon: it is useful to have such pointers but once we find the moon, we do not need to keep using our fingers to find it. Similarly, texts and linguistic teachings in general can lead us to the truth but should not be confused with the truth. For Buddhists, it is the truth that sets us free.

THE BUDDHIST CANON

Buddhism has a problematic relationship to language. In part this difficulty results from the fact that Buddhism involves numerous languages (Sanskrit, Pali, Chinese, Japanese, Tibetan, etc.) and uses technical terms that are difficult to translate into Western languages such as English. Ultimately, however, the problem stems from a certain philosophical understanding of language itself. In general, Buddhism has a rather anti-authoritarian view of "sacred word." Such a view seems to go back to the historical Buddha himself, who maintained that his own words (and by extension, the words *of any* teacher) should not be considered authoritative just because of their source. Rather, they should be carefully examined

Statue of Buddha giving his first sermon,
Sarnath, India. Courtesy of the American
Institute of Indian Studies.

and deemed true when borne out by a practitioner's own reasoning and experience. This pragmatic and existential view of verbal teachings has been
honored more in theory than in actual practice. Moreover, the Buddha also
hesitated initially to teach what he had discovered in his own awakening
because he realized that words would not be able to convey the full truth.
Eventually, of course, he did set out to teach, but he always claimed that
certain aspects of his teachings (such as the character the state beyond suffering, *nirvana*) were beyond the reach of language. His insistence on this
point has fostered a view among Buddhists that language works well for
simple, everyday life but cannot express the ultimate nature of reality.[2]

Nonetheless, words and texts have always been important in Buddhism.
During his lifetime, the Buddha explicitly told his followers to preach the
Dharma in any language (thus further distinguishing his movement from
the Brahmanical traditions of early Hinduism, where Sanskrit is the sacred
language). Again, this injunction demonstrates the practical, commonsense character of early Buddhism, in which the primary aim was to spread
the teachings in the most suitable manner available. Obviously, words were
needed to convey the basic truths and to guide seekers on the path. Right
before his physical death, the Buddha told his followers to take the Dharma

as their refuge, for it would serve as their teacher from then on. It was in light of this command that the monastic community began the practice of meeting regularly to recite the teachings and thus maintain their common bond. For all intents and purposes, the teachings *were* the Buddha, defining the Buddha's followers as the community entrusted with the body of knowledge and practices needed to lead to full awakening. In either oral or written form, texts convey Dharma needed to become Buddha.

Throughout the Buddha's preaching career and for centuries afterwards, all discourses existed only in oral form. Buddhist tradition maintains that the entire body of teachings was recited at the First Council held after the Buddha's passing, and from then on, this collection was memorized by all members of the community and recited at regular intervals. This oral tradition was passed down to each succeeding generation, thus establishing a clear line of transmission from the Buddha's first sermon. Although scholars agree that this traditional account is idealized, the basically *oral* nature of Buddhist texts clearly shows even in the written texts we have today. Buddhist texts tend to be in dialogical form, contain various numerical lists (e.g., the Three Marks of Existence, the Four Noble Truths, the Eightfold Path), have a great deal of repetition from passage to passage, and often begin and end with certain stock formulas. Such features are obviously meant to aid memorization, and very early in Buddhist history certain monks became essentially professional reciters specializing in specific parts of the canon. Even today traditional Buddhist study requires that texts be memorized and recited before they are explained and analyzed.

The Tripitaka

The authoritative collection of Buddhist texts is known as the Tripitaka (Three Baskets). This term comes from the tradition that the texts were written on palm leaves stitched together by threads (from which the term *sutra*, the term designating a sermon by the Buddha, comes) and then kept in three baskets. The division into "baskets" was not done haphazardly but reflected the nature and content of the texts themselves; texts of a similar nature were placed in the same "basket" while those of a different sort were relegated to other "baskets." Briefly, these are:

Vinaya (Discipline)—This "basket" includes texts on personal and social morality, precepts of monastic orders, regulations governing the entire Buddhist community *(sangha)*, and rules concerning the consequences of breaking monastic precepts. Perhaps the oldest section of the canon, Vinaya texts are of great sociological interest, as they define the *sangha* as a distinct group following a set way of life. The most important part of the Vinaya is the Code of Discipline, a body of rules covering all aspects of monastic life designed to promote the peaceful, orderly way of conduct necessary for attaining *nirvana.* It is supposed to be chanted twice a month by the community during which time anyone who has violated a rule is obliged to confess to the entire assembly. The current standard version of the Code of Discipline comprises some 227 rules for men and 311 for women.[3]

Sutras (Discourses)—These texts appear to be the closest to the Buddha's "original teachings." The *sutras* set forth the Buddha's teachings through stories, illustrations, anecdotes, and so forth. Often delivered in response to specific questions and addressed to specific audiences, the *sutras* do not present a systematic philosophy but are the best sources for the Buddha's biography. *Sutras* typically open with the stock phrase "Thus I have heard," hearkening back to the tradition that during the First Council, Ananda, the Buddha's attendant, recited all of the discourses from memory. This section of the Tripitaka is the most famous and by far the largest of the "three baskets."

Abhidharma (Further Teachings, elaborations on *sutras*)—Perhaps the most controversial of the "baskets," Abhidharma texts attempt to formally systematize the teachings found in the *sutras.* As the most philosophical of the "baskets," the Abhidharma likely developed from the necessity of explaining and defending Buddhist teachings and were gradually expanded over time. Many Abhidharma texts examine and refine the Buddha's teachings on the "factors" *(dharmas)* that make up the phenomena of our experience. Typical Abhidharma themes include the process of perception, the psychology of Buddhist practice and attainment, and various mental states that arise in certain situations.

The earliest surviving references to the Tripitaka come from inscriptions dating to the second century B.C.E. that refer to groups within the *sangha* responsible for memorizing and reciting three distinct categories of texts. Certainly several early Buddhist schools had their own Sanskrit versions of the sacred canon, but these original no longer exist except as fragments found at various central Asian sites. For the most part these early Sanskrit editions survive only in Chinese and Tibetan translations.

Today there are three complete versions of the Buddhist canon (Pali, Chinese, and Tibetan), each associated with one of the three main branches of Buddhism (Theravada, Mahayana, Vajrayana).[4] Although there are differences in content between the three versions of the canon, most of the discrepancies come down to differences in language and culture, not doctrine. Each version of the canon includes all three "baskets" of texts. We might draw a rough analogy here to the Christian Bible: although all Christians hold the Bible as sacred, various Christian denominations use distinctly different versions.[5]

Pali Canon

The Pali canon is held as authoritative by the adherents of the Theravada, who are concentrated in Sri Lanka and Southeast Asian countries such as Cambodia, Laos, and Thailand. As its name indicates, this version of the canon is written in Pali, a language derived from Sanskrit and one that many Theravadins claim was the Buddha's own language.[6] According to legend, the Pali canon was brought from northern India to Sri Lanka in the third century B.C.E. and was eventually written down some two centuries later by five hundred enlightened monks assembled at a cave temple. It is doubtful, however, that the Pali canon we now have is the same as what was originally brought to Sri Lanka.

The Pali canon is generally considered the oldest complete version of the Buddhist canon. Many Theravadins regard it as the literal "word of the Buddha," but it shows evidence of later editing by scholar-monks. Like the other two surviving versions, the Pali canon comprises a vast corpus of texts, including more than 10,000 of the Buddha's discourses. It fills more than 50 volumes in its printed Western edition. Despite its ancient origins, most of the manuscripts upon which modern editions are based date back only to the eighteenth and nineteenth centuries.

The Pali canon is far more complex than a simple assortment of texts that can be easily filed into three "baskets." For example, the Pali Vinaya falls into three major divisions and includes an early commentary that is obviously a later addition. The Sutra section is by far the largest of the three "baskets" and consists of more than 30 volumes that encompass several thousand individual texts. This "basket," in turn, is divided into five collections according to length of *sutra* and topics covered. The fifth of these subsections is a miscellaneous collection that not only includes various discourses and sermons but stories about the Buddha's previous lives, known as Jataka tales, ghost stories designed to drive home basic lessons on *karma*, and verses attributed to early monks and nuns. The third and last section of the Pali canon, the Abhidharma, consists of seven separate works, all devoted to detailed classification and analysis of *dharmas.* As the most systematic and abstract section of the canon, the Abhidharma has long been the province of only the most scholarly and devout members of the *sangha,* although Abhidharma texts are said to be so powerful that even laity who cannot comprehend them can benefit from hearing them recited.

Like the Bible or the Qur'an, the Pali canon is closed, meaning that no new texts can be added to it. Scholars generally agree that this is one indication that the Pali canon attained written form before the Chinese and Tibetan versions. Most of the texts in the Pali canon have their equivalents in the other existing versions, although there are some discrepancies. Other versions of the Vinaya, for instance, give different numbers of monastic rules, and other *sutra* collections do not include the material in the fifth section of the Pali Sutra "basket." The divergence is most obvious, however, when it comes to the Abhidharma collections, where no individual texts included are held in common.[7]

In addition to texts officially included in the Pali canon, there is also an extensive collection of commentaries written in Pali. Although they do not enjoy canonical status, these texts have helped define Theravada Buddhist tradition and, like the Tripitaka itself, are said to date back to the First Council. Like the canonical texts as well, these commentaries were transmitted orally for centuries. One of the most important Pali commentaries, the Great Chronicle, dates back to the fifth century C.E. Several of these early commentaries appear to have originally been written in Sinhalese, the indigenous language of Sri Lanka, but they were translated into Pali and reorganized by Buddhaghosha (4th–5th century C.E.), a commentator whose works remain authoritative for Theravadins to this day.

Some Well-Known Pali Texts

Several Pali *sutras* are quite famous. These include the short Turning of the Wheel of Dharma, commonly regarded as the Buddha's first sermon, delivered to the five ascetics in the deer park near Varanasi, as well as the much longer Great Passing, which relates the Buddha's final words and physical death. The Buddha often used parables to illustrate important points of his teachings, and many of these have been preserved as part of longer *sutras.* Perhaps the best known of these the parable of the poisoned arrow, in which the Buddha responds to a monk who insists that the Buddha answer his questions on the nature of the universe, the ultimate fate of the soul, and other such esoteric matters. Rather than answer directly, the Buddha compares the hostile monk with a man shot with a poisoned arrow who refuses treatment until he learns particulars about the archer who shot him, the bow used, the arrow itself, the type of poison, and similar details. This parable reflects the practical orientation of Buddhism in general and the Buddha's insistence that his followers concentrate on what was most important: suffering and how to overcome it.

One of the most famous Pali texts is the Dhammapada (Verses of the Teaching), a collection of 427 excerpts from the Buddha's sermons in verse form. Monks often use the Dhammapada when teaching the laity, and novices memorize all of it early in their careers. The Dhammapada was one of the first complete Buddhist texts translated into Western languages and has been well known in Europe and North America since the nineteenth century.

The Pali canon includes as part of the Sutras "basket" a compilation of more than five hundred Jataka tales, detailing the Buddha's various previous lives in many different forms (king, nobleman, deer, bird, monkey, tree-spirit, etc.). The Jatakas not only reinforce the singular character of the Buddha-to-be, they also vividly depict the importance of basic Buddhist teachings concerning morality and *karma*, and thus are frequently used by monks when instructing the laity. Scenes for the Jataka tales are often depicted in Buddhist temple paintings and statues, much as Biblical stories are depicted in stained-glass windows in Christian churches.

Two other texts in the Pali canon have also gained some renown, the Songs of the Elder Monks and Songs of the Elder Nuns. These are verses attributed to some three hundred of the early monks and nuns, and were most likely written down sometime in the third century B.C.E. Although some scholars doubt these works are entirely factual, they have an immediacy typically found in first-person accounts and, as such, give us an important insider's view on the early *sangha*.

Yet another well-known Pali text is the Questions of King Milinda, a noncanonical text purporting to be a record of a conversation between two historical persons, a monk named Nagasena and King Milinda (Menander, ~155 B.C.E.). Milinda was a Bactrian Greek king who ruled over a territory covering what is now Afghanistan down through Pakistan and into central India. This region had been conquered by Alexander the Great in 327 B.C.E. and became a major center of borrowing between Hellenistic and Indian cultures. According to tradition, Milinda was converted to Buddhism through his conversation with Nagasena. The Questions of King Milinda is one of most accessible works of Theravada in prose and remains perhaps the clearest introduction to major points of Buddhist teaching.

Chinese Canon

The Chinese canon resembles the Pali version in many respects, although there are some important differences. The most obvious of these differences is linguistic. Because it is written in classical Chinese, the Chinese Buddhist canon is read and studied in societies where Chinese cultural influence has been strong: Japan, Korea, Vietnam, and other regions of East Asia. In fact, Buddhism was adopted in many of these areas because it was seen as the primary vehicle of Chinese civilization.

The title of the Chinese canon is Great Storehouse of Scripture (Dazangjing) and seems to derive from terms used to refer to imperial libraries. More importantly, whereas the Pali canon preserves the Theravada understanding of the Dharma, the Great Storehouse of Scripture preserves a Mahayana understanding and includes various texts that present a broader, more transcendental version of Buddhist teachings. Furthermore, unlike the Pali Canon, the Great Storehouse of Scripture is an *open* canon, meaning that it can be added to. Nonetheless, although this distinction is important (as it indicates that from a Mahayana perspective the Dharma is not strictly confined to a finalized set of writings), the open nature of the Chinese canon (and Tibetan canon for that matter) is more theoretical rather than actual.

The Chinese canon is considerably younger than the Pali canon, although written versions of Chinese Buddhist texts were in existence from at least the second century C.E.[8] Certainly, Chinese scholar-monks were cataloguing handwritten versions of the Chinese Buddhist canon as early as 515 C.E., and it seems clear that these early versions of the canon were considerably shorter than the ones we have now. The first printed edition of the Chinese canon was produced in Sichuan in 972–83 C.E. and consisted of 1,076 texts in 480 bound volumes.

The standard modern version of the Chinese canon is the Taisho Shinshu Daizokyo ("Taisho" for short), which was compiled by a team of Japanese scholars during the Taisho period (1912–25). It was published in 1924–29 and includes 2,184 texts gathered in 55 volumes. In addition, there is a supplement of 45 volumes. The contents include those found in the Pali canon (Vinaya, Sutras, Abhidharma). However, the Taisho also contains numerous commentaries, treatises, and histories—material generally regarded as extracanonical in Theravada tradition. Furthermore, the Taisho edition (and earlier Chinese versions on which it is based) is arranged very differently from the Pali canon. Volume 54 of the Taisho even includes eight texts on non-Buddhist teachings.[9]

Some Well-Known Chinese Buddhist Texts

The Chinese canon is so vast that it would be impossible to choose a truly representative sample of texts for discussion. In addition, it includes several versions of the same texts that were translated into Chinese at different times by different groups of monks. Nonetheless, a brief look at a select number of texts helps provide a sense of the Chinese canon's range and scope.

The first Mahayana texts are the Perfection of Wisdom (Prajnaparamita) *sutras.* As a rule, the Perfection of Wisdom texts are quite lengthy (running anywhere from 8,000 to 100,000 lines), although later ones are often considerably shorter. Like other *sutras,* the Perfection of Wisdom texts purport to be dialogues between the historical Buddha and his various disciples. They are filled with soaring rhetoric, especially about the powers and practices of the "wisdom beings," or *bodhisattvas* (those who are actively seeking to become enlightened and are replete with paradoxical language. Thus, for instance, in one *sutra* the Buddha speaks of an aspiring *bodhisattva:*

> He has gone beyond all that is worldly, yet he has not
> moved out of the world;
> In the world he pursues his course for the world's weal,
> unstained by worldly taints.[10]

Perfection of Wisdom texts also make extensive use of negation, often seeming to deny all statements concerning reality, including the basic teachings of early Buddhism. Why such extreme rhetoric? The basic idea behind such denial seems to be to unsettle the intellect and to provoke confusion and skepticism, thus making it practically impossible to become attached to any established doctrine. From a Buddhist standpoint, it is very easy to get attached to certain teachings (even Buddhist ones) and accept them as unquestioned dogma. Merely accepting teachings, though, is almost always a mistake; at best it evinces a partial understanding of the Dharma, a "lower wisdom." Such partial understanding, however, is not True Wisdom *(prajna),* the transcendent realization of Emptiness *(shunyata),* the true nature of reality, that a Buddha has attained. It is this "highest wisdom" that the Perfection of Wisdom texts aim at.

Some of the most well-known Perfection of Wisdom texts are the Diamond Sutra and the Heart Sutra. The Diamond Sutra enjoins one to maintain a nondualistic attitude in all activities, including the practice and cultivation of key virtues such as generosity, and it has been particularly valued in the Chan/Zen schools of Buddhism.[11] The brief Heart Sutra amounts to a distillation of *prajna* teachings (the "heart" of Buddhist wisdom). It is extremely popular in East Asia and Tibet (perhaps being the single most-recited text in the entire world aside from the Qur'an of Islam) and contains one of the most famous lines in all of Asia: "Form is emptiness, Emptiness is form."[12]

Another famous *sutra* that is in the *prajna* vein (while also including most major aspects of Buddhist teachings) is the Vimalakirti Nirdesha Sutra (Sutra Expounded by Vimalakirti). The Vimalakirti, although Mahayana in orientation, encompasses early Buddhism, instructs its audience in meditation techniques, and provides basic guidance for the laity. Many passages in the Vimalakirti also demonstrate typical Buddhist dialectics, and even contain hints of Tantric practices. Although Shakyamuni, the historical Buddha, and various other Buddhas appear in this *sutra*, most of the teachings come from the mouth of the title character, Vimalakirti, a wily Buddhist layman whose knowledge of the Dharma and miraculous powers dwarf those of the Buddha's monk disciples. The Vimalakirti was especially influential in China and Japan, where the charismatic layman seemed to exemplify the wise, scholarly ideal so prized by Confucian scholar-officials yet also demonstrated the humor so characteristic of Daoist sages.

However, perhaps the single most influential Buddhist text in all of East Asia is the Lotus Sutra. The Lotus Sutra claims to have been preached by Shakyamuni Buddha at Vulture Peak, one of India's holiest mountains, yet from the opening scene, the historical figure reveals his transcendent, eternal nature that manifests continually at all times in all worlds. According to the Lotus Sutra, in reality there are myriad Buddhas, each preaching the same essential Truth while appearing in specific human forms such as Siddhartha Gautama. Apparent differences in Buddhist teachings are really the result of certain manifestations of Buddha using "skillful means" to pitch their message in ways best suited to their audience. The Lotus Sutra illustrates this principle of "skillful means" in a famous parable in which a father saves his children from a burning house. Knowing that his children have different likes, the father coaxes them all out of the house with the promise of goat carts, deer carts, or bullock carts. Enticed by the offer of such fine toys, the children rush out, only to find that they all receive carts more wondrous than they could have imagined. So, too, although there seem to be different ways ("vehicles") within Buddhism, in fact the different ways are all the One Buddha Way (vehicle). Moreover, by holding out this One True Way, the Lotus Sutra also proclaims the universal nature of Buddhahood, offering the possibility that all sentient beings will attain Highest Perfect Enlightenment. Perhaps more than any other single Buddhist text, the Lotus Sutra has been a focus of popular veneration in East Asia, with the Japanese Nichiren sect being the most extreme example.

There are also several well-known treatises in the Chinese canon that have been the subject of much study over the centuries. Of these, perhaps the most notable is the Treatise on the Awakening of Faith in the Mahayana, most often known in English as the Awakening of Faith. Attributed to Ashvaghosa (second century C.E.), a monk who also wrote a famous biography of the Buddha, this treatise is a systematic outline of Mahayana thought and has played a major role in the development of East Asian Buddhist schools.[13] An excellent example of the traditional question and answer style of Buddhist teaching, the Awakening of Faith speaks of the universal Buddha-nature of all beings, the "One Mind" that is the source of all the universe. Although this Mind is One, it has two aspects:

1. Pure Suchness (what is actually there), *nirvana*, the Dharma itself; and
2. the world of suffering, defilement and experience, or *samsara*.

From an unenlightened perspective, Suchness and *samsara* appear to be radically different, but in reality they are the same except that they are perceived differently. The text explains their relationship through a famous analogy to the relation between water (Pure Suchness) and waves (*samsara).*

Tibetan Canon

The Tibetan Buddhist canon, like the Pali and Chinese canons, is a massive collection of texts brought primarily from India and translated over the course of several centuries. The earliest edition was compiled in the fourteenth century by Buton, author of the first definitive history of Buddhism. Buton divided the canon into two parts: the Kanjur (Translation of the Word of the Buddha) and the Tenjur (Translation of Treatises). The earliest printed version of the Kanjur was made in 1411 in Beijing, while the first complete printings of the entire Tibetan canon (Kanjur and Tenjur together) were done in Narthang in 1742.

The Kanjur contains the words of Shakyamuni as well as other Buddhas. In the standard modern version, the Kanjur numbers 98 volumes containing more than 600 individual texts. It is divided into four basic parts: Vinaya, Perfection of Wisdom Sutras, other Sutra texts, as well as 22 volumes of Tantras. The Tenjur is more vast and eclectic in nature. In its most recent edition the Tenjur comes to 224 volumes and contains more than 3,600 texts. It includes a host of commentaries as well as hymns, dramas, and technical treatises on such diverse subjects as logic, grammar, medicine, astrology, and chemistry. This tremendous breadth of subject matter reflects the curricula taught in Tibet's great Buddhist universities during the time when the Tibetans were compiling their canon. Beyond these collections there is an enormous amount of extracanonical Tibetan material, much of which has been very influential in Tibetan history. Among these extracanonical works are groups of texts that Buton and his collaborators left out, such as the Tantras of the Nyingma school ("Ancient School," a Tibetan lineage relying heavily on older Tantric texts and practices). In the fifteenth century a Nyingma scholar remedied this situation by collecting all of this texts and publishing them under the title One Hundred Thousand Nyingma Tantras.

Some Well-Known Tibetan Buddhist Texts

Since the Tibetan canon is essentially Mahayana in orientation, it includes most of the texts in the Chinese canon. For example, the Heart Sutra, the Diamond Sutra, and the Vimalakirti all exist in Tibetan as well as Chinese. Most annotated English translations of these texts make use of both Chinese and Tibetan versions, as well as surviving Sanskrit remnants and commentaries. This great overlap in content between the Chinese and Tibetan canons is only to be expected, since China and Tibet have had a long history of interaction. Nonetheless, there are parts of the Tibetan canon that distinguish it from the Chinese and Pali versions.

The Tantras warrant special attention. Often regarded as the secret teachings of the Buddha, the Tantras primarily refer to sacred writings most likely composed more than a thousand years after the historical Buddha's passing. These texts mark no real philosophical development beyond Mahayana but have a distinct practical and ritual focus. The term *tantra* itself is Sanskrit for "fabric/woven," and refers to powerful Hindu and Buddhist practices that weave together body, speech, and mind in order to transcend the world of *samsara*. These practices combine meditations and rituals, and aim at enabling the practitioner to attain Buddhahood as quickly as possible. A decidedly esoteric (secret) body of knowledge, the Tantras are written in an intentionally oblique style ("twilight language") that requires extensive oral explanation by a master. As such, true understanding of the Tantras is open only to those who have undergone special initiations. Most Tantras are preserved in Tibetan and to this day, Tantric Buddhism (technically known as Vajrayana) is the most common form in the Tibetan region.[14]

The Tantras themselves outline complex ritual procedures involving lengthy recitations, devotions to and visualizations of particularly deities, and yogic meditation. These practices draw on ancient Indian theories in which a yogi learns to manipulate physical and mental energies in order to transform the body, climaxing in a blissful state of total union with Pure Mind. The Tantras, thus, are spiritual instruction manuals that, because of their power, have been closely guarded. Most scholars believe that the Tantras found in the Tibetan canon reflect the ongoing influence of Bon, the indigenous pre-Buddhist religion of the Tibetan people.

The most famous Tibetan Buddhist text does not appear in either the Chinese or Pali versions of the canon. In fact, it is a noncanonical text drawn from Nyingma traditions and teachings, and is most commonly known in the West as The Tibetan Book of the Dead. The Tibetan title of this work (Bardo Thol Dro) translates as "Liberation through Hearing in the *Bardo*" and refers to the intermediate state *(bardo)* between death and rebirth, said to last 49 days. During this time, a deceased being is said to encounter terrifying and peaceful images based upon his own *karma.* It is the duty of the living to recite the Bardo Thol Dro into the ear of the dead or dying person in order to guide them through the *bardo* by reminding them that the visions are not real but are rather manifestations of the deceased's mind. An important, ritually powerful text in the best sense of Tantra, the Bardo Thol Dro is recited to the deceased for the entire 49-day *bardo* period. Its primary aim is to help the deceased understand the workings of *karma* and so attain a better rebirth or even, perhaps, liberation from the cycle of death and rebirth. Contemporary scholars have also noted that the Bardo Thol Dro comforts the bereaved by providing a channel for their grief while educating and preparing them for their own death.

BUDDHIST TEACHINGS

The term *Buddha,* as noted in the previous chapter, means "awake." According to Buddhist tradition, Siddhartha "woke up" to the true nature of reality and so became Buddha. The implication here, of course, is that the rest of us are asleep. The state of attaining such an awakening is known as *nirvana* or sometimes "enlightenment," and refers to a state of being beyond the cycle of life and death. The historical Buddha is sometimes called "Shakyamuni Buddha" in honor of his clan of origin, but most Buddhists agree that he is not the only Buddha. Rather, Buddhists hold that Siddhartha merely realized the eternal truths that have always been present and had been realized before by others. In a sense, the term *Buddha* names the Truth that Siddhartha Gautama embodied and sought to pass along to his followers. Most systems of Buddhist thought hold that we *all* can follow his example, that all sentient beings can manifest or become Buddha. Such ideas are particularly stressed in later schools of Buddhism.

As a self-conscious tradition, Buddhism arose during the sixth century B.C.E. alongside other ascetic movements such as Jainism. This was also the time when the Indian philosophical texts known as the Upanishads were composed. Each of these ascetic movements accepted the basic Indian view of the universe as a beginningless cycle of creation, destruction, and rebirth in which beings are continuously being recycled through different lives. This view of the cosmos was laid out in the Vedas, the oldest and most sacred Hindu texts, and most Indian traditions have accepted it as well. However, Buddhism and the other ascetic movements of the time were united in the view that this cosmic cycle of death and rebirth is overwhelmingly marked by disruption and pain (suffering). The only way to overcome this suffering was to attain true knowledge, which would enable one to free oneself from the wheel of suffering. Indeed, all of these ancient ascetic movements lay out paths by which one moves skillfully toward liberation through a disciplined life of strict ethics, meditation, and spiritual cultivation.

The original Dharma has long been the subject of debate. As noted, the Buddha himself taught orally on specific topics, pitching his message to the level of his audience. Only later were his teachings written down. Although there are some discrepancies between different texts, we can be fairly sure of some things. The Buddha's teachings were essentially pragmatic and experiential, not based on idle speculation. He repeatedly stressed that his followers should test out his teachings rather than accept them on his authority. For the Buddha, if people practice his teachings, they will learn firsthand what reality is, come to terms with it, and thus will free themselves from suffering. In the simplest terms, the Buddha viewed most people as living out of a fundamental ignorance of the nature of reality. Moreover, he saw that people generally acted in self-destructive ways, being motivated by hatred, delusion, and greed. These "three poisons" are basic manifestations of the fundamental ignorance underlying human life, and are perhaps similar to the way the "seven deadly sins" in Christianity are prominent manifestations of the fundamentally sinful nature of humanity.[15] According to the Buddha, when we "wake up" (attain *nirvana*), we will understand existence and, as a result, *not* act in so destructive a manner. In fact, the Buddha seems to have taught that upon awakening one will spontaneously act out of compassion. This great spiritual goal of Buddhism comes from a disciplined life of good conduct and intention, characterized by mindful attention to experience in all its forms.[16]

Before examining the most important Buddhist teachings, it is important to emphasize how very practical in nature they originally were. The teachings may seem very abstract when first studied, but they come from specific, concrete situations—situations we *all* can relate to, and that express the Buddha's own wisdom and compassion. One of the best illustrations of this practical, existential character of Buddhist teachings can be found in the story of Kisa Gotami, a poor young wife whose only son dies while still a child.[17] Blinded by grief, she clings to his body and begs everyone she meets to give her medicine for her son. Finally, a wise man directs her to the Buddha. When she comes into his presence, she repeats her plea. Understanding her situation at a glance, the Buddha assigns her a task before he gives her the medicine: she is to make the rounds throughout a nearby city, asking for mustard seeds from any house where no one has died. Buoyed by hope, she rushes to the city and begins knocking on doors. Unfortunately, at each house she finds the same thing: all have had someone in the household die. At this point she realizes the Buddha's lesson in her task, and leaves the city. Coming to the burning ground, she says to her dead boy, "Dear little son, I thought that you alone had been overtaken by this thing which men call death. But you are not the only one death has overtaken. This is a law common to all mankind."[18] She then lays his body down where it will be properly taken care of and returns to the Buddha, who accepts her into his order.

Core Teachings

Buddhist teachings are interrelated and overlapping, making it difficult to discuss them one by one. Perhaps the easiest way is to follow traditional Buddhist pedagogy and proceed in a numerical fashion. Thus, we will begin with the Three Marks of Existence, continue with the Four Noble Truths and the Eightfold Path, and conclude with an overview of Dependent Origination, which is typically laid out in 12 interrelated steps. Before beginning, however, it is also important to emphasize that Buddhist teachings have never been merely intellectual. One needs to grasp them intellectually, of course, but this is only part of full comprehension. The teachings themselves are, in fact, related to meditation exercises, and perhaps can only be understood in the context of a life founded upon meditation practice. For Buddhists, authentic religious and philosophical training requires both study and meditation, since the aim of Buddhism is not just to know the true nature of reality but to integrate this knowledge into one's life so as to become free from suffering.[19]

The Three Marks of Existence

In an early discourse on the nature of existence, the Buddha tells his disciples, "Whether Buddhas arise, O monks, or whether Buddhas do not arise, it remains a fact that ... all [the world's] constituents are [1] transitory ... that all its constituents are [2] dissatisfactory ... that all its constituents are [3] lacking a permanent self."[20] In this passage, the Buddha describes *samsara* as "marked" by three characteristics: impermanence, suffering, and "no-self." These Three Marks of Existence are a good way to get an idea of the basic Buddhist worldview.

1. **Impermanence *(anitya)***
   The most basic Buddhist insight is that all of reality is constantly changing. From moment to moment, nothing remains stable or permanent. Our bodies, thoughts, feelings, and all the things of the world are all in an ongoing process of change. For Buddhists (and most Indian thinkers), since all things are always changing, no thing we ever encounter is truly real (to be real is to be permanent, unchanging). What we normally consider to be stable "things" are, in fact, just causally related processes moving through time. We can compare this notion to a viewing a motion picture—when the film runs through a projector we perceive what appear to be images of people and things moving about and interacting with each other. In reality, however, the images are the result of light being projected through the film's various "stills" that run through the projector in rapid succession.

   For Buddhists, this constant process of change *is* reality. If we can adjust to this state of affairs, we can live well and *not* suffer. The problem is, however, that we do not see how impermanent things really are. In a sense we even refuse to see it, much as those whom psychologists diagnose as neurotic refuse to accept life as it actually is. In truth, from a Buddhist perspective most people are habituated by their societies to *not* see impermanence. The Buddhist path, by contrast, aims at training us to see the basic impermanent nature of reality, to realize it fully, and integrate this realization into our lives. Our basic notions of "things" as real and abiding are projected fictions, the result of our deluded understanding.

This basic Buddhist teaching on the thoroughly impermanent nature of reality is often hard to grasp for those not raised within a Buddhist monastic environment. The difficulty is even greater for people raised in a culture premised on notions of permanent (or lasting) substances, a typically Western metaphysical view that goes back to very early stages of Greek philosophy. In truth, there really is no "substance" in Buddhism. Ironically, however, the Buddhist teaching of impermanence has intriguing parallels with the views of contemporary physics, in which reality ultimately is comprised of various configurations of energy.

2. Suffering *(duhkha)*

The mark of impermanence leads directly to the "second mark" of existence— suffering. "Suffering" is an unfortunate but common translation of the Sanskrit term *duhkha* and has, perhaps, more than anything else given rise to the misconception of Buddhism as "pessimistic." In actuality, Buddhism is no more pessimistic than any other world religion; a better translation of *duhkha* might be "dissatisfactoriness" or even "frustrating."[21] Because things are impermanent, always changing, they are necessarily going to produce emotional and psychological reactions from people and other beings.

The Buddha outlined three senses in which ordinary life is marked by suffering, all of which are due to impermanence. First, life is marked by suffering in the most obvious, physical sense. The constant changes of our physical environment and our own bodies inevitably result in pain and discomfort. Early Buddhist texts are replete with passages describing giving birth, getting sick, growing old, and dying as examples of the fundamentally painful nature of human life. No one escapes from these, as even casual reflection shows. Second, life is marked by suffering in that happiness and enjoyment, even when attained, are fleeting and do not last. We all experience happiness at various times, but inevitably it does not last, leaving us with a sense of sadness and loss. Third, life is marked by suffering because of the very nature of the human mind. Our minds naturally respond to life's pains and disappointments by giving rise to certain unwholesome and painful states, such as hatred, fear, greed, and anger. Thus, in the Buddhist analysis, human existence in marked by suffering.

One often overlooked dimension of the Buddha's teaching on suffering is that it applies on both the individual and social level. The inevitable pain and dissatisfaction experienced by individuals tends to produce unwholesome states of mind (hatred, greed, envy, etc.) that individuals, in turn, often act upon. Thus, individual suffering leads to acts that inflict suffering on others. Moreover, unwholesome states of mind and the actions to which they give rise contribute to political and social institutions and practices that further spread suffering; war, poverty, and political repression are all examples of suffering on the social level.

3. **"No-self"** *(anatman)*

The final of the Three Marks of Existence and one of the hallmarks of Buddhist doctrine is the teaching of "no-self," a feature that follows directly from impermanence and suffering. The Sanskrit term here, *anatman* (literally "no *atman*"), is sometimes rendered "no soul," although this translation does not capture the truly radical nature of the Buddha's teaching. Nowhere does Buddhism show more clearly how far it departs from mainstream Hinduism than with the teaching of "no-self." Many Brahmanical thinkers of the Buddha's time agreed with the teachings of impermanence and suffering but maintained lasting happiness could be found within the depths of one's own being. Here, at the very core beneath the superficial layers of "self" (material body, life force, consciousness, rationality), the sages of the Upanishads taught that one can find a permanent, unchanging being of limitless bliss and knowledge. From a Buddhist standpoint, however, the quest to find this *atman* that is misguided, even futile. According to the Buddha, when you examine experience, you never actually find an *atman.* Furthermore, the *atman* is an illogical idea that serves no real purpose. Certainly we all have a notion of a "self" based upon our experience but when we pay attention, we see that this "self" is constantly changing and is marked by suffering. Thus it cannot be an *atman.* The notion of a permanent "self," like an *atman,* is really a projected fiction, not an abiding "thing." Indeed, it is much like our ideas of other permanent "things."

There are lots of analogies by which Buddhist teachers seek to convey this essential yet deeply perplexing teaching of "no-self." One of the best examples is in the Questions to King Milinda, where the monk Nagasena explains the notion of "self" by way of analogy to a chariot. The chariot "exists," but when we look closely we see that it is really just a collection of parts (wheels, axle, platform, etc.) to which we apply the label *chariot.* Personal identity through time here is not supplied by a permanent material or metaphysical substance but rather through causal connections and, of course, the label conventionally applied to the various pieces. Similarly, the Buddha elsewhere suggests that when it comes to a human being, the body (and name) supplies a pragmatic unity through life.[22]

Of course, in light of the "no-self" teaching, Buddhists have had to redefine rebirth. Rebirth for Buddhists is not due to a "reincarnating soul" but is rather a continuous, moment-by-moment process of creation and destruction, death and rebirth. A useful analogy is a candle flame: although it may at first appear to be a substantial "thing," in reality the flame is a chemical process that changes moment to moment. The flame can also be passed from one candlewick to another, but there is no "thing" being passed, and the flame on the second wick, although in some sense connected to the first, is not the same.

The "no-self" teaching, like other Buddhist teachings, is very much tied to meditation practices. Much Buddhist meditation involves paying careful attention to experience in order to see what it actually there. In large part this comes down to systematically deconstructing assumptions we have concerning a "self" that exists apart from experience. One well-known teaching that assists such analysis involves breaking experience down into five categories (*skandhas*, meaning "aggregates" or "heaps") of processes: material forces, raw sensations, sensory perceptions, habitual tendencies and impulses, and conscious awareness. From a basic Buddhist perspective a "person" just is a collection of these Five Aggregates, nothing else. Moreover, the Five Aggregates are constantly changing mental and physical processes, and so none of them can be considered a permanent "self" either.

The Buddha did, however, teach that the last aggregate, conscious awareness, has particular importance because, due to the cumulative force of *karma*, this conscious awareness continues for some time after death until it gives rise to a new conscious life. This means that the negative and positive qualities of consciousness follow the individual into his or her next life. Note however, that even this view of karmic conditioning does not entail a permanent "soul" taking on a new body.

The Four Noble Truths

The Buddha himself laid out the Four Noble Truths in his very first sermon. They rank among the most famous of Buddhist teachings and can be considered the foundation of Buddhist practice. Ultimately, the Four Noble Truths come down to a way of formulating the Buddha's basic insights into the Three Marks of Existence (impermanence, suffering, no-self) and applying them directly to human life. These truths are:

1. **Existence is suffering.** The First Truth merely restates the second of the Three Marks of Existence. Ordinary human life is suffering *(duhkha)* in the sense that to varying degrees it is full of pain, disappointment, and unhappiness. Certainly there are the gross sufferings of disease and death, but there are also the more subtle sufferings and irritations of everyday life. Even joys

and good times end, bringing about some degree of suffering. For the Buddha, no matter how hard we try, we always end up being frustrated, anxious, and insecure.

2. **Suffering is caused by desire.** The Second Truth states that the basic unsatisfactory nature of human life is due to our incessant desire (literally, "craving" or "thirst") to acquire things. This is an insatiable drive for material possessions or intellectual and emotional gratification provoked by our clinging to things in ignorance of their essentially impermanent, unsatisfactory, and insubstantial natures. According to the Buddha, most people delude themselves that possessions, attachments, and relationships are the sources of a secure and stable life when in fact they simply cause more suffering.

3. **Suffering can be overcome.** The Third Truth makes the fundamentally positive nature of Buddhist teachings clear—we do not have to suffer. We are not necessarily trapped by our desires and attachments, and we can in fact find true peace. To reach such tranquility, we need only eliminate desire and selfish craving. If we do this, we will be free from suffering.

4. **The way to overcome suffering is by following the Eightfold Path.** The Fourth Truth concerns the path that leads to freedom from suffering. This is sometimes known as the Middle Way between the extremes of self-indulgence and self-denial, a way of life marked by calm detachment and wisdom.

The Four Noble Truths are a very simple summary of how Buddhist teachings have direct bearing on human life. In many respects they resemble a doctor's prescription for the ills of life: like a doctor, the Buddha assesses the illness and its symptoms (suffering), finds the root cause (desire), proclaims that it can be cured (suffering can be overcome), and outlines a regimen of treatment (the Eightfold Path).

The Eightfold Path

The Eightfold Path is the final of the Four Noble Truths outlined above. It is basically a series of "factors" or steps laying out how one should live in a Buddhist fashion. This is a way of living in accordance with the Buddha's teachings stressing wisdom and compassion. As such, the Eightfold Path constitutes a total guide to life, thereby underscoring the fact that Buddhism is not so much a matter of what you know as *what you do.* Briefly, these eight steps are:

1. **Right understanding.** Correctly perceiving and having faith in the Four Noble Truths, the Buddha's teachings on *karma* and rebirth, and so forth.

2. **Right intention**. Sincerely aspiring to live according to Buddhist teachings. For monks and nuns this means renouncing worldly life and accepting the "homeless" lifestyle.

3. **Right speech**. Taking great care that one's words are marked by compassion and consideration for others. Among other things, this means abstaining from lies, slander, abuse, and gossip.

4. **Right action**. Living an upright and moral life. At the very least this means abstaining from killing, stealing, lying, adultery, and using intoxicants.

5. **Right livelihood**. Being very careful not to engage in occupations that cause harm or that may be morally questionable. These typically include professions based on trickery and greed, or that involve trading in weapons, living beings, intoxicants, and so forth.

6. **Right effort**. Conscientiously striving to seek after and promote what is good while avoiding and even discouraging evil.

7. **Right mindfulness**. Learning to discipline and control one's mind. By controlling one's mind, one becomes finely attuned to mental and physical phenomena, and remains calm even in the midst of joy, sorrow, or fear.

8. **Right concentration**. The culmination of meditative training. Through rigorous training, one gradually learns how to gather one's attention on a specific object, achieving deep levels of calm, focused awareness.

Although it is customary to enumerate the eight individual "steps" sequentially, they do not necessarily follow one another in numerical order. Rather, each step is related to and supports the others, in much the same way that spokes on wheel all join together at the hub, thus providing the support for the wheel itself. This way of understanding the Eightfold Path is graphically illustrated by the image of the Wheel of Dharma that the Buddha began spinning when he preached his first sermon.

Sometimes Buddhists explain the Eightfold Path in an abbreviated fashion, as the Three Trainings: wisdom, moral conduct, and concentration. In this scheme, wisdom embraces the first two steps (right understanding and intention), moral conduct covers steps three through five (right speech, action, and livelihood), while concentration includes steps six through eight (right effort, mindfulness, and concentration). Buddhists also view each of the steps as having both an ordinary and an ultimate level.

To tread the Buddhist path is to carefully follow these eight steps in the hope that they will lead one to *nirvana*. Advancing along the path is not usually understood as linear but may rather be described as more of a spiraling progression. That is, one moves along the path by progressively getting deeper and deeper into each of the stages, thereby gaining more and more skill in living a wholesome Buddhist life. In so doing, one also acquires more and more wisdom, and so becomes more and more compassionate toward others. Attaining *nirvana,* thus, is not about reaching a final resting place but perfecting one's Buddhist practice.

Dependent Origination

Although many Buddhists would not even attempt to describe what the Buddha actually realized when he sat under the "tree of enlightenment" (*bodhi* tree), it seems clear that it amounted to a radically new vision of reality. The understanding that he awoke to required him to coin a new term to convey the contents of his enlightened perspective: Dependent Origination *(pratitya-samutpada).* The notion of Dependent Origination is the closest thing there is to an absolute metaphysical truth in Buddhism. Indeed, some scholars say that the history of Buddhism is a history of reinterpretations of Dependent Origination. So important is this teaching that in an early text the Buddha says, "Whoever sees Dependent Origination see Dharma, whoever sees Dharma sees Dependent Origination."[23]

Dependent Origination actually is based on a simple insight that is related to the teachings of impermanence, suffering, and "no-self." Essentially, Dependent Origination is the teaching by which the Buddha described the complete interdependence (and impermanence) of all things in our experience. All phenomena we encounter are conditioned by various factors (physical and mental) and these, in turn, are conditioned by other factors, and so on. The Buddha's vision of reality, thus, is of an ongoing, ever-changing web of relationships through which all things come into existence, abide, decay, and are destroyed. Moreover, by paying close attention we can perceive the thoroughly interdependent nature of reality both in the immediate present and as it occurs over time.

In its most general formulation, Dependent Origination can be summed up in the following statement: "this arising, that arises; this not arising, that does not arise." Nothing stands alone; all are interrelated and connected. Dependent Origination is a general principle of conditionality that describes the nature of all things, but the Buddha's primary focus was on how the teaching applies to the human condition. To this end, he taught a specific version of Dependent Origination that explains how certain basic constituents of experience work together to give rise to suffering, and how these same constituents can be modified to reduce and even end suffering.

This specific version of Dependent Origination as a description of human life is most commonly laid out in a series of 12 stages, each of which conditions the one following it:

1. **Ignorance:** not knowing the Four Noble Truths and their implications concerning the basic dissatisfactory nature of human life.
2. **Mental formations:** habitual tendencies and impulses; negative and unwholesome mental states or attitudes (e.g., greed, rage) that are conditioned by ignorance.
3. **Consciousness:** the state of mind that is conditioned by one's habitual tendencies and impulses. For example, a disposition toward ill tends to result in one being aware only of others' faults as opposed to their positive qualities.
4. **Mind-and-body:** literally "name and form," this link refers to the fact that the status of one's physical and mental being is conditioned by consciousness.
5. **Senses:** the orientation of one's senses to the surrounding world. Such basic sensory orientation is conditioned by the state of one's mind-and-body.
6. **Contact:** the sensory connection one has with the world, made possible by the fact that one has a particular sensory orientation.
7. **Sensation:** the raw feelings and emotions (pleasant, unpleasant, neutral) that arise from sensory contact with the surrounding world.
8. **Craving:** the self-centered "thirst" (the drive described in the Third Noble Truth) to prolong a pleasurable sensation or get rid of an unpleasant one.
9. **Attachment:** the active clinging to the things of this world and the pleasures they evoke or the aversion to unpleasant feelings these things evoke. In many respects, attachment is the natural result of intense cravings conditioned by the orientations and unwholesome mental states that arise as a result of our basic ignorance of the Four Noble Truths.
10. **Becoming:** the manner in which one's personality forms throughout life, primarily due to one's attachments. Such attachments condition the continuation of an existence founded on ignorance, unwholesome mental states, self-centered orientations, and cravings.
11. **Birth:** how one is reborn after death or, more importantly, the way one "gives birth" to one's identity through the actions and attitudes that comprise one's becoming.
12. **Old age and death:** the culmination of life. Really this link refers to the whole mass of suffering that comes from being born of a process that, in turn arises from attachments that are ultimately founded on ignorance.

Although each of the stages is said to depend upon the previous one, in a real sense they mutually condition each other, and can be analyzed both forward and backward. In an early *sutra* the Buddha explains:

> On ignorance depends mental formation; on mental formations depends consciousness; on consciousness depends mind-and-body; on mind-and-body depends senses; on senses depends contact; on contact depends sensation; on sensation depends craving; on craving depends attachment; on attachment depends becoming; on becoming depends birth; on birth depends old age and death, sorrow, lamentation, misery, grief and despair. Thus does the entire mass of *duhkha* arise.[24]

The 12 stages of Dependent Origination are often diagramed in a circular pattern reminiscent of a clock, with each stage corresponding to an hour, or a 12-spoked wheel, the Wheel of Becoming. The Wheel of Becoming is often depicted as within the jaws of Mara, the demon who tempted Siddhartha when he sat beneath the *bodhi* tree.

Although the twelve stages culminate in the arising of suffering, this teaching of Dependent Origination as it applies to human life is not pessimistic. In fact, the Buddha taught that attaining *nirvana* could break the complex chain of circumstances leading to the arising of suffering. As the Buddha says,

> On the complete fading away and cessation of ignorance ceases mental formations; on the cessation of mental formations ceases consciousness; on the cessation of consciousness ceases mind-and-body; on the cessation of mind-and-body ceases senses; on the cessation of senses ceases contact; on the cessation of contact ceases sensation; on the cessation of sensation ceases craving; on the cessation of craving ceases attachment; on the cessation of attachment ceases becoming; on the cessation of becoming ceases birth; on the cessation of birth ceases old age and death, sorrow, lamentation, misery, grief and despair. Thus does the entire mass of *duhkha* cease.[25]

It may at first appear from this passage that the Buddha is advocating the extinction of human life itself but he actually is describing the process by which suffering, one of the basic "marks" of ordinary (unenlightened) human life, is overcome. In other words, the process of Dependent Origination can also be understood as something like "Dependent Cessation," in which one gradually eliminates the negative conditions leading to suffering and so attains *nirvana*.

With the rise of the Mahayana movement at the beginning of the common era, Dependent Origination underwent a reinterpretation. The earliest Mahayana writings, the Perfection of Wisdom texts, speak of phenomena as "empty" *(shunya)* of any and all inherent existence. The true nature of reality, in this perspective, is usually translated as "Emptiness" or "Void" *(shunyata)*. Emptiness in itself is not a "thing" but the nature of all things (including the *dharmas* or momentary "factors" of existence). The teaching of Emptiness does not mark a radical departure from early Buddhist teachings, and can be understood as the logical implication of the doctrines of impermanence, "no-self," and Dependent Origination.

The Perfection of Wisdom texts use various metaphors to describe the "empty" nature of existence: a banana plant (substantial in appearance but hollow in the middle), bubbles on surface of a stream (temporary and fragile), images in a dream (seemingly real but actually the illusory products of our own minds). Buddhist thinkers take great pains to emphasize that Emptiness does not exist by itself nor does it have any positive attributes. It is, rather, a term designating the Buddhist truth that everything is "empty" of true, permanent being. For Buddhists, this is true even though from our naive, unenlightened perspective, everyday objects (chairs, desks, even ourselves) seem solid and substantial.[26]

Later Philosophical Movements

As the Buddha himself said, all compounded things are impermanent, subject to constant change. This is nowhere more evident than with the Dharma itself. The processes of change within Buddhism led, ironically, to the institutionalizing of teachings that seem quite different from what the historical Buddha actually taught. These later schools are more philosophical and systematic than what we see in the earliest Buddhist discourses, often including a lot of speculation and metaphysical analysis of such topics as the origin of the universe and the differences in spiritual achievement between various Buddhists adepts. Such elaboration is common in all religious traditions, although it does tend to mark a growing separation between the laity and religious professionals. Sometimes such movements even serve as catalysts for calls to "return to the original message" of the founder, as occurred, for example, with the rise of Protestantism in Medieval Europe. There are many important schools of Buddhist thought; here is a brief overview of some of the most prominent.

"Scholastic" Buddhism

The first recognizable Buddhist philosophical schools arose among the more intellectual members of the *sangha* who were drawn to the study of the Abhidharma. Most of these Abhidharma specialists engaged in the painstaking analysis of human experience into their momentary constitutive "factors" *(dharmas)*, enumerating vast lists of these "factors." Several of the more astute became involved in arcane discussions on the varying lengths of time these *dharmas* lasted and, at times, even speculated about transtemporal dimensions of existence. In their esoteric and highly technical intellectual pursuits, these scholastic Buddhists resemble the monastic theologians of Medieval Europe, who engaged in high-level debates on such abstruse topics as the number of angels who could dance on the head of a pin.

There were quite a few of these early philosophical schools (the traditional number is 18) but most of them gradually died out.[27] The writings of these schools are truly impressive in scope and are still studied by Buddhist philosophers. One can get a taste of their analyses in passages such as the following:

> The substance called eye is of the nature of that which sees [a "seer"]. In it is produced an action of seeing, when its power is awakened on account of the emergence of the totality of its causes and conditions. The eye does not apprehend independently of consciousness *(vijnana)*, nor does the eye-consciousness know the object unsupported by the active eye. The eye as well as eye-consciousness, with the help of such accessories as light, cooperate simultaneously toward bringing the perception of a given object. The object, the eye, the eye-consciousness, and the light, all manifest their power, i.e., become active and flash forth simultaneously. The object appears, the eye sees, and the eye-consciousness knows it. This is called the direct knowledge of an object.[28]

Such careful, painstaking analysis of the factors involved in the process of perception reveals just how complex experience actually is, and helps one realize just how blind we often are to the various dimensions of our world.

Despite the great analytic skill and philosophical profundity found in the treatises of these "scholastic" Buddhists, their writings do differ (if only in style) from what we see in the teachings attributed to the Buddha. Most Abhidharma analysis is far beyond the reach of anyone who is not pursuing *nirvana* full-time. In addition, it does seem that in some cases the speculations of "scholastic" Buddhist thinkers do go beyond original Buddhist teachings. Furthermore, the meticulous enumeration and analysis of *dharmas* seems somewhat foreign to the original spirit of Buddhism, which was focused on attaining *nirvana,* not the exhaustive cataloguing of human psychology. Critics charged these thinkers with being too austere and selfishly attached to their analytic pursuits. It was these schools that were derided as "Hinayana" (small vehicle) for their excessively narrow, "monkish" concerns by later Mahayana thinkers.

Madhyamika

The first truly Mahayana philosophical school is the Madhyamika (School of the Middle Way). The Madhyamika school is a systematic presentation of the teachings found in the Perfection of Wisdom texts and provides a strong critique of "Hinayana" dogmatism. Madhyamika thinkers stress the Emptiness of all things, including our ideas and opinions. Madhyamikas repeatedly invoke the common Buddhist notion that there are two levels of Truth: ordinary/conventional and ultimate. Most of our daily lives involve opinions and assertions concerning the conventional level. Here, they are perfectly valid and useful. However, no actual ideas or teachings can hold true at the ultimate level, which is beyond the reach of thought and language.

Because they maintain that Ultimate Truth is inconceivable and ineffable, Madhyamika thinkers rely on the rhetorical technique of negation to drive their points home. Many Madhyamikas claim they proclaim no thesis of their own, and instead attack their rivals' views through arguments that attempt to refute an opponent by demonstrating the internal contradictions of his/her position (*reductio ad absurdum* arguments). The intention behind such Madhyamika criticisms is to push one beyond the point of clinging to *any* verbal teaching about reality. From a Madhyamika perspective, any clearly defined philosophical position results in attachment and hence, suffering. Thus, we need to break free of any and all "views" of reality. However, Madhyamika thinkers are not nihilists. Rather, they claim merely to follow the example of the Buddha and steer a "middle way" between affirmation and negation.

The most famous Madhyamika and perhaps greatest Buddhist thinker of all time was Nagarjuna (~150–250 c.e.), to whom several important treatises are attributed. Nagarjuna's best known work, the Middle Stanzas, is a brilliant refutation of "Hinayana" views. His opening dedication gives a good sense of his thinking:

I prostrate to the Perfect Buddha,
The best of teachers, who taught that
Whatever is dependently arisen is
Unceasing, unborn,
Unannihilated, not permanent,
Not coming, not going,
Without distinction, without identity,
And free from conceptual construction.[29]

In this passage Nagarjuna makes full use of Madhyamika negation while still demonstrating his abiding faith in the Buddha's teachings. Later in the same treatise Nagarjuna provocatively states that there is no real difference between *samsara* and *nirvana,* at least from the standpoint of Ultimate Truth.

Nagarjuna's disciple, Aryadeva (~170–270 C.E.), continued his master's polemical tradition and he was followed by many others. Among the most prominent later Madhyamikas were Candrakirti (~600–50 C.E.), a major commentator on Nagarjuna's works, and Shantideva (~695–743 C.E.), one of the foremost Buddhist poets. The Madhyamika school has long been a major school of thought in Buddhism. All later important Buddhist thinkers have been trained in Madhyamika thinking and it has attracted the interest of many Western philosophers as well.

Yogachara

The second major school of Mahayana thought arose in response to what some thinkers perceived as the streak of nihilism within Madhyamika. Without denying the validity of Nagarjuna's logic, several thinkers sought to articulate a more positive view in light of some of the teachings found in the *sutras.* These thinkers also did not wish to abandon Abhidharma analysis of human experience entirely but were interested in how the mind functions and even generates our experiences. It seems likely, as well, that these thinkers were deeply involved in Buddhist yoga and meditation, hence the name of this school: Yogachara (The Practice of Yoga).

Whereas the Madhyamika school focuses on Emptiness, Yogachara concentrates on the nature and functioning of the mind. As a result, Yogachara is also referred to as Vijnanavada (School of the Mind). Yogachara thinkers claim that whereas Abhidharma philosophers maintain that consciousness arises when the senses come into contact with their objects (essentially a "commonsense" view), what is actually the case is that a fundamental process of consciousness produces both sensations and their objects. Most Western scholars have considered Yogachara to be a form of Idealism (a theory that the world is produced by the mind) but it seems that Yogacharins may be advancing a more subtle view. For instance, it could be that Yogachara thinkers mean that the world *as we experience it* is produced by the mind rather than existing in and of itself. Yogachara thinkers push us to realize that most of our lives are not real but are, rather, mental constructions of reality, "ideation only." This more subtle interpretation makes sense given the Yogacharin stress on yoga and meditation—practices that often reveal the subtle workings of our mental processes.

According to the Yogachara philosophy of mind, consciousness itself manifests through six senses (sight, hearing, smelling, tasting, feeling, mental awareness) and their objects. Behind these six sense-consciousnesses is a seventh consciousness that unites the previous six and serves as the basis for reflection and self-awareness. Beneath all seven of these consciousness lies an eighth and final level of consciousness, the "Storehouse Consciousness" *(alaya-vijnana)*. It is this Storehouse Consciousness that ultimately generates the subjective and objective aspects of experience, just as the ocean's water takes form as waves. The Storehouse Consciousness also explains our apparent continuity in this life through periods of unconsciousness (sleep, fainting) as well as previous and future lifetimes.

For Yogacharins, the Storehouse Consciousness explains how *karma* functions. Each action and experience deposits a karmic "seed" that is stored in the Storehouse and influences how it generates later experience. Some time in the future (perhaps the next moment, perhaps years later), the "seed" matures with the help of our attachments and habitual mental formations, ripening until they manifest as new events within the flow of experience. These experiences, in turn, deposit their karmic "seeds" into the Storehouse, and so on.

Along with their theory of the many levels of consciousness and karmic "seeds," Yogachara thinkers also distinguish Three Natures within experience. These are:

1. **The "imagined" nature:** ordinary experience in which oneself and objects appear to be independent entities. Such independence, however, is only an imagined construction, a superimposition of the mind.
2. **The "interdependent" nature:** the real nature of experience, that is, the fact that the "imagined" independent entities actually arise interdependently on the basis of the processes of consciousness.

3. **The "perfected" nature:** experience when one has purified oneself from the
   ignorance that continually superimposes a view of reality in which we imagine ourselves and objects as independent. In other words, the perfected nature of experience is the realization of *nirvana*.

These Three Natures of experience are not distinct "things" but rather
describe stages of spiritual growth one goes through when following the
Buddhist path. We begin essentially living in a fantasy world of our own
construction, but through diligent study and practice, we gradually come
to realize the difference between our imaginings and how life actually is.
Accepting life on its own terms rather than what we would like it to be enables us to eliminate our insatiable grasping at "things" and live in a more
productive and happier way.

The greatest Yogachara thinkers were the brothers Asanga and Vasubandhu (~400 C.E.), who authored several important treatises of Yogachara
philosophy. Vasubandhu was the more prolific of the two, and in his Thirty
Verses he provides an excellent overview of Yogachara teachings that clearly
shows how they aim at awakening. In the last verses he writes:

> When consciousness is without an objective support, then consciousness
> is established in "ideation only," since in the
> absence of anything to grasp, there is no grasping.
>
> When [he] is without thought, without objective support, his
> knowledge is supramundane. There is "turning away" from the
> object, through the abandonment of the two kinds of weakness [i.e.,
> the belief in a "self" and the belief in "real things"].
>
> That is the realm without defilements,
> inconceivable, good, permanent, happy with released body;
> this is what is called the Dharma-body of the great Sage.[30]

Yogachara teachings spread among Buddhist intellectuals in the years following Asanga and Vasubandhu. Prominent later Yogachara thinkers included the great Buddhist logician Dinnaga (~600 C.E.) and Dharmapala
(~600 C.E.), who headed the great university of Nalanda.

Yogachara philosophy is probably the most abstruse and complex system
in all of Buddhism, yet in recent years it has generated increasing interest
among Western scholars, many of whom appreciate the keen psychological
insights found in Yogachara texts. Certainly the Yogachara analysis of mind
as being composed of multiple levels and its role in constructing our expe-

Ruins of the great Buddhist university of Nalanda in India. Courtesy of the American Institute of Indian Studies.

rience of life uncannily parallels Sigmund Freud's theories of personality. Moreover, Yogachara's emphasis on the necessity of yogic practice alongside the philosophical study of Buddhist doctrine continues to exert tremendous influence on Buddhist thought. In this sense, at least, Yogachara seems fully in keeping with the animating spirit of early Buddhism.

Tathagatagarbha Thought

Neither Madhyamika nor Yogachara exhaust all aspects of Buddhist thought. Another major line of Buddhist thinking (although it never was a formal, institutionalized "school") speaks of an inner reality that is always already Buddha. This inner reality is known as the Tathagatagarbha (womb/embryo of Buddha). It is like a "womb" in that it contains the potential to become Buddha and it is like an "embryo" in that it can develop into Buddha. Perhaps the best way to describe it is as one's "Buddha-nature."

The Buddha-nature is inherent in all beings, thus everyone has the capacity to become awakened. The reason people are unaware of their inherent Buddha-nature is because it is concealed by defilements such as ignorance, hatred, and greed. When these unwholesome thoughts and emotions are removed, the Buddha-nature shines forth, naturally luminous. One has, then, attained *nirvana.*

We must beware of equating the teachings of Buddha-nature with the positing of some universal, substantive "self." Although some texts may speak of the Buddha-nature as eternal and unchanging, it is not a permanent "soul" that manifests in all things. Rather, the Buddha-nature is our latent potential for awakening that can be developed through conscientious Buddhist practice and study. Buddha-nature thought is universal and all-embracing; all beings can (and perhaps will) become fully enlightened. The idea, thus, is positive and encouraging to those embarking on the Buddhist path.

There are a number of important texts that elaborate on Buddha-nature ideas. One of the most famous of these treatises, *Analysis of the Jewels and Lineages* (Ratnagotra-vibhanga), states:

> Because Buddha knowledge is contained in all beings, because it is pure and non-dual in nature, because those who belong to the lineage of the Buddha advance towards it as their goal, therefore all living beings have the "Buddha nature" within them.
>
> Like a Buddha in a faded lotus flower, like honey covered by bees, like a fruit in its husk, like gold within its impurities, like a treasure hidden in the dirt ... like a valuable statue covered with dust, so is this [Buddha-nature] within all beings.[31]

Buddha-nature literature has been very influential in East Asia, particularly in the Chan/Zen schools, which proclaim the paradoxical idea that we are all Buddha, we just do not know it yet.

Buddhist Schools as Interpretive Traditions

Although these four philosophical movements differ considerably, they are all rooted in basic Buddhist texts (particularly the *sutras*) and claim in essence to go back to the earliest layer of Buddhist teachings. We might do better to understand them as "interpretive traditions" rather than separate philosophical schools. Moreover, all four traditions of thought were the work of devout philosophical thinkers who may have profoundly disagreed but still recognized each other as rival Buddhists, not "outsiders." In addition, the relationship between these philosophical schools is not one of mere succession. In fact, historical sources indicate that different Buddhist schools existed side by side, sometimes within the same monasteries. The fact that groups of monks could coexist despite doctrinal differences underscores the *practical* focus of Buddhist teachings. The Dharma is first and foremost a guide to awakening, marking out the path that all Buddhists follow. Buddhists have generally understood themselves as united in practice, particularly in their adherence to the Code of Discipline (Vinaya).

This tendency toward coexistence does not mean that there were not conflicts between philosophical schools or that interaction between schools was necessarily peaceful. However, generally speaking no Buddhist school has been declared "heretical" in the sense that some Christian movements have been. In East Asia, Buddhist schools have taken particular pains to present unified systems of teachings, in large part because of the stress on harmony that is so prominent in East Asian societies. As a result, East Asian schools often concoct schemes in which they "rank" the teachings from the most basic level on up to what they consider the "final" (ultimate) teachings. Although such schemes do not fully mask philosophical rivalries, they do recognize a plurality of versions of the Dharma even while seeking to put the teachings into a coherent order.

NOTES

1. Roger J. Corless, *The Vision of the Buddha: The Space under the Tree* (New York: Paragon House, 1989), 217.

2. This distinction, usually referred to as the Two Truths (relative and ultimate), plays an important role in later Buddhist philosophy.

3. This disparity reflects the basic gender hierarchy found in Buddhist traditions. No nun can reprove a monk, and all nuns are subordinate to monks, even those ordained after them. However, such institutional hierarchy does not mean women are spiritually inferior to men.

4. The differences between these three major branches of Buddhism are discussed in Chapter 3. Technically, there are five versions of the Buddhist canon—Pali, Chinese, Tibetan, Korean, and Mongolian. However, the Korean and Mongolian Buddhist canons are derived from the Chinese and Tibetan versions.

5. For example, all Christian Bibles contain both the Old and New Testaments. However, Roman Catholic and Eastern Orthodox Bibles also include a group of 14 books known as the Apocrypha (literally, "things that are hidden") that were composed during the intertestamental period. Because the authenticity of some of these texts is disputed, Protestant Bibles generally omit them.

6. The resemblance to Sanskrit clearly shows in Theravadin Buddhist terms such as *dhamma, sutta,* and *nibbana* (the Pali equivalents of *dharma, sutra,* and *nirvana,* respectively) and many books on Buddhism use Pali terms instead of Sanskrit. Like Sanskrit, Pali survives today only as a literary language.

7. The variant Abhidharma collections clearly show the philosophical differences that arose between branches of Buddhism in the centuries after the Buddha's passing. One of the Pali texts, for example, even aims at refuting the "wrong" views of other Buddhist schools.

8. The translation of Buddhist texts into Chinese was the largest and most complex translation project in history, involving centuries and requiring the efforts of thousands of people. For details see Kenneth Ch'en, *Buddhism in China: A Historical Survey* (Princeton, NJ: Princeton University Press, 1964), 365–86.

9. These other schools of thought represented include two schools of Hindu philosophy, Manichaeism (an ancient religion that arose in Persia), and Nestorian Christianity (an early, heretical form of Christianity that was present in China since the eighth century). The inclusion of such non-Buddhist material underscores the truly Mahayana (i.e., all-inclusive) nature of the Chinese Buddhist canon.

10. E. A. Burtt, ed., *The Teachings of the Compassionate Buddha* (New York: Penguin Books, 1982), 132.

11. The oldest surviving printed book in the world is a copy of the Diamond Sutra found in central Asia and dated May 11, 868 C.E.

12. Some scholars have suggested that the Heart Sutra was originally composed in Chinese. Aside from being so famous, it is also a notoriously puzzling text in that the Buddha himself never speaks in it (most of the teachings are given by the great *bodhisattva* Avalokiteshvara) and the text itself ends in a powerful "spell," or *mantra.*

13. Many scholars maintain that the Awakening of Faith, although claiming to be an Indian treatise, was composed in China, perhaps by its alleged translator, a south Indian monk named Paramartha (sixth century C.E.)

14. Tantric Buddhism was never very popular in China, but it rose to great prominence in Japan as part of the Shingon (True Word) school, still one of the major forms of Japanese Buddhism.

15. The "three poisons" and are often represented in Buddhist art by the snake (hatred), the pig (delusion), and the rooster (greed).

16. As in Christianity, Islam, and many forms of Hinduism, in Buddhism the key to a spiritual life is the intention by which one performs one's actions.

17. Also called "the parable of the mustard seed," this story appears in many traditional sources. This version comes from E. A. Burtt, ed., *The Teachings of the Compassionate Buddha,* 43–46.

18. Ibid., 45.

19. We might compare Buddhist teachings on this account with the teachings of Jesus Christ, who, for example, is alleged to have said, "If you

continue in my word, you are truly my disciples; and you with know the truth, and the truth will make you free." John 8.32 (NRSV)

20. Anguttara-nikaya, III, 134; quoted in Donald W. Mitchell, *Buddhism: Introducing Buddhist Experience* (New York: Oxford University Press, Inc., 2002), 34,

21. Using the famous Buddhist analogy of a chariot, we can explain *duhkha* as what happens when the chariot has an improperly made axle hole (too small, too large, off-center, etc.). Driving such an off-centered wheel will result in a wobbly or bumpy ride—a rather apt description of much of human life.

22. We can perhaps get a sense of what the Buddha means by reflecting on certain ideas in contemporary American society. For instance, it is common when meeting an old acquaintance to say, "you're not the same person." Similarly, medical science tells us that our bodies renew themselves at the cellular level every seven years. Thus, in a sense, we do hold to something like a "no-self" doctrine in certain instances.

23. Quoted in Peter Harvey, *An Introduction to Buddhism: Teachings, History, and Practices* (Cambridge: Cambridge University Press, 1990), 54 (bracketed material added by the author).

24. From the *Samyutta-nikaya*, II, 90. Quoted in Donald W. Mitchell, *Buddhism: Introducing the Buddhist Experience* (New York and Oxford: Oxford University Press, 2002), 40 (bracketed material added by the author).

25. Ibid., 42 (bracketed material added by the author).

26. One scholar, Richard Payne, Dean of the Institute of Buddhist Studies, has summed up the teaching of Emptiness very simply: "Everything exists; nothing is real."

27. One of the most influential of these early schools was the Sarvastivada (Teaching that All Exists) school, which seems to be the primary group singled out by Mahayana critics as "Hinayanists." The contemporary Theravadin school of Buddhist was also one of these 18 early schools.

28. From the Abhidharmipa, quoted in David J. Kalupahana, *Buddhist Philosophy: A Historical Analysis* (Honolulu: University of Hawaii Press, 1976), 102–3.

29. Jay L. Garfield, trans., *The Fundamental Wisdom of the Middle Way: Nagarjuna's Mulamadhyamakakarika* (New York: Oxford University Press, 1995), 2.

30. Trimsika (Thirty Verses), 28–30. Quoted in Kalupahana, *Buddhist Philosophy*, 149 (bracketed material added by the author).

31. Ratnagotra-vibhaga, I, 27 and 97. Quoted in Mitchell, *Buddhism: Introducing the Buddhist Experience*, 140 (bracketed material added by the author).

3

BRANCHES

Like most religious traditions, Buddhism encompasses a wide variety of styles and practices. Indeed, some scholars argue that "Buddhisms" (plural) is more appropriate than "Buddhism" (singular). Although there is some truth to this notion, it can lead to confusion. Buddhism is most easily understood as encompassing three different traditions or branches: Theravada, Mahayana, and Vajrayana. All three derive from the original movement founded by the historical Buddha, and all three share the core teachings laid out in Chapter 2. However, each of these branches reflects distinct historical and cultural developments, and there are some important differences between them.[1] In a sense, they comprise three separate paths, each claiming to lead to *nirvana*, the state beyond suffering. Drawing a parallel to another great world religion, we can consider these branches of Buddhism to be analogous to the major divisions (Eastern Orthodoxy, Roman Catholicism, Protestantism) within Christianity.

THERAVADA

Theravada is the oldest of the three branches of Buddhism. It is one of the 18 schools formed as a result of the second great council of the Buddhist order held some hundred years after the Buddha's passing. According to traditional accounts, that council engendered a major schism in which one sect calling themselves the "Members of the Great Order" (Mahasangikas) split off from the rest of the Buddhist community *(sangha)* because of differences in monastic discipline and doctrine. The remaining monks, claiming to maintain the true tradition transmitted from the days of Siddhartha Gautama, referred to themselves as those who followed the "Teaching of the Elders," a title that was eventually rendered into Pali as *Theravada*.[2]

Although other early schools of Buddhism spread along with Theravada, only the latter survives. Theravada spread from India to Sri Lanka under the reign of Emperor Ashoka, the legendary Buddhist ruler, during the third century B.C.E. (Theravadins claim that Ashoka's son Mahinda was the monk who brought Buddhism to Sri Lanka, making him the first Theravada missionary). It rapidly became the state religion. Several early Sri Lankan kings became active sponsors of Theravada, allowing the sect to consolidate its teachings and practices, and eventually render them into written form. From Sri Lanka, Theravada spread to other parts of Southeast Asia, where it still predominates in the countries of Burma (Myanmar), Thailand, Cambodia, and Laos.[3]

As its name suggests, Theravada is considered the most conservative of Buddhist sects. Many Theravadins maintain that they are the keepers of the "original" Buddhism as taught by the historical Buddha and his disciples. However, scholars of Buddhism have concluded that such sectarian claims are historically unfounded. Theravada Buddhists consider the Pali canon to be the only authoritative collection. To this day Theravadins resist straying from the early Pali texts, exhibiting at times an almost "un-Buddhistic" adherence to the traditional scriptures.

Theravada accepts all the common core teachings of Buddhism (the Three Marks of Existence, Four Noble Truths, Eightfold Path, etc.) and has a strong tradition of study of the Abhidharma, or systematic elaborations on various topics discussed in the sacred discourses *(sutras)*. As with other traditions of Abhidharma, in Theravada the aim of such study is to train the mind to see through the mental constructions we typically project onto the outer world. Skill in Abhidharma study leads to a type of wisdom that we might conceive as an acute discriminative awareness of reality. Unlike other schools, however, Theravadin Abhidharma focuses less on speculative metaphysical issues and more on carefully observing human psychology.[4]

Theravadins generally hold that the attainment of the state beyond the cycle of life and death *(nirvana)* can only come about through self-effort, without any outside supernatural aid. For them, the Buddha thus serves primarily as a saint and great teacher who laid out the path his disciples should follow. In the Theravada perspective, the Buddha was a great man, a model for all Buddhists, and a clear witness to the potential for all people to become enlightened. However, once the historical Buddha passed on, his direct influence on the world ceased. The Buddha knows nothing of the world now and cannot come to our aid.

One of the hallmarks of Theravada is the upholding of the *arhat* as the ultimate spiritual ideal. Meaning "worthy" or "deserving one," the term *arhat* refers to persons who have reached the goal of enlightenment, or *nirvana*. At its simplest, an *arhat* is a wise monk, perfect in knowledge and in conduct, who has mastered all meditative states and has removed all defilements. An *arhat* can recognize things as they truly are and thus is beyond all pain and suffering.[5] Because of his attainments, an *arhat* is thought to possess great supernormal powers. In popular Theravada Buddhism, many *arhats* have become the focus of their own cults, much like Christian saints, and claims of *arhat* status are continually being made on behalf of especially holy monks. Devout laypersons seek them out to ask for favors and may wear protective amulets bearing their images. The monasteries of such monks may even become centers of holy pilgrimage during and after their lifetimes.

Upholding of the *arhat* ideal means, among other things, that Theravadins make a sharp distinction between the monks and the laity. Both monks and laity are members of the larger Buddhist community *(sangha)*, but they have distinct although not entirely separate roles. In fact, in Theravada society, monks and laity exist in a symbiotic relationship in which each benefits the other. This relationship is one in which the lay community provides material support for the monks (food, clothing, property, perhaps money to purchase necessary items) while the monks provide spiritual and moral guidance. Commonly, monks are said to provide a "field of merit" (good *karma*) by which members of the laity further themselves in the spiritual if not material sense. This relationship is marked by ritual exchanges of gifts. Such exchanges occur daily (e.g., food given to monks on their begging rounds) and on special occasions (e.g., the annual presentation of new robes to the monks by the local villagers) and attest to a common Buddhist social order that has held sway throughout Southeast Asia for centuries.

Monks also have fulfilled basic ministerial roles in Theravadin societies. That is, monks will typically preside at funerals (rarely birth ceremonies or weddings) and at certain festivals connected with the annual growing cycles of rice and other crops. Monks may also be called upon to conduct special protective rituals *(parittas)* to mark special occasions such as the building of a new house, the start of a long journey, or in times of illness, drought, famine, or other disasters. In all such ceremonies, the monks are drawing on their reservoir of spiritual power to ward off evil forces and invite blessings. Comparable duties, of course, are commonly performed in Western societies by priests, ministers, or rabbis.

Because of their training and spiritual power, monks have traditionally been highly esteemed in Theravadin societies. Indeed, becoming a monk often represents a decided elevation in social status for males from poor backgrounds. It is not uncommon for laypeople to assume monastic vows for limited periods of time to get a basic education, to repay debts to their parents and ancestors, or to receive simple meditation training.[6] Becoming a monk does not necessarily involve a lifetime commitment as it usually does in the West. In Burma (Myanmar), for example, it has long been customary for all young boys to spend a short period of time (three months or so) as a monk as a way of marking their entrance into manhood.[7] However, pursing *nirvana* is a lifelong vocation that requires a disciplined monastic setting; it is essentially impossible for a lay person to attain *nirvana,* according to Theravada teachings.

Being a Theravada monk does not necessarily require severe ascetic practices other than a vow of celibacy and rules against acquiring material goods, and most monks live in reasonable comfort. Still, a monastic lifestyle involves making drastic changes. Upon joining the order, a new monk must give up his name, clothes, and all former possessions. His head is shaved, and he is given a new Pali name and a simple yellow robe. Typically, he will remain a novice for a period of two to four years, at which point he may seek full ordination or return to lay life.

Daily life in Theravada monasteries, as in all Buddhist monastic communities, is highly regimented and follows a basic pattern that was established by the Buddha's earliest followers. A monk usually rises at daybreak, washes himself, lights a candle before the image of the Buddha, and spends a set period of time chanting and meditating before leaving the monastery. Outside the monastery grounds, the monk walks silently to the nearest village, begging bowl in hand. There, he makes his daily rounds, stopping at every door to receive whatever food the villagers have to offer.[8] After making his rounds, the monk returns to the monastery to eat breakfast before joining other monks in the assembly hall for prayer, instruction, and more meditation. The main (and last) meal of the day is eaten before noon in a communal dining room. In the afternoon the monks devote themselves to scriptural study and meditation. At sunset the monks gather in one final assembly for more instruction and then retire to bed. Following this daily routine enables the monks to gain merit toward their liberation.

Theravada monks in procession. Courtesy of Ronald Y. Nakasone.

Nuns provide an interesting contrast to monks in Theravada, in that they have far less social prestige. From the very beginning, the order of nuns has been subordinate to the order of monks in all Buddhist traditions, with nuns generally living under many more rules. For a number of reasons, the nuns' community had almost died out in most Theravadin societies.[9] However, in recent years the number of nuns has been increasing. Like monks, nuns have their heads shaved, take a Pali name, and wear special robes (white, brown, or yellow). Traditionally most nuns were permanently ordained (often they were older women) and spent much of their day doing domestic chores around the monastery, with less time for study and meditation than monks. Sometimes nuns' upkeep came from family support, personal savings, or surplus alms from lay donors. Only rarely did nuns themselves go on daily begging rounds.

MAHAYANA

Sometime near the beginning of the common era, a major cultural movement began to sweep through Buddhism that resulted in remarkable changes for both monastics and laity. Called Mahayana (Great Vehicle), this new form of Buddhism spread northwest into central Asia and then eastward into China. From China, the Mahayana form of Buddhism eventually spread to Korea, Japan, and Vietnam—areas where it still dominates today.[10] In contrast to Theravada, Mahayana Buddhism encompasses far greater variety from sect to sect. Whereas Theravada can be described as conservative, Mahayana is decidedly more liberal, particularly when it comes to the laity and their capacity for spiritual development. Mahayana Buddhists also include new scriptures in addition to those in the Pali canon, new forms of teaching, new rituals, and new meditational practices.

Although its exact origins remain unclear, historical evidence suggests that Mahayana arose from the early schisms within the *sangha* (most scholars think it originated from the Mahasangika, one of the earliest Buddhist reform movements, and other related sects). It seems likely that early Mahayana does not mark a sharp break with older forms of Buddhism but rather was the product of tendencies already present in Buddhist tradition that were encouraged by the major social changes in India at that time. Certainly by the third and fourth centuries, there were new Buddhist ordination lineages that distinguished themselves from older forms of Buddhism, which they referred to pejoratively as "Hinayana" (small vehicle). Nonetheless, Mahayana tradition continued to be practiced side by side with these older forms of Buddhism for centuries.

The Mahayana movement in all its forms has distinct reformist roots. In particular, it seems that early proponents of Mahayana were critical of the "Hinayana" emphasis on monks and their personal spiritual development (best exemplified in the attention many "Hinayana" orders gave to dogmatic Abhidharma teachings and analysis). Mahayanists perceived such "monkish" pursuits as not in keeping with the compassionate spirit of the Buddha, whose aim was to aid *all* beings. For followers of Mahayana, this meant that the laity needed to have a larger, more active role in Buddhism. In the earliest forms of Buddhism, laypeople essentially had the role of supporting the *sangha* through food, alms, or other donations. Anyone wishing to become more actively engaged in following the Buddhist path had to "leave home" and join a monastic order. Advocates of Mahayana, however, maintained that even laypersons could make serious spiritual progress and perhaps even attain enlightenment without necessarily renouncing ordinary life. In practice this meant an elevation in status for devout laity, especially for women.

Coupled with this elevation in status for the laity was a deeper emphasis on the veneration of shrines *(stupas)* housing the relics of the Buddha or other particularly holy persons. Such veneration had been a long-standing practice among Buddhists since the historical Buddha's passing, but by the beginning of the common era, lay Buddhists had developed a tradition of making pilgrimages to such holy sites. Over time, some devout lay Buddhists attached themselves to specific *stupas* as unofficial caretakers and guides. Gradually, a widely accepted view rose that the merit accrued by making pilgrimages to these shrines could prove very beneficial for one's future *karma*.

The rise of *stupa* veneration also reflects an important development in the Mahayana understanding of merit. Early Buddhist teachings on *karma* and merit stressed that good or bad *karma* was purely the result of one's own actions and no outside agent could affect it. Nevertheless, as Buddhism became an institutionalized religious tradition, most Buddhists allowed that merit could be transferred to another person in certain circumstances, usually through specific rituals honoring one's deceased relatives, or, more rarely, rites aimed at the welfare of all beings. In the Mahayana, this notion of transferring merit became much more widespread.

Another Mahayana development that had far-reaching consequences concerned the idea of "skillful means," the notion that Buddhist teachings are pragmatic and thus can be tailored to meet people's capacities and/or needs. Again, there is evidence of this idea at the very beginning of the Buddha's preaching career, but in the Mahayana tradition the notion of "skillful means" becomes even more important, as witnessed by the famous parable of the burning house in the Lotus Sutra, one of the most beloved Buddhist scriptures. Buddhists have generally held that Ultimate Truth is always somewhat obscured to people, particularly those just embarking on the spiritual quest. Therefore, they must be led gradually with provisional formulations. As people progress, earlier views are rejected as being inadequate, and subtler, more complex teachings are given.[11] Mahayana texts such as the Lotus Sutra even put forth the idea that the historical Buddha's entire teachings were merely provisional devices to get humans started on the way. This trend, in turn, led many followers of Mahayana to focus on

Stupa at Sanchi, India. Courtesy of the American Institute of Indian Studies.

other heavenly Buddha figures and attaining a truly cosmic wisdom as the ultimate goal.

Related to such developments, and a major feature of Mahayana that sets it apart from Theravada and the other "Hinayana" schools, is a far more transcendent view of Buddha. As early Buddhism came into contact with non-Indian theistic traditions, it absorbed some of their views, although it remained uniquely Buddhist. "Buddha" became more of an absolute essence of reality rather than merely a historical person, with the corresponding idea that there are many different Buddhas presiding over different worlds (Buddha-realms). Such teachings were formalized through a doctrine of the Three Bodies of the Buddha. These are:

1. **The Appearance or Transformation Body**: an earthly manifestation such as Shakyamuni Buddha (Siddhartha Gautama).
2. **The Body of Bliss:** a heavenly Buddha presiding over a particular Buddha-realm. The Body of Bliss can communicate directly with other celestial Buddhas and is the focus of popular devotion among Mahayana Buddhists.
3. **The Dharma Body:** the One Absolute, Cosmic Reality.

This doctrine of the Three Bodies explained both the oneness of all Buddhas everywhere and the unity of the Buddha-nature, the potential for enlightenment that all beings share. According to this teaching, the One True Buddha (Dharma Body) manifests as compassionate heavenly deities (Body of Bliss) and as human beings who become enlightened on earth (Appearance Body), such as the historical Buddha. Clearly, with such a teaching Mahayana took on much more of a theistic dimension than we see in early Buddhism or in Theravada.

However, the most distinctive feature of Mahayana that sets it apart from Theravada is the role played by "wisdom beings," or *bodhisattvas*. A *bodhisattva* is a particularly devout follower of Buddhism who conscientiously vows to aid all other beings in becoming enlightened. Some Mahayana texts even claim that out their great compassion for all suffering beings, *bodhisattvas* voluntarily postpone their own entry into *nirvana* until all beings have attained enlightenment. The *bodhisattva* ideal is present in early Buddhism (particularly in the case of stories of Siddhartha's previous lives, the Jataka tales), but Mahayana greatly expanded upon it. *Bodhisattvas* share their merit with all beings. Those who are highly advanced along the path are reborn in the heavens, from which they can come to the aid of any and all who call upon them, in some respects resembling saints in popular Christianity.[12] At such high levels, *bodhisattvas* are almost indistinguishable from full Buddhas in that both *bodhisattvas* and Buddhas, out of their inexhaustible compassion, stand poised to bestow grace upon those who have faith

For followers of Mahayana, the *bodhisattva* becomes the spiritual ideal, as opposed to the *arhat* of Theravada. According to Mahayanists, *arhats* are selfishly focused on their own liberation rather than on relieving the suffering of other sentient beings. To emphasize this high ideal, Mahayana encourages all Buddhists, male or female, monastic or lay, to take *bodhisattva* vows. This is typically done in a special ritual in which the aspirant formally vows both to become Buddha and to strive actively for the liberation of all who suffer. In practice, this amounts to vowing to live as devout and holy a life as possible in the understanding that one will eventually be reborn in a heavenly realm, from which one can transfer merit to others. There also was a sense that one could, in certain circumstances, be reborn on earth in human form if that would further other beings on their spiritual journey.

Mahayanists have always regarded taking *bodhisattva* vows as a serious matter, for it means dedicating oneself to a great spiritual journey for the sake of all living beings. The *bodhisattva* path is a great journey involving the practice of six virtues (Giving, Morality, Patience, Vigor, Meditation, and Wisdom). According to the earliest Mahayana texts, the Perfection of Wisdom Sutras, it is the last of these Six Perfections (Wisdom) that is the most important. With Perfect Wisdom the *bodhisattva* realizes the truth of Emptiness and no longer distinguishes between "self" and "other." The *bodhisattva* can then perform all other virtues "perfectly" with no selfish motive, and so attain Buddhahood. As Mahayana tradition developed, the teaching of the Six Perfections was expanded through the addition of four more virtues (Skillful Means, Vows, Power, and Omniscience). *Bodhisattvas* at the highest level were understood as having mastered each of these Ten Perfections. Over time, Mahayana thinkers devised a systematic outline of the *bodhisattva* path that they divided into Ten Stages (sometimes known as the "Ten Stages of Attainment") with each stage corresponding to one of the Ten Perfections. The *Bodhisattva* path, thus, can be understood as follows:

Ten Perfections	Ten Stages of Attainment
Giving	Joy
Morality	Purity
Patience	Brightness

Vigor	Radiance
Meditation	Difficult to Conquer
Wisdom	Facing *Nirvana*
Skillful Means	Far-going
Vows	Immovable
Power	Spiritual Intelligence
Omniscience	Dharma Cloud

Progressing through all Ten Stages has traditionally been considered a truly compassionate venture, worthy of great admiration. Mahayana teachers also stress that it can be an arduous undertaking, requiring eons to complete. It has also been understood that an aspiring *bodhisattva* will need the aid of the great heavenly Buddhas and *bodhisattvas* to reach this goal.

Because of the popularity of the *bodhisattva* ideal and the necessity of aid for those traveling the *bodhisattva* path, various heavenly Buddhas and *bodhisattvas* play major roles in Mahayana Buddhism. Indeed, Mahayana history is marked by innumerable devotional cults dedicated to myriads of these heavenly beings. Of these, a few stand out as especially important. One of the earliest *bodhisattvas* in Mahayana records is Maitreya (the Friendly One), the *bodhisattva* destined to be the next Buddha of our world. Currently, many Buddhists hold that Maitreya resides in a heavenly realm awaiting the time when the Buddha Dharma needs renewal. He will then be reborn here to teach the Dharma anew.[13] Some Buddhists pray to Maitreya to hasten his arrival or to be reborn when he comes, since it is believed that it is easier to become enlightened when one has the example of a living Buddha. Another well-known *bodhisattva* is Manjushri, the guardian of Perfect Wisdom, who is a patron of those Buddhists devoting themselves to monastic life.

Far and away the most popular *bodhisattva*, however, is Avalokiteshvara (the Lord who Looks Down [from Above]), perhaps the most venerated figure in all of Buddhism. Avalokiteshvara is the very embodiment of Great Compassion and has a long history of devotion throughout the Buddhist world. He is a prominent figure in many texts, and his image is found in India and Southeast Asia, particularly in the great temple complex of Borobudur, Indonesia. Avalokiteshvara undergoes an intriguing shift in China, where he manifests in female form as the *bodhisattva* Guanyin.[14] In the guise of Guanyin, this *bodhisattva* can be found throughout East Asia, and because of her great tenderness, she is a particular favorite among women seeking children or who have had children die in infancy. Another form of Guanyin is Tara, who is particularly revered in Tibet.[15]

With the rise of the *bodhisattva* ideal, Mahayana Buddhism was able to spread among the general populace in Asian lands far more effectively than the more monastically focused "Hinayana" sects. *Bodhisattvas* have had and continue to have enormous appeal, becoming great savior figures for millions of people. In their enduring compassion and self-sacrifice, they have often been compared with Jesus Christ. An importance difference, however, is that whereas Christ is held by Christians to have been historically incarnate as Jesus, the historical character of many *bodhisattvas* is doubtful. In this respect, Buddhism remains very much an Indian religious tradition, since Indians have generally not emphasized the historical nature of many of their most important religious figures.

Other major changes that Mahayana ushered in concern new meditation techniques and practices, artwork, and different philosophical interpretations of Buddhist teachings. With the rise of cults to various *bodhisattvas* residing in numerous celestial realms, the technique of special visualizations became more widespread. By concentrating on a particular *bodhisattva* or Buddha (often with the aid of elaborate paintings or statues depicting them in their wondrous realms), a meditator sought to attain a

Painting of a *bodhisattva*, perhaps Avalokiteshvara. Courtesy of the American Institute of Indian Studies.

vision of that figure. Through intense training and devotion, a practitioner could achieve an altered state of consciousness in which he or she would see the *bodhisattva* or even "join" the figure in his heavenly realm. Such visualization practices informed later philosophical developments (especially the Yogachara school) and were taken up in earnest in the Vajrayana movement.

As for philosophical developments, there have been a number of major Mahayana schools throughout Buddhist history. Madhyamika and Yogachara (discussed in Chapter 2) are certainly the dominant philosophical schools, but other schools arose as time went by, and Mahayana spread to other countries such as China, Tibet, and Japan. Two schools in particular, however, have had great popular appeal and tremendous influence: Pure Land and Chan/Zen.

Pure Land

Pure Land Buddhism has deep roots in Buddhism's Indian homeland and Mahayana teachings and practices. Some five hundred years after the historical Buddha's passing, Mahayana Buddhism was spreading among India's Buddhist population, many of whom developed intense devotion to various *bodhisattvas.* Pure Land arose from these devotional cults and is essentially a religion of faith and grace, one in which the faithful rely on *bodhisattvas* and other heavenly figures for salvation. The major figure in Pure Land is the *bodhisattva* Dharmakara, a young prince who lived before Siddhartha Gautama and who, through devout practice and compassion, became the Great Buddha Amitabha.[16] According to Pure Land *sutras,* Dharmakara made 48 great vows when aspiring to become enlightened. One of these vows established a paradise (a Buddha-realm) where his followers could be reborn. Once in this Pure Land, the faithful will be uplifted by Amitabha's great merit and so go on to attain *nirvana.* Traditionally, this Pure Land is said to be in the western heavens or even somewhere in distant western Asia.[17]

Sutras describe the Pure Land as a paradise, free of the pollution and decay of this world. The Pure Land was said to be paved with precious jewels, a place where one's basic necessities (food, water, etc.) could be obtained merely by wishing. Best of all, the texts promised that the faithful would dwell in this land of bliss in the presence of a true Buddha and so

Giant bronze statue of Amida (Amitabha) Buddha, Kamakura, Japan.
© Corbis.

learn the Dharma firsthand. The Pure Land idea, thus, stood in marked
contrast to much of the everyday reality of peoples' lives. It also picked up
on certain notions in some Buddhist texts that the Dharma itself reaches
a point where it decays. Many Buddhists who lived several centuries after
the passing of the historical Buddha were convinced that they were living in
this age of decay, when people could no longer practice Buddhism properly.
For the uneducated laity (and even for many monastics), Buddhism at that
time was not clearly defined, and few could master its complex doctrines
or devote themselves to intense rituals and meditations. With social and
political changes on the rise, many saw evidence that such degeneration
was spreading, and that they were in need of "other" help. Pure Land *sutras*
spoke to such a situation, explaining how Amitabha promises to help all
who meditate or call upon him. Pure Land, thus, was the "easy path," the
way for those with faith in the salvific power of Amitabha. The main practice of the school involved chanting a sacred formula *(mantra)* to express
their faith: "Homage to Amitabha Buddha." Although the most important
time to chant the *mantra* was on one's deathbed, followers began to repeat
the phrase many times as a means of keeping their minds focused on Amitabha. Calling the name of Amitabha quickly became a common practice
among laity and monastics alike.

Pure Land teachings became very widespread after Buddhism came to China. This is not too surprising, since this simple faith in a type of savior deity closely resembled traditional Chinese folk beliefs. Although separate Pure Land schools were established in China, Pure Land ideas and practices were not confined to one sect. They became widespread in the temples and monasteries of all Chinese Buddhist schools, along with elaborate paintings and altarpieces depicting Amitabha and his attendants. Reciting the Pure Land *mantra* was common in China, where it was known as "remembering the Buddha," or *nianfo* (in Japanese, *nembutsu*). Often, the practitioner fingers beads while reciting the chant. Tanluan (476–542), one of the great patriarchs of Chinese Pure Land, stressed the importance of having faith, fixing the mind on Amitabha for rebirth, and constantly repenting one's failures and shortcomings. Other Pure Land patriarchs emphasized how some *sutras* claim that only one sincere repetition of *nianfo* was necessary for salvation. Such views prompted one Pure Land thinker to write, "If just one instant [of recitation has such power], how much more must it hold true for those who practice constant recollection and recitation *(nian)*! Indeed, this is a person who is constantly repenting."[18]

Chinese Pure Land was also marked by the particular prominence of Guanyin, Amitabha's main attendant and helper. While Amitabha essentially aided the faithful in passing on to the Pure Land after death, Guanyin became even more popular in China as an agent who would aid them in life. As the goddess of mercy, Guanyin gained great devotion from women and eventually became the "giver of children." Statues of Guanyin—graceful, clad in white, often holding a child in her arms—strongly resemble depictions of the Virgin Mary with child, and may have been inspired by Christian missionaries to China during the late Middle Ages.[19]

Pure Land teachings and practices were exported from China throughout East Asia, and caught on among the general populace in both Korea and Japan. It was in the latter especially that Pure Land developed into a major school. Under the guidance of Honen (1133–1212) and Shinran (1173–1262), two Tendai monks who were critical of what they perceived to be the magical and superstitious nature of Buddhism in their day, Pure Land became a large movement that found great support among the masses and eventually split into a number of different lineages. To this day most Buddhists in Japan and elsewhere are followers of Pure Land. Its strong resemblance to Protestant forms of Christianity have both intrigued and puzzled Westerners for years, and much Buddhist-Christian dialogue has involved Pure Land thinkers.[20]

Chan/Zen Buddhism

Chan, the great "meditation" school, seems almost diametrically opposed to Pure Land. Like Pure Land, however, it has Indian roots, specifically Indian meditation practices known in Sanskrit as *dhyana*. Such techniques came to China with the early Buddhist missionaries, and had a ready audience among Chinese Daoists, who also engaged in meditation. Indian techniques, however, were often complex and proved difficult to teach. Gradually, as Buddhism became more and more adapted to Chinese culture, there emerged a form of simple, quiet meditation designed to still the mind and body and thereby serve as means of attaining an intuition of Truth beyond all thoughts and concerns. The Chinese called such meditation *chana*, or more simply *chan*, the closest they could come to pronouncing the Sanskrit term *dhyana*.

For quite some time Chan was not a separate "school" but, like Pure Land, was practiced by Buddhists from various monasteries and lineages. Only later did it become a self-conscious movement. Chan is the most iconoclastic, individualistic, and puzzling of all Chinese Buddhist schools. Although it was actively forming during the Tang dynasty (618–906), Chan really came into its own during the Song dynasty (960–1279). Along with Pure Land, Chan was the only major Buddhist school to survive the great persecution of 841–45 relatively intact.

Chan styles itself as mysterious teaching that can only be passed along by qualified masters. Nowhere is this more evident than its great motto attributed to one of its legendary patriarchs: "A separate transmission outside the scriptures, not relying on words and phrases, directly transmitted from mind to mind."[21] According to Chan tradition, the school began with the historical Buddha, Shakyamuni, and his famous Flower Sermon. One day the Buddha took his seat before all the assembled monks and, instead of speaking, remained silent while holding a single flower aloft in his hand. Of all those assembled, only his disciple Mahakashyapa understood. The Buddha publicly recognized Mahakashyapa's realization and he, in turn, passed the wordless teaching along to his disciples. Eventually the transmission passed to Bodhidharma (470–543 C.E.), who, it is said, brought the teachings from India to southern China, crossing the great Yangtze River on a reed. From Bodhidharma, the transmission passed through several more patriarchs until it was inherited by Huineng (638–713), the legendary Sixth Patriarch. All later Chan masters have cited Huineng as the source of their received transmission.

This mythic account of Chan's origins cannot be corroborated by actual historical evidence. We do know that sometime in the late fifth century a shadowy figure named Bodhidharma was actively teaching some form of meditation in southern China. After his death, his followers set up various lineages but most of them faded away. By the late eighth century, we seem to have two main branches of this school: northern Chan and southern Chan. Over time the latter came to dominate, mainly through the efforts of a monk named Shenhui (684–758), who claimed to have received transmission from Huineng. Southern Chan eventually split into numerous subschools, all tracing themselves to Huineng. Only during the Song dynasty, when the various Chan schools were well established, did an actual account of the various schools and their origins get hammered out into a coherent line.

The Tang persecution of Buddhism left many Chan temples in the provinces untouched, especially in northern China, where the local rulers tended to be great supporters. One Chan master rose to prominence here, Yixuan (d. 867), who established the Linji school of Chan, which dominated Chinese Buddhism for centuries. As time passed, various new forms developed from this line (Chinese texts speak of "Five Schools" and "Seven Houses"). By the eleventh century, there were two main schools of Chan: Linji and Caotong. The latter split off from the Linji school over matters of practice and how realization comes about.[22]

During the Song dynasty, Chan had a strong lay following, particularly among the elite of Chinese society. Some Song Chan masters were highly educated and very influential in intellectual circles. This resulted in one of the great ironies of Buddhist history: many Chan masters were great scholars, and Chan tradition has produced a vast amount of literature—more than any other school of Buddhism. Yet Chan prides itself on the claim of *not* relying on words.

Chan's Main Features

The aim of Chan is "to see into one's nature and become Buddha." It is based on the paradox that is central to Buddha-nature teachings: we are all Buddha, we just do not know it. Essentially Chan accepts Huayan ("Flower Ornament") metaphysical teachings but it stresses direct realization and practice over intellectual study. Chan pushes its adherents to an immediate, intuitive apprehension of Truth. This is not a deliberate, rational conclusion but a sudden awakening (in Japanese, *satori*) that can only be achieved through a regimen of strict, rigorous discipline. For this reason, Chan traditionally required a monastic setting.

Different techniques developed in the various Chan schools to lead students to awakening. The centerpiece of Chan practice is seated meditation, or *zuochan* (in Japanese, *zazen*). Chan practitioners would spend long hours sitting cross-legged (usually in the lotus posture, with heels resting on the inner thighs), following their breath as a way of stilling the mind. A common image used to describe the mind in Chan meditation is water. Ordinarily, our minds are stirred up and opaque, like turbulent water sloshing around. If we still ourselves and our minds, we will become clear, just as water naturally clears itself when held still. As one Chan master writes:

> This one teaching of meditation is our most urgent business. If you do not practice meditation and enter *dhyana,* then when it comes down to it, you will be completely at a loss. Therefore, to seek the pearl, we should still the waves; if we disturb the water, it will be hard to get. When the water of meditation is clear, the pearl of the mind will appear of itself.[23]

Chan monasteries also stressed physical labor as part of the monks' daily routine. Such labor not only supported the community (Chan monasteries were on the whole self-sufficient), it served as a way to extend meditation into monks' daily lives; work itself became a moving meditation.

The most distinctive aspect of Chan training, though, involved the use of "public cases," or *gongan* (in Japanese, *koans*). *Gongan* are brief, paradoxical stories or statements, almost like riddles. They are designed to lead a student to a realization of truth beyond the reach of words and thought. Some of the more famous *gongan* are: "If clapping two hands produces a sound, what is the sound of one hand clapping?" and "Show me your original face before you were born!" Such perplexing questions and statements obviously do not have rational answers, which is precisely the point. A Chan master gives a *gongan* to his student to solve. The *gongan* becomes the focus of intense mental effort on the part of the student, who meditates on the *gongan* day and night in an effort to find a solution, some sort of proper response that demonstrates insight. Finally, after numerous failed attempts, the student exhausts his rational mind and, in effect, gives up. At this point the student will then have a breakthrough and realize the solution. Often *gongan* cannot be solved verbally—the student's "answer" may be a gesture, a shout, or some other action demonstrating his awakening. According to some accounts, meditation on a *gongan* left the student's mind so sensitive and receptive that sometimes a master could awaken student with a scream, a blow, a nonsensical phrase, or even a facial expression. Generally the student is rewarded for solving a *gongan* by being given another one to solve. The Linji school, in particular, makes great use of *gongan,* with the Caotong school using them to a lesser degree.

The Chan master is central to the entire regimen of training. He personally directs students, and the monks in the monastery are subservient to him. The master verifies students' progress, acknowledges their understanding, and transmits the teachings that he received from his own master. To study Chan is to study under a specific master. Such direct, face-to-face connection is absolutely essential for a Chan lineage to live on.

According to the great Chan masters, when all is said and done, awakening—although it is sudden, immediate, and miraculous—is very natural and ordinary. Awakening is nothing special, for then one realizes just what is always already the case. Chan does not claim to transform the practitioner into something new, just what he or she truly is. As Master Linji wrote long ago: "Followers of the Way, the Law of the Buddha has no room for elaborate activity; it is only everyday life with nothing to do. Evacuate, pass your water, put on your clothes, eat your food; if you are tired, lie down. The fool will laugh, but the wise man will understand."[24]

Chan is Buddhism but it is a *Chinese* form of Buddhism: spontaneous, practical, very this-worldly. There is no doubt that it borrowed heavily from Daoist philosophy and practice and, in turn, influenced Daoism. Chan had tremendous impact on Chinese culture from the Song dynasty on, becoming a major inspiration for the arts of calligraphy, poetry, and painting (all of which demonstrate spiritual as well as aesthetic insight, in the traditional Chinese view). Almost all Chinese intellectuals during the later Middle Ages had some familiarity with its teachings and expressed their admiration for it to varying degrees. We can see this Chan influence clearly with the rise of Neo-Confucianism, a late medieval reinterpretation of Confucianism that stressed seriousness, self-effort, and meditative practices. Even the Neo-Confucian practice of compiling the recorded sayings of the great Confucian masters is a direct borrowing from Chan.

Chan has been deeply influential outside of China, going to Korea (where it is known as *Son*) and Vietnam (where it is called *Thien*). However, Chan has exerted its greatest influence in Japan, where it was known as *Zen.* The Linji school (Rinzai Zen) was introduced into Japan, where it flourished during the Kamakura period (1185–1333), by a monk named Eisei (1141–1215). Rinzai temples became great centers of artistic and cultural achievement. The Caotong school (Soto Zen) was introduced into Japan by

Dogen (1200–1253), one of Japan's greatest philosophers and Zen masters. Soto Zen was never as popular as Rinzai, but its focus on silent meditation *(zazen)* as the means to awakening has had great impact on Japanese art.

In addition to the Rinzai and Soto schools, a third school of Zen also arose in Japan. Called *Obaku,* it was introduced to Japan in 1654. Always smaller than either Rinzai or Soto, Obaku Zen combines aspects of both. It advocates sudden, violent enlightenment for those who are naturally "gifted," who generally are to be trained through rigorous *zazen* and *koan* practice. Obaku, however, also reserves a quieter, more gradual path for other practitioners. This gradual path involves *zazen* as well as the Pure Land practice of *nembutsu.*[25]

VAJRAYANA

The most recent and, in many ways, most exotic of the major branches of Buddhism is Vajrayana. Followers of Vajrayana often describe it as the "third turning of the Wheel of Dharma," with Theravada and Mahayana being the first and second turnings respectively. The idea is that Vajrayana is the culmination of the previous two turnings. Historically, there is some truth to this view, since Vajrayana emerged much later than either Theravada or Mahayana. Sometime around the third century C.E., Vajrayana teachings and techniques rose to prominence in India and spread to other regions of the Buddhist world. It eventually disappeared in Theravada lands and developed only a minor following in Mahayana areas, but it came to dominate in the Himalayan region. Vajrayana Buddhism still is the majority religion in Nepal, Bhutan, Tibet, and Mongolia.[26]

Vajrayana is the secret-ritual vehicle of Buddhism. The name *Vajrayana* can be translated as "diamond vehicle," emphasizing the diamond qualities of hardness, clarity, and indestructibility. The term is also sometimes translated as "thunderbolt vehicle," in reference to thunderbolt scepter *(vajra)* of the Vedic god Indra. The *vajra,* like Indra's scepter, symbolizes cosmic power. It is usually rendered as an hourglass-shaped wand that Vajrayana adepts use in rituals. Its various prongs represent different Buddhas, and its power is enlightenment itself: unbreakable yet capable of shattering all spiritual obstacles.

Vajrayana draws on Indian elements, both Hindu and Buddhist. As a strongly ritual tradition, it makes great use of magical chants and syllables *(mantras)* thought to evoke great spiritual power when properly uttered.[27] Because of this reliance on *mantras,* Vajrayana is also known as Mantray-

Vajrayana ritual implements (*vajra* and bell). Courtesy of John C. George.

ana (the *mantra* vehicle). In Vajrayana, *mantras* have traditionally been considered closely guarded, secret teachings passed along from master to especially qualified pupils. Thus, scholars sometimes speak of Vajrayana as "esoteric" (secret) Buddhism. In addition, Vajrayana is often popularly known as "Tantric Buddhism" because of the prominent role of Tantric texts and rites. Tantrism describes a complex movement that appears in both Hindu and Buddhist forms. It arose in India in the early centuries of the Common Era as a critical response to institutionalized forms of religion. Tantrism employs special ritual techniques to tap into mysterious cosmic forces that Tantric practitioners often conceive of in both masculine and feminine forms. These techniques aim at uniting with and harnessing such forces for spiritual transformation. Such rites tend to be available only through secret initiation and training by a master who belongs to a specific lineage.

In addition to *mantras,* Vajrayana Buddhism also employs other ritual devices. Some of the more important are symbolic gestures made by the hands and fingers *(mudras),* and visual aids using pictures, diagrams, or magical circles *(mandalas)* designed to help a devotee attain mystical union with a particular *bodhisattva* or Buddha. Some of the most spectacular examples of Tibetan art are the great wall hangings *(thanghas)* that usually portray one or more Buddhist deities geometrically arranged in chartlike *mandalas.* Such *mandalas* are often the focus of complex visualization meditations preceding major rituals.

Vajrayana rites include practices of sexual yoga. Some Vajrayana texts state that since the world is bound by lust, it must be released through lust.

How this was to be done varied. "Right-hand" Tantra interpreted discussion of masculine and feminine powers and their accompanying rites symbolically, while "Left-hand" Tantra tended to act such things out. Tantric rites included ritual unions where the partner was visualized as a deity; a noncelibate couple would envision themselves as divine being and consort. The goal of such practices, when undertaken properly and with enough preparation, was to confront lust, master it, and transcend it. "Left-hand" Tantric practices earned a bad reputation in various quarters, encouraging Tantric Buddhism to go underground and become a secret tradition.

The texts laying out such secret techniques in Vajrayana were the Tantras, which are included only in the Tibetan canon. The Tantras classify the myriads of *bodhisattvas* and Buddhas into family groups that Vajrayana Buddhists use in their practices. These pantheons can get quite large, since each individual Buddha may include various emanations and will be accompanied by a *bodhisattva* and even a female counterpart.[28] In a typical ritual, the head of a particular Buddha family will be situated in the center of a *mandala* with the other family members placed in specific spots surrounding him. The placements in the *mandala* correspond to the deities' cosmic connections. Through guided meditations on these various deities, Tantric practitioners can gain a vision that, in turn, helps them achieve enlightenment.

Meditations involving visualizations play a major role in Vajrayana tradition. These practices are often quite complex and require extensive training.[29] Typically, a devotee trains his attention on a chosen figure (Buddha, heavenly *bodhisattva*, or other deity) with the aid of a *mandala*. At the first stage, the devotee may, for instance, envision rays of light emanating from the deity as it resides in its heavenly realm. Having achieved this stage, the practitioner advances to a stage in which he identifies with the spiritual being to the point where his consciousness is entirely absorbed into the entity's being. Such intense visualizations may lead the devotee to sense the cosmic powers flowing through the various "wheels" of energy *(chakras)* located at certain points of his body, and even perceive himself to be residing at the center of a pure Buddha realm defined by the *mandala*. The meditation concludes by carefully dissolving the vision into nothingness, thus graphically encouraging the release from one's ego-attachment.

The numerous deities invoked through such visualization exercises are themselves very complex figures. Like Hindu deities, they have dual aspects (peaceful or fierce) according to the functions they are required to perform; usually a deity will be invoked in its peaceful form to bestow blessings but

in its fierce form to repel evil forces. Vajrayana practitioners are particularly concerned with invoking and uniting Compassion and Wisdom, keys
to achieving enlightenment, which are usually depicted in the "father-
mother" image in which the deity is locked in sexual embrace with its consort. Ritually enacting such union (usually the province of "Left-handed"
Tantra) requires a series of special initiations involving baptism and other
such rites.

Vajrayana rites often involve the practice of magic, usually with the help
of chanted *mantras* and special *mudras*. The *mantras* do not necessarily
have to be spoken orally to be effective, and they are often written on banners hung from trees and lines or on slips of paper that are rotated in cy-
lindrical containers called prayer-wheels. The most famous *mantra* is the
Sanskrit phrase *Om mani padme hum* (Hail the Jewel in the Lotus). Vajrayana practitioners interpret this *mantra* in various ways, most commonly as
an invocation of the female form of the *bodhisattva* Avalokiteshvara, "the
lady of the jewel lotus."[30]

A distinctive feature of Vajrayana Buddhism is the role of the *siddha* (accomplished one), an adept in Tantric teachings and practices. Between the
eighth and twelfth centuries, tradition holds that there were 84 Mahasid-
dhas (Great Accomplished Ones)who helped spread Vajrayana teachings
in India and injected a dynamic, lay-centered spirit into the Buddhism of
the time. Their teachings were continued by their disciples, many of whom
became *siddhas* in their own right. *Siddhas* take their name from the miraculous powers *(siddhi)* they develop through meditation, yoga, and secret
rituals. They usually have been portrayed as wild, long-haired lay-people
who lived unconventional lives as wandering holy figures.[31] *Siddhas* have
often been rather eccentric "wizard-saints," shaman figures who could contact gods, cure illness, promote good harvests, or even bewitch enemies.
One of the greatest *siddhas* in all of Buddhist history was Milarepa (1040–
1123), a charismatic Tibetan poet and hermit who could withstand freezing
temperatures in his mountain cave with complete equanimity.

Because of the wondrous tales of the various *siddhas,* certain superficial
readings of some Tantric texts as well as some widely publicized accounts
of the actions of several contemporary gurus, Vajrayana has a reputation
for encouraging wild and immoral behavior. There is some justification for
this popular view. Passages in some of the Tantras speak, through oblique
"twilight language," of practitioners eating meat, drinking liquor, committing murder, having sexual intercourse, and even devouring human flesh.
Certainly the rites of "Left-handed" Tantric communities have often raised

eyebrows, particularly among noninitiates. Some Vajrayana practices are regarded as karmically dangerous and hence call for special training, as Vajrayana devotees intentionally engage in passionate acts. The rationale behind such rites, however, is well tested over centuries. By using the passions rather than fighting them, Tantric practitioners can overcome them, rather like fighting fire *with* fire. A famous Tantra states, "Those things that bind people of evil conduct, others use as a skillful means to gain freedom from the bonds of *samsara*. The world is bound by passion, but by passion too it can be freed!"[32]

Vajrayana spread throughout India and into other Buddhist lands. There were Vajrayana monasteries, for example, throughout Southeast Asia before Theravada's rise to dominance. A major Vajrayana center was located Indonesia, and its influence can still be seen at Borobudur on the island of Java, where the famous temple complex is laid out in the shape of an elaborate *mandala*. In the eighth century Vajrayana Buddhism was introduced into China, where it was briefly in vogue during the Tang dynasty when Buddhism was at its height. The exotic nature of Vajrayana's artwork and Tantric rites had tremendous appeal for the imperial court, but the tradition eventually died out. From China Vajrayana was transmitted to Korea, where it flourished until the fourteenth century. However, the Tantric tradition enjoyed far greater success in Japan, where, as the Shingon school, it has prospered down to the present day. Generally speaking, the Tantrism of Shingon is of the "Right-handed" type.

Vajrayana achieved its greatest success, though, in the Tibetan region. Introduced there by the great guru *rinpoche* (precious teacher) Padmasambhava, it quickly came to dominate the indigenous shamanistic tradition of Bon, absorbing much of the latter's magic lore in the process. As the dominant religion in the region, Vajrayana was able to shed much of its clandestine status, although it has maintained the notion of transmitting its most powerful teachings through esoteric lineages. From the sixteenth century until very recently, the Gelugpa school of Vajrayana, the lineage to which the Dalai Lamas belong, has dominated Tibet.

Vajrayana was relatively unknown in the West before the 1950s. Since then, however, many Tibetans have fled their homeland for India or the West, and Tibet itself has become somewhat more accessible. Tibetan texts have been widely studied and translated as well. Thus, although Vajrayana came to the United States later than Zen and Pure Land forms of Buddhism, it rapidly established a foothold in the latter half of the twentieth century. The spread of Vajrayana in the West has been encouraged by the many public appearances of the Dalai Lama, the charismatic leader of the Tibetan community in exile, and prominent celebrity followers such as Richard Gere. Because of its perceived exotic nature and the high profiles of some of its spokespeople, Vajrayana promises to continue to attract popular attention around the world.

DIFFERENT PATHS TO THE SAME GOAL

All three of the major branches of Buddhism differ greatly from each other. Nonetheless, they also have many similarities, the most obvious being that they all revere the same founder and all mark out paths by which one can overcome suffering. A shorthand way of differentiating them is to say that Theravada lays out the path of self-purification, Mahayana lays out the path of compassion, and Vajrayana lays out the path of passion. A well-known Buddhist allegory describes how these paths are similar and yet distinct. Imagine that a yellow-robed Theravada monk is walking down a path in a forest when he comes across a poisonous plant. Realizing the danger it poses to himself and any other traveler, the monk uproots the plant, discards it, and continues on. Now imagine a blue-robed Mahayana monk walking the same path. When he sees the plant, he, too, recognizes the danger it poses, both to himself as well as others. However, he also realizes that the poisonous plant can be of use. Therefore he picks it and makes a medicine from it to cure disease. Finally, imagine a red-robed Vajrayana monk coming down the same path. He spies the poisonous plant, and recognizes it for the danger it poses. He then picks the plant—and eats it.

It would be a mistake to view Theravada, Mahayana, and Vajrayana as completely distinct traditions. The analogy to the main branches of Christianity (Eastern Orthodoxy, Roman Catholicism, and Protestantism) proposed earlier in this chapter is useful, provided it is not pushed too far. Certainly all three Buddhist traditions are the products of different historical and cultural conditions. Yet their differences tend not to be substantive and may be more matters of degree rather than kind. Theravada, for example, does teach compassion and the ultimate Emptiness of all things. Mahayana generally accords monastics higher status than the laity. All three branches of Buddhism involve elaborate magical rites in which various deities and other spiritual beings are invoked. Perhaps most importantly, all three branches have produced many great religious leaders who have sincerely sought to lead others beyond a life of suffering. Theravada,

Mahayana, and Vajrayana Buddhism continue the teachings, practices, and spirit of Siddhartha Gautama, the historical Buddha. All three mark out different paths to *nirvana.*

NOTES

1. Some scholars argue that doctrinal differences between Theravada and Mahayana in particular have diminished over time. See Huston Smith, *The World's Religions* (New York: HarperCollins, 1991), 127.

2. The Sanskrit title for "Teaching of the Elders" is *Sthiravada.* This became *Theravada* when translated into Pali, an Indic language derived from Sanskrit that has become the sacred language of Theravada tradition.

3. Because it is concentrated in southern areas of Asia, Theravada is sometimes also called the "southern School."

4. Theravadin philosophy of mind includes a subconscious level that serves as a repository for karmic forces—an idea very reminiscent of Yogachara teachings concerning the Storehouse Consciousness.

5. *Arhat* is also one of the titles of the Buddha.

6. It has been observed that many sons of poor families in Thailand seek ordination as a way of getting an education, sometimes all the way through college. Often these young monks will serve as teachers or administrators in monastic communities for a year or two before disrobing and returning to the secular world. See Donald K. Swearer, *Buddhism and Society in Southeast Asia* (Chambersburg, PA: Anima, 1981), 25.

7. In this regard, appropriate Western parallels might be the Christian rite of confirmation or the Jewish rite of bar mitzvah.

8. Contrary to popular belief, monks are not necessarily vegetarian. Monks must take anything that is placed in their bowls. The Buddha himself seems to have accepted meat that was placed in his begging bowl, and he explicitly allowed monks to eat meat as long as there was no evidence that the creature had been killed specifically for them.

9. The nuns' ordination line died out in Sri Lanka in the eleventh century following an invasion; it died out in Burma about two hundred years later.

10. Because it is geographically concentrated in East Asia, Mahayana is sometimes known as "eastern Buddhism."

11. A famous analogy illustrates this point: Buddhist teachings are like a raft to ferry one across a body of water *(samsara).* The raft is necessary for the crossing, but once on the far shore, the traveler must abandon it because it is no longer required. Similarly, when one reaches certain advanced stages

along the spiritual path, one should discard previous teachings because they have served their purpose and will now only hinder further progress. Upon attaining full enlightenment *(nirvana),* of course, one abandons *all* teachings.

12. Mahayana Buddhists regularly pray to *bodhisattvas,* petitioning them for blessings, good fortune, and help in times of severe distress.

13. In this respect, the cult of Maitreya closely resembles some of the millennial sects within Christianity that eagerly anticipate Jesus' Second Coming.

14. This gender shift can be understood as a prominent example of "skillful means," since the *bodhisattva* has the power to assume any shape needed by believers.

15. Tara is alleged to have been born from one of Guanyin's tears.

16. Amitabha means "Infinite Life," and is often equated with the name Amitayus (Infinite Light).

17. This western connection has led some scholars to speculate that Pure Land may have been influenced by Western traditions such as Zoroastrianism, Gnosticism, or even early Christianity.

18. From Compendium on the Happy Land by Daochuo (d. 645), a great Pure Land patriarch. Quoted in William Theodore de Bary and Irene Bloom, eds., *Sources of Chinese Tradition, Volume I: From Earliest Times to 1600,* 2nd edition (New York: Columbia University Press, 1999), 486.

19. It has been pointed out that, like devotional Christianity, Pure Land has a God-figure (Amitabha), a mediator (Guanyin), is based on faith and grace, and includes a devotional practice that resembles the rosary. See Julia Ching, *Chinese Religions* (Maryknoll, New York: Orbis Books, 1993), 142.

20. There is a story that when Jesuit missionaries came to Japan in the sixteenth and seventeenth centuries and found various forms of Pure Land flourishing, they became incensed, convinced that Lutheran "heretics" had beaten them there.

21. Traditionally attributed to Bodhidharma, an Indian prince credited with bringing Chan teachings to China in the sixth century.

22. Among other things, Caotong insists on a more quietistic and gradualist approach to meditation that cannot be forced, in contrast to the Linji practice of provoking an awakening through unorthodox techniques such as shouts or slaps. Some Caotong masters have claimed that "just sitting" *is* the Buddha-mind.

23. Changlu Zongze, Principles of Seated Meditation. Quoted in William Theodore de Bary and Irene Bloom, eds., *Sources of Chinese Tradition, Volume I: From Earliest Times to 1600,* 2nd ed. (New York: Columbia University Press, 1999), 524.

24. Linji Yixuan, Seeing into One's Own Nature. Quoted in William Theodore de Bary and Irene Bloom, eds., *Sources of Chinese Tradition, Volume I: From Earliest Times to 1600,* 2nd ed. (New York: Columbia University Press, 1999), 504.

25. Such mixing of Pure Land and Chan/Zen practices, although officially rather rare in Japan, was common in China and is still the norm among most Chinese Buddhists.

26. Some people refer to Vajrayana as "northern Buddhism," since its areas of dominance are north of the historical Buddha's native region.

27. In this respect, Vajrayana picks up the ancient Vedic idea that the sacred rituals performed by brahmin priests were ways of harnessing tremendous cosmic power.

28. The presence of both male and female deities is necessary for conducting the visualizations required as part of Tantric sexual rites.

29. In the following description I use masculine pronouns *(he, his)* in keeping with the fact that most Tantric texts are addressed to a male audience. It is important to note, though, that there have always been well-known *female* Vajrayana adepts.

30. Some Vajrayana Buddhists interpret the six syllables of the *mantra* as referring to the Six Perfections or the Six Realms of Rebirth (hells, hungry ghosts, animals, humans, fierce gods, heavenly gods).

31. *Siddhas* are similar to the early wandering holy men *(shramanas)* of ancient India. They are also reminiscent of some of the Chan and Zen masters, who were famous for their unconventional behavior.

32. Hevajara Tantra, II, 2.50–51. Quoted in Mitchell, *Buddhism: Introducing the Buddhist Experience,* 162.

4

PRACTICE WORLDWIDE

Although teachings are important in Buddhism, the religion stresses *practice* over *belief*.[1] Many Buddhist practices were established in ancient times but are still observed today. Moreover, there are specific rituals that mark each of these practices, and much of Buddhist literature is devoted to detailing them.

EMBARKING ON THE PATH

As a universal religion not tied to race, ethnicity, or national origin, Buddhism is open to all people. Becoming a Buddhist is commonly done by "Taking Refuge," a formal profession of faith in the Three Jewels (Buddha, Dharma and *sangha*—the teacher, teachings, and community, respectively).[2] Taking Refuge is an important step in a Buddhist's life—it may be the culmination of childhood education (much like a bar mitzvah or bat mitzvah in Judaism) or a new commitment to the pursuit of the state beyond life-and-death *(nirvana)*. There are differences between the three main branches of Buddhism (Theravada, Mahayana, and Vajrayana) on the ramifications of Taking Refuge, but all Buddhists agree that it has positive karmic effects.

Taking Refuge is the closest thing to a universal rite of passage in Buddhism. At its simplest, this rite involves reciting out loud three times the following formula: "I take refuge in the Buddha; I take refuge in the Dharma; I take refuge in the *sangha*." Often a monk recites each "refuge" first, and a group of initiates repeats his words in unison. Most Buddhist ceremonies begin and end with such communal affirmations of allegiance. Sometimes the recitations are accompanied by a series of bows and prostrations as a way of physically enacting the practitioners' dependence.

After Taking Refuge, most Buddhists vow to follow the Five Precepts. The Five Precepts are derived from the steps of the Eightfold Path (especially those concerning right action, right speech, and right livelihood), and constitute Buddhism's basic moral code. They are chanted regularly in rituals by both monks and laity. The Five Precepts are

1. To abstain from intentionally harming life.
2. To abstain from taking things not explicitly given.
3. To abstain from illicit sexual activity.
4. To abstain from harmful speech (lying, gossip, etc.).
5. To abstain from indulging in intoxicants (liquor or other drugs).

As one can see, the Five Precepts are vows to abstain from potentially destructive actions, thus setting boundaries for leading an orderly life. For the most part, actions that do not run counter to the precepts are perfectly acceptable. The Five Precepts are open to a wide range of interpretation. For example, some Buddhists view the fifth precept concerning intoxicants as allowing occasional consumption of alcohol so long as it does not lead to intoxication. Members of monastic orders take far more restrictive vows in addition to these five.

The first precept on avoiding harm does *not* require Buddhists to be vegetarians. Vegetarianism is encouraged, but many Buddhists eat fish or meat except on special occasions. Theravada monastic codes do not prohibit monks and nuns from eating meat, only from eating creatures specifically slaughtered for them. Monks and nuns are to follow the Buddha's example and eat whatever food they receive, with the idea that overcoming desire and attachment is more important than avoiding meat. Most Mahayana lineages, though, require their members to be vegetarians on the understanding that eating meat causes animal suffering. Monastics in Nepal, Tibet, and other Himalayan regions, however, do not have to eat a vegetarian diet.

Mahayana Buddhists may follow an expanded version of the Five Precepts known as the Ten Good Actions. In addition to abstaining from harming, stealing, and illicit sexual activity (covered by three of the Five Precepts), the Ten Good Actions include prohibitions on certain types of speech (lying, using harsh words, using words designed to cause enmity, engaging in idle talk) as well as prohibitions on being greedy, becoming enraged, and holding "wrong views." Abiding by such prohibitions helps purge the mind of unwholesome thoughts and dispositions, thus removing any motivation to commit harmful deeds.

The Buddha encouraged his followers to engage in beneficial actions and to develop helpful attitudes and virtues. Generally speaking, members of the *sangha* are enjoined to be content with life as it is (to counteract selfishness and desire) and to cultivate compassion for other beings. One way this can be done is through systematic meditation on the Four Divine Abodes (loving-kindness, compassion, sympathetic joy, and equanimity). Through carefully guided meditations, practitioners develop goodwill, empathy, and joyful sympathy with others and extend these attitudes to all living beings while gradually becoming detached from selfish concerns. Nurturing such dispositions helps break down feelings of separation from others, allowing one to embrace all beings, be they lovable or unlovable, friends or enemies.

Mahayana Buddhists often take *bodhisattva* vows as part of their spiritual path. *Bodhisattvas* are beings who, out of compassion, postpone their achievement of *nirvana* to aid other beings.[3] This is a path based on altruistic motivation and can be taken by lay and monastic followers. Traditionally, Mahayana teaches that becoming a *bodhisattva* entails many lives and takes eons to accomplish. Usually this journey begins after the aspirant has earned a high level of merit and, with the guidance of a teacher, experiences "the thought of Enlightenment" *(bodhichitta).* During a special ritual, the aspirant vows to attain Awakening *for the sake of all living beings.* For Buddhists, undertaking the *bodhisattva* path is way of taking full advantage of one's precious human birth; the vows are powerful forces that guide one to ever deeper levels of compassion and wisdom.

All Buddhist practice is predicated on a strict but flexible ethical code. Common stereotypes that Buddhism is an otherworldly mysticism that ignores matters of morality are grossly misleading. Fundamental to all Buddhist teaching is the cosmic law of cause and effect *(karma)* and its consequences. One simply cannot accumulate the positive balance of *karma* needed to advance toward *nirvana* without maintaining ethical integrity. Moreover, cultivating compassion requires living a moral life as well.

The Buddha Dharma comprises a comprehensive moral blueprint for living. Although Buddhism includes exacting meditation exercises, most of these have very practical applications. One of the goals of such practice is to instill a thorough understanding of *karma.* By training practitioners to observe *karma*'s subtle effects, these meditations enable them to choose actions designed to lead to the most beneficial outcome possible.

MONASTICISM

Monasticism is found in many religions and refers to living a secluded and ascetic life dedicated to spiritual matters. Monastics (monks and nuns) renounce ordinary life to live in poverty and celibacy apart from mainstream society. Buddhist monasticism does not require a lifelong commitment, and to this day many people (especially in Southeast Asian countries where Theravada, the most conservative branch of Buddhism, dominates) join a monastic order for a brief period, often as a way of getting an education. Although most Buddhists are lay people, monasticism has been central to Buddhism since its beginning.

At first, the Buddhist monastic community wandered from place to place (except for a three-month retreat during the rainy season), relying on gifts of food and clothing from local people. This was not a new way of life, since there was a long-standing tradition in India of devout people renouncing village life to dedicate themselves to spiritual pursuits. Eventually, however, the monastic order received gifts of land and property. In response, Buddhist renunciates established settled communities of monks and nuns who lived together to study, teach, and practice the Dharma.

In Buddhism, becoming a monastic is called "leaving home" because aspirants literally leave their homes and join a community of fellow religious seekers. This does not mean, however, that monastics are cut off from the world. Rather, the relationship between monastics and laity is based on an informal social contract of spiritual and material exchange: monks and nuns teach, perform rituals, and in general offer themselves as a "field of merit" for the laity to use in developing virtues, thereby insuring a better rebirth. The laity, for their part, provide food, clothing, and other necessities for the monks so that they may live in full-time pursuit of *nirvana*. This relationship is epitomized in the daily alms round. Monks walk from door to door, holding their begging bowls in calm, meditative detachment. The laity show their gratitude by placing food into the monks' bowls and bow to demonstrate their respect.

Joining a monastic order involves a series of steps. Although the Buddha stated that he was establishing a "middle way" between asceticism and indulgence, he stressed that monks and nuns were to live "depending on little" for their existence. Traditionally, the Theravada branch requires that a candidate be old enough to "scare away the crows" (about seven or eight years of age). At the first level, the candidate's head is shaved and he is given a monastic name and a set of robes with a few other articles.[4] Novitiate or-

Buddhist monk begging for alms, Kyoto, Japan. Courtesy of the author.

dination only requires that the candidate repeat his vows of Taking Refuge and accept Ten Precepts (the usual abstentions with the addition of five more: abstention from wearing perfumes and flowers, singing and dancing, using a large bed, taking regular meals, and acquiring personal wealth). Novices may advance to full ordination after a time of intensive training lasting weeks or even months. During this ceremony, the novices take their full monastic vows, kneeling for hours as the entire content of the Code of Discipline, the section of the canon covering monastic life, is read to them. At the conclusion of ordination, new monks are informed of the "four resources" available to them to secure their basic needs: the foot of a tree for shelter, robes made of rags for clothing, alms for food, and fermented cow's urine for medicine.

In Mahayana orders, monks often undergo a third ordination in which they take *bodhisattva* vows. The day before taking their vows, candidates kneel to receive the special marks of a fully ordained monk or nun: 9 or 12 scars on their heads. These marks are made by placing small cones of incense in lines of three on the candidates' heads and allowing the cones to burn down to the scalp. Initiates overcome the pain by chanting sacred verses *(sutras).*

All Buddhist monks and nuns must abide by the Code of Discipline. From the very beginning, the Buddha specified that the monastic community was bound by state laws, and he prohibited criminals, escaped slaves, and debtors from joining. He also set out rules and principles governing communal life. In Theravada tradition, monks are bound by 227 rules, but this number differs in other branches: Tibetan monks follow 258 rules, whereas Japanese monks follow 250. Penalties for violating monastic rules vary depending on the nature of the infringement. The most serious violations are having sexual intercourse, stealing, killing, and claiming false levels of spiritual attainment. These four are known as "defeats" and call for expulsion from the community. Less serious violations require public confession and vows of repentance. Often, violators engage in specific austerities, in much the same way that some Christians take on penances after confessing their sins. Monastic communities as a rule have a distinct hierarchy determined by seniority from the time of ordination. In addition, in accordance with the Buddha's instructions, every two weeks (on the new and full moons) the entire community assembles to chant the Code of Discipline, confess any violations, and reconfirm their monastic commitment.

All branches of Buddhism clearly differentiate between the order of monks and the order of nuns. From an institutional point of view, nuns are inferior to monks (even newly ordained novices), and are bound by many more rules. This comparatively inferior role for nuns reflects misogynistic attitudes prevalent in Asia from ancient times up to the present. Still, the Buddha, although originally reluctant, did admit women into the monastic order—a truly radical policy in his day.[5] Moreover, nuns have long taken active roles in the operation of the *sangha* and ministering to the public. Although there is no longer an order of fully ordained nuns in Theravada tradition, fully ordained nuns are still found in Mahayana countries, especially in East Asia. Both South Korea and Taiwan have notably large communities of nuns.

Buddhist monasteries range in size from small village temples housing only a few monks to grand teaching institutions.[6] Monasteries are usually walled compounds containing a mound housing sacred relics *(stupa)*, an image house or shrine, and a *bodhi* tree similar to the one under which the Buddha attained enlightenment. Typical monasteries also house a library, residential buildings (single cells arranged around a central court), refectories, clinics, and bathing and toilet areas. Most Buddhist monasteries follow the pattern established with the founding of Jetavana monastery near the city of Sravasti, India: a hilltop location surrounded by trees and supplied with abundant water.[7] According to tradition, such a setting helps to maintain the discipline needed to attain enlightenment.

Although the Dharma governs all of monastic life, it is most clearly embodied in the central Dharma Hall, where meetings take place and major ceremonies are held. Libraries are important as well, as they are where scriptures and commentaries are stored, copied, studied, and translated. Several monasteries were widely known for their collections of texts and became great centers teaching and learning. One of the most famous was at Nalanda in northern India, which in its heyday was one of the greatest scholarly centers in all of Asia.

Daily life in a monastery can vary widely across the different branches of Buddhism and even from community to community. Nonetheless, all monasteries are dedicated to living according to and spreading the Dharma. Theravada monasticism claims to be the closest to the earliest way of life outlined by the *sangha,* and it remains a small but vital part of most Southeast Asian societies.[8] Monastic life changed, however, as Buddhism spread to other cultures. The most drastic changes occurred in China. Chinese culture had been family centered from prehistoric times, so "leaving home" proved particularly difficult. Over time Chinese monasteries took on familial features, with the master becoming a new monk's "father" and the other monks becoming his "elder brothers." The Chinese government regulated monastic communities, limiting the number of monasteries offering ordination and issuing official ordination certificates. A fully ordained monk had an unusual amount of freedom in China. He could serve at a local temple, where he could earn a comfortable living performing rites for local cli-

Typical Theravada monastery. © Getty Images/32095.

ents (some even earned enough to establish their own private temples), or join a large, public monastery and advance through the institutional hierarchy, perhaps even to the level of abbot. Particularly devout or ambitious monks would travel to famous monasteries (where they received free lodging) to study with renowned Dharma masters—a wandering life symbolic of detachment from worldly affairs. However, most Chinese monks never advanced beyond the level of novice.

Of all Chinese Buddhist schools, monasticism was most central in Chan (*Zen* in Japan). As Chan spread to Korea, Japan, and Vietnam, it brought a distinct monastic style that still dominates East Asia. Specific rules for Chan monasteries date back to the early seventh century but were first laid out by Baizhang Huaihai (720–814), who is famous for requiring that all monks work. As Baizhang put it, "A day without work is a day without food."

Chan monks are supposed to live lives based on humility and discipline. They are allowed only a few possessions (a razor, a set of bowls, a set of black robes and white vestments, cotton leggings, a large bamboo hat, and straw sandals). Daily life is divided between work, study, ritual, and meditation. A typical day begins at 3:30 or 4:00 A.M. and ends at 9:00 P.M., although this is sometimes followed by compulsory "night sitting" (meditation). Usually monks meditate for two hours in the morning and three to five hours in the evening. This schedule is punctuated by monthly intensive meditation sessions that may entail 8 to 15 hours of daily meditation and may last from five to seven days. Such sessions often attract monks and laypeople from outside the monastery.

Generally Chan monks do not engage in alms rounds but work for their upkeep. Typical tasks include cleaning, gardening, building maintenance, or cooking. Such physical labor offsets the lethargy resulting from long hours of meditation, allows the monastery to be self-supporting, and helps focus the mind. Even simple assignments afford opportunities for extending the concentration attained in meditation into other areas of life. The ultimate goal of Chan training is not to escape the world but to be fully awake in any situation.

Since Chan is so physically and psychologically demanding, it has traditionally been the practice to deny someone's initial request to enter monastic life. Usually, an applicant must demonstrate his sincerity by waiting outside the monastery for two days and then spending three to five days in a small room, alone. When admitted, the would-be-monk goes to the meditation hall and prostrates himself three times before the image of the Buddha or *bodhisattva* there. He then is assigned one mat (about three feet by six feet in size) on which he will live, sleep, and meditate. After a few days he has a private interview with the Chan master (the first of many) and officially begins monastic training.

Becoming a hermit, although rare, is still practiced in Buddhism. This form of monasticism calls for extreme discipline, since ideally, hermits should dwell far from society. The Buddha and his earliest monks set the pattern for hermit life, but many great figures in Buddhist history lived solitary lives dedicated to religious cultivation. Over the years, these hermits included various Tibetan yogis (some of whom lived alone in mountain caves), and certain Chan and Zen masters (famous for their mountain huts). Usually Buddhist hermits have been associated with larger communities, receiving occasional visitors or disciples bringing food and seeking instruction. A more common practice is for devout monks to opt for "sealed confinement" in a room on monastery grounds. This period (typically three years) begins with a formal ceremony to which friends and lay supporters are invited. The monk declares his intention and the purpose of his confinement, as well as the exercises he will perform (meditation, chanting, prostrations, etc.) The door to the room is then sealed. The hermit remains alone for the specified period, receiving only food and water. Such periods of solitude have long been regarded as the ultimate way to cultivate wisdom and detachment.

MEDITATION

Many people associate Buddhism with meditation, but meditation itself is often poorly understood. To begin with, there are problems in defining "meditation," as it can cover many practices involving sustained concentration. Moreover, although meditation is central to Buddhism, one cannot attain *nirvana* merely by meditating. Attaining deep levels of meditative trance is not possible without proper physical and ethical discipline. Physical discipline requires training to achieve and maintain proper posture (e.g., the lotus position, in which both legs are crossed so that the heels rest upon the inner thighs) and to regulate one's breathing. Proper ethical discipline is harder. In addition to scrupulously following the precepts, one must remove all impure or selfish thoughts. A practitioner should also learn to suppress the Five Mental Hindrances (sensual desire, ill will, lethargy, agitation over lapses in concentration, and doubt). Overcoming these disruptive forces allows one to focus the mind and gradually enter ever deeper states of concentration.

Most Buddhist meditation aims at instilling "mindfulness," an attitude of general attentiveness to a particular object. Mindfulness meditation is also known as "recollection" (in that one learns to "re-collect" one's normally scattered thoughts). Developing mindfulness requires focus and concentration but is useful for cultivating patience and detachment from habitual reactions to the world. Becoming more mindful is an important step in learning how to enter the higher stages of meditative trance and attaining wisdom.

The most basic style of meditation is a twofold practice known as "calming and insight" *(samatha-vipashyana)*. It begins by calming the mind's incessant jumping from thought to thought, usually by focusing on a simple bodily movement such as walking or, more commonly, breathing.[9] Once a level of calm is established, a practitioner turns to developing insight, usually by contemplating the breath itself, bodily postures, and sensations, the elements that compose the body. In insight meditation, the practitioner maintains simple awareness of an object as it is. By developing this power of sustained observation, the practitioner learns to see what reality actually is like. Through much practice of calming and insight, the practitioner learns to observe the Three Marks of Existence as well as the way in which things arise and depart, moving on to perceptions, emotions, and other states of mind. Such practices enable the practitioner to realize Buddhist teachings directly in his or her experience.

A particularly powerful insight meditation involves contemplating corpses. As part of their training, monks may visit charnel grounds to observe bodies in varying states of decay. Such training forces monks to come to grips with their own mortality and provides a visceral experience of impermanence and "no-self." Corpse meditation may also help monks learn to understand and overcome disgust and fear, and it is an effective antidote for lust and sensual desire. Today, some monks augment this practice by observing autopsies.

Other types of meditation include visualization. Visualization involves the carefully controlled imagining of a particular image while avoiding the flighty and delusional aspects of such activities as daydreaming. Often aided by artistic images, visualization grew very popular as Mahayana spread through Asia. Some well-known visualization practices involve picturing "Lady Perfect Wisdom" (Perfection of Wisdom personified as a beautiful goddess), the "Mother of the Buddha." Others involve calling to mind a Buddha or *bodhisattva* residing within his celestial abode, usually in exquisite detail. One Pure Land text describes a procedure in which practitioners concentrate on the Pure Land day and night for a week, after which it will appear right there before their eyes. Visualization practices are particularly prominent in Vajrayana Buddhism, where they often serve as a way to empowerment. For instance, in many Tantric initiation rituals, the aspirant is required to gaze upon or even sit within a sacred diagram *(mandala)* depicting Buddhist deities situated within their particular realms. The initiate concentrates on a particular deity's image, enabling it to come alive in his mind. He then mentally approaches it, perhaps even "joining" with it. Over time, the initiate memorizes the deity's form and is able to construct (physically or in his imagination) the *mandala* for other, more advanced visualizations.

Perhaps the best-known Buddhist meditation is the "seated meditation" *(suochan* in Chinese, *zazen* in Japanese) so characteristic of Chan/Zen tradition. It is a simple practice derived from the calming and insight technique and takes up much of a monk's day. Seated meditation usually begins with practitioners sitting on cushions, their legs crossed, backs straight, hands resting in their laps. With eyes half-open (to ward off sleep and maintain contact with the external world), they focus on their breathing. Meditators in the Linji/Rinzai school sit facing each other, drawing strength from communal effort. Members of the Caotong/Soto school, in contrast, face the wall of the meditation hall with their backs to each other. In both schools, it is common for one monk to parade up and down between the rows of monks, armed with a special stick to strike the shoulder of anyone whose attention seems to be flagging. Through long practice under the watchful eye of the master, the student's mind gradually stills, allowing the Original Mind to flash into the open. Such sudden insights *(satori)* do not signal full enlightenment but herald the beginning of true cultivation. Typically, the student progresses to ever deepening experiences of insight. Most Chan/Zen schools maintain that seated meditation is not merely the means to Awakening but is the essence of Wisdom itself. Meditation is a dynamic state, the active awareness of present reality, Buddha-mind within the everyday world.

A Tibetan meditation similar to seated meditation is "Great Perfection" *(dzogchen)*, a practice associated with the Nyingma school in which the practitioner comes to experience the pure nature of Mind itself. Guided by a guru in calming the mind, the *dzogchen* student gradually gains awareness of the inherently "empty" (impermanent and evanescent) nature of all mental and emotional states. From there one moves on to a state of pure awareness, the innately still and luminous essence of mind that is the Buddha-nature. As such experiences of Mind's essence deepen, Buddhahood spontaneously manifests itself in the practitioner's life.

The highest states of meditation are trances *(dhyana, samadhi)*, extreme levels of concentration long associated with progress toward *nirvana*. One who attains such exalted states has achieved such an advanced spiritual condition that all desires have been eliminated and further advancement to *nirvana* is easy. Some early texts refer to four states of trance that culminate in a state of pure awareness beyond all forms of sensation and conceptualization. It is at this level that *arhats* and *bodhisattvas* are said to enter *nirvana*. In Mahayana traditions, some trances are accompanied by visions and supernatural experiences (e.g., extrasensory perception) by which one can confirm one's spiritual attainments.

CHANTING

Chanting is common to all forms of Buddhism and can be a highly effective meditation technique, a way of invoking helpful deities or a means of protection from negative forces. Oral recitation of liturgical texts has been practiced since the earliest days of the *sangha*, and most Buddhist practitioners (lay and monastic) engage in it to some extent. The power of chanting derives from both the sacred nature of the words themselves and the mental focus of the person chanting. Chanting is especially common in Vajrayana and Pure Land Buddhism, where services may last for hours, but even Chan/Zen schools chant texts such as the Heart Sutra.

Usually, practitioners will chant a sacred syllable or series of syllables *(mantra)* or a somewhat longer passage from scripture *(dharani)*. These are repeated over and over continuously as a way of harnessing the power of speech to focus the mind. The use of sacred speech is so prominent in Vajrayana that this branch of Buddhism is often referred to as "the *mantra* vehicle" (Mantrayana). Practitioners often accompany their chanting by fingering small beads strung together on a string. These strings of beads, which can vary in length, help the practitioner keep track of the number of recitations and prevent the mind from wandering.[10]

Most Buddhist chants are in Sanskrit, the sacred language of India, although in East Asia scriptures are chanted in Chinese or Japanese. Even there, however, practitioners still chant *mantras* and *dharanis* in Sanskrit. As Mahayana developed, certain texts composed specifically for ritual chanting appeared—the "Buddha-name *sutras*." These texts, little more than lists of the names of various Buddhas, were thought to create when chanted great merit that the practitioner could transfer to another being, usually someone recently deceased. Because of this, priests will chant these *sutras* at funerals in hopes of helping the dead attain a favorable rebirth. Chanting also is thought to change the situation for the living, generating favorable *karma* as, for example, in the chanting of the formula when Taking Refuge.

Chanting is popular because the constant repetition of words and phrases has a powerful effect on a practitioner's psyche. Usually the *mantras* or other passages recited are short, symbolic phrases. The Heart Sutra is one of the most popular texts for chanting in its entirety or for its concluding *mantra: gate gate paragate parasamgate bodhi swaha* (Gone, gone, gone beyond, gone way beyond, Enlightenment, All Hail!). It is recited in Chan and Zen temples before meditation sessions, at funerals, and even at weddings.

Followers of Pure Land Buddhism repeatedly chant the holy name of Amitabha Buddha to attest to their faith. Called "remembering the Buddha" (in Chinese *nianfo*, in Japanese *nembutsu*), this practice is ideal for lay Buddhists who cannot devote themselves to the pursuit of *nirvana* although it is popular with monks and nuns as well. To this day the phrase "I take refuge in Amitabha Buddha" (in Chinese *Nianfo Amituo Fo*, in Japanese *Namu Amida Butsu*) is among the most recited lines throughout East Asia. The Japanese Pure Land priests Honen (1133–1212) and Shinran (1173–1263) maintained that one need only recite *nembutsu* once in true sincerity to attain rebirth in Amida's Pure Land.

DEVOTION

The desire for a personal relationship with a deity is common in many religious traditions. Buddhism has a strong devotional side as well. This is true even in Theravada, where the Buddha is understood to be a person who died and can no longer aid his followers. Devotion has been primarily the province of the laity, but monastics are often deeply involved in it. Archaeological and historical sources indicate that Buddhist devotion goes back to the Buddha's first followers. According to traditional accounts, the Buddha's cremated remains were divided into eight portions and distributed to local rulers who enshrined them throughout northern India. These eight sites quickly became major places of worship.

Most Buddhist devotion takes place at temples and shrines. Temples range in size from small neighborhood shrines to large complexes encom-

Offerings at Buddhist temple, Xian,
China. Courtesy of the author.

passing many compounds. The latter often serve as great monasteries and
may house hundreds of monks and nuns. Although most crowded on important holidays and festivals, temples are open at all hours of the day. Visitors typically come to offer prayers and incense but may also consult with
monks on religious matters or to hire them to perform certain rituals. At
temples visitors can sometimes hear Dharma talks, receive meditation instruction, or even stay for a short period.

The most important Buddhist shrines are domelike mounds *(stupas)*
housing sacred relics (bits of bone, teeth, or ashes of the Buddha and important saints), texts, and other precious articles. In one early text the Buddha
tells his followers, "Whoever lays wreathes of flowers, or puts perfumes, or
adds color [to the *stupas*] with a devout heart will reap benefit and happiness for a long time."[11] *Stupas* can be found in most temple complexes. *Stupas* were probably based on the burial mounds of ancient kings and rapidly
became places where Buddhists could honor the Buddha and the Dharma.
Emperor Ashoka (274–236 B.C.E.) saw to the construction of many *stupas*
across his realm. As Buddhism spread into East Asia, the form of the *stupa*
changed, becoming the pagoda, a tower having an odd number of stories
(three, five, or seven) that is often a temple's most prominent landmark.
Many scholars surmise that the Mahayana movement began at such sites,

with the first *bodhisattvas* being particular devout lay persons who took it upon themselves to maintain the *stupas* and deliver sermons to those who came to worship. In addition, lay Buddhists often worship at small in-home shrines and altars similar to the altars traditionally reserved for ancestor veneration.

Most devotional practices entail veneration of holy relics and sacred images. The basic idea behind such veneration is the accumulation of merit by instilling beneficial mental states, such as gratitude and a sense of obligation, and motivating worshippers to perform good deeds. Buddhist relics and images are channels for imparting sacred power and healing, much like relics and images of holy figures in other religions. Worshippers typically pray, prostrate themselves before the image, and offer tokens of incense, candles, or money. As in Hinduism, venerated images are not "idols" but *icons* that serve as sites where worshippers can meet the deity in person. Buddhist images may even be bathed and paraded through the neighborhood on festival days.

Although Pure Land is the most obvious devotional form of Buddhism, over the years a number of cults to certain Buddhas and celestial *bodhisat-*

Statue of Maitreya in the form of the jolly fat monk (Budai/Hotei) so popular in East Asia. © Getty Images/32127.

tvas have arisen. Relatively early on, there was a large cult dedicated to Maitreya (the Friendly One), who currently is waiting in the lowest heaven to be reborn on earth. Until then, Maitreya is said to respond to all who call upon him. Popular legend maintains that he even appeared on earth as a jolly, fat Chan monk who carried a large bag and was particularly fond of children; his image is often found in Chan temples or Chinese shops and restaurants. Manjushri (Sweet Glory), is a great *bodhisattva* renowned for his wisdom. Depicted as a prince brandishing a sword (to cut through ignorance), his image is found in many meditation halls. Avalokiteshvara, (the Lord who Looks Down [from Above]), is probably the most popular Buddhist deity. Known for his great compassion, he resides in Amitabha's Pure Land, from whence he responds to the cries of the world. Avalokiteshvara appears in numerous forms, one of which is the Dalai Lama. In East Asia, he appears as a female, Guanyin in China and Kannon in Japan. Another popular *bodhisattva* is Kshitigarbha (Earth-store), who appears in the hell realms to aid the afflicted. Known as *Jizo* in Japan, he guides travelers and is especially concerned with protecting dead children.[12]

Devout Buddhists also practice fasting. Monks and nuns typically fast for much of the day and during retreats, but laity fast on certain occasions or during pilgrimages. In Theravada tradition, lay Buddhists often visit

Shrine to the *bodhisattva Jizo*, Nara, Japan. Courtesy of the author.

temples on the day of the full moon, bringing special offerings. There, they ritually take Eight Precepts (the usual Five Precepts with the addition of three others in which the devotee vows to abstain from taking solid food after noon, engaging in dancing or other improper shows, and resting on seats or luxurious beds). Many don white robes and spend the entire day at the temple listening to sermons and studying devotional literature. Such days of special observance increase faith as well as allow the laity to get away from their usual distractions and sample a bit of monastic life.

DONATION AND PATRONAGE

Donation has been crucial to Buddhism's spread and its survival. Making donations is a way to develop and demonstrate generosity, one of the most important Buddhist virtues. The Buddha himself embodied this virtue through his many sacrifices during his previous lives and in his preaching career. Buddhists regard generosity as essential to overcoming desire and cultivating gratitude and compassion.

Lay people are the ones who usually give donations, and it is through their giving that they accumulate merit. The most obvious means of giving donations has been through food given to monks on their daily alms rounds, but gifts can also be given at temple services, in payment for the performance of rites, or on special occasions. Generally monastics do not handle money, so most alms are given in the form of food, clothing, or property. Although they accumulate merit through such donations, laypeople are repeatedly counseled to give freely and joyously, rejoicing at the benefit of others.

This stress on the intention that informs donation has led to a particular practice known as "merit transfer." Although most Buddhist teaching stresses that one's deeds (both good and bad) only directly influence the future course of one's own existence, the practice of transferring merit to benefit other beings became widespread in many communities, particularly with the rise of Mahayana. It is quite common for Buddhists to dedicate the merit from their good deeds to all beings, but especially to the deceased. Merit transfer is a regular part of Buddhist funerals and commemorative rites to help the departed gain a better rebirth. Transferring merit also benefits the living by placating evil spirits who are thought to cause havoc and misfortune.

Throughout history, the monastic order has received gifts of enormous value, a fact that challenges their aim of leading simple lives dedicated to spiritual cultivation. In addition, some gifts run directly counter to monastic precepts. For example, the Code of Discipline prohibits monks and nuns from enjoying shows of music and dancing, yet there is an ancient tradition in Sri Lanka of making musical offerings (especially drumming) to the Buddha, much as such offerings were made to great kings in the past. Usually, making such musical offerings is the province of a special caste whose members, in exchange, receive the right to farm monastic lands.

Just as in other religions, donations in Buddhism express great disparities in wealth and prestige in the larger society. Inevitably, the rich and powerful make the largest donations and thus have great influence on the *sangha*. Indeed, the Buddha himself originally came from the ruling class and often consorted with kings and princes. Such patronage, whether by royalty or particularly wealthy and influential merchants, attests to the strong political side of Buddhism. The most famous patron in Buddhist history was Emperor Ashoka, who established the ideal all other Buddhist rulers sought to emulate. Other famous patrons include the wealthy merchant Anathapindaka (~sixth century B.C.E.), who purchased the land for the first Buddhist monastery; the devout Wendi (r. 581–604), who founded the Sui dynasty and reunited China after centuries of disunity; and Prince Shotoku (574–622), who is credited with bringing Buddhism to Japan. Various powerful Buddhist rulers and patrons commissioned many great works of art, founded vast monasteries and temples, and helped enforce Buddhist values and practices in their societies. Moreover, sponsoring the *sangha* was a good way for a monarch to establish the legitimacy of his rule in the eyes of his subjects.

Ideally Buddhist political rule is predicated on nonviolence (*ahimsa,* one of the virtues a Buddhist swears to live by). Buddhist rulers were forbidden to mete out unduly harsh punishments and were supposed to administer justice fairly to all persons. Many pious kings released prisoners on festival days, and even today certain rituals centered on nonviolence continue to be celebrated on special occasions. Sometimes caged birds and other animals are released on Buddhist holidays with the idea that imprisoning any being inflicts harm on it.

In practice, rule by nonviolence has proved difficult. Buddhist rulers were expected to maintain armies and a police force to protect their people from criminals and foreign enemies. As a rule in Buddhism there is no justification for wars of aggression, but some Buddhist thinkers have argued that defensive wars may be necessary to maintain order. Although Buddhism has overwhelming spread by peaceful means, there have been many territorial wars between Buddhist kingdoms in Southeast Asia. In addition, Buddhist monks have served as army chaplains and advisers in China, while in Japan, some monasteries employed armies of soldier-monks who engaged in military struggles "for the Dharma."

PILGRIMAGE

Pilgrimage, the practice of visiting holy sites, has a distinguished history in Buddhism. Right before he passed on, the Buddha encouraged his followers to visit four sites associated with major events in his life: Lumbini (where he was born), Bodh Gaya (where he achieved Enlightenment), the deer park in Sarnath (where he gave his first sermon), and Kushingara (where he passed from the world). These sites evoke powerful emotions of joy, faith, and gratitude, and those who die while en route to them are assured rebirth in a heavenly realm.

In Buddhism, pilgrimage is as much *internal* as external. Pilgrims should participate with proper intention and disposition and maintain physical and mental purity; they often wear distinct clothing. Buddhist pilgrims sometimes make additional vows to local gods and spirits at certain sites. At most sites, pilgrims circumambulate clockwise, keeping their right side facing the object of veneration as a sign of respect. Many Tibetan pilgrims cover their entire pilgrimage routes by making thousands of consecutive full-body prostrations.

Pilgrimage is intimately bound up with devotion. Historical sources attest to various Buddhist pilgrims since ancient times. One of the earliest was Emperor Ashoka, who commemorated his visit to Lumbini by erecting an inscribed pillar and saw to the construction of numerous *stupas*. Many later Buddhist rulers sought to emulate his devout actions. As Buddhism spread, pilgrims came to India from all over Asia. An early Chinese pilgrim was Faxian, a monk who traveled along the Silk Road to India in 399 C.E. On his return he visited Sri Lanka and Java, leaving detailed accounts of the sites there. Even more famous was the monk Xuanzang (596–664), who spent 14 years traveling to important sites throughout central Asia before reaching India. There he studied with the greatest Buddhist thinkers of his day, returning to China with an entire caravan of Buddhist relics, artworks, and texts.

The holiest place in all of Buddhism and the destination for many pilgrims is Bodh Gaya, the site of the Buddha's Enlightenment. The earliest known structure there was erected in the third century B.C.E. by Ashoka.

Mahabodhi Temple, Bodh Gaya, India. Courtesy of the American Institute of Indian Studies.

Over time other structures were built, including the magnificent Mahabodhi (Great Enlightenment) temple, which has been restored numerous times. Bodh Gaya is the site of numerous inscriptions left by devotees and now includes several monasteries and related shrines as well as small *stupas* containing the ashes of earlier pilgrims. The *bodhi* tree stands at the center of the site, underneath which is the Buddha's seat, the "diamond throne." According to legend, Ashoka's daughter took a cutting from the *bodhi* tree and transplanted it to Sri Lanka, a practice repeated by other missionaries when establishing new tree shrines.

Sacred mountains have also been sites of Buddhist pilgrimage. Sri Lanka, for example, contains 16 important sites, the most famous being "Adam's peak," said to be the site of one of the Buddha's footprints. Sacred mountains are found in other Buddhist countries as well. Some of the more notable include Mount Wutai in China, Mount Fuji in Japan, and Mount Kailish in Tibet.

Pilgrimages can be lengthy and may encompass numerous shrines and sites. The Japanese pilgrimage circuit at Shikoku, a large island in Japan's Inland Sea, includes 88 temples associated with Kukai (774–835), the founder of the Shingon school. To this day, Buddhist pilgrims from around the world travel this circuit, donning white garments and journeying on foot for a period of up to 60 days.

Buddhists have also engaged in pilgrimages to sacred sites in the West. One of the most inspiring in recent decades was performed by two American Buddhist monks, Heng Ch'au and Heng Sure. Beginning in May 1977, they started out from Gold Wheel Temple in Los Angeles and walked some 800 miles to the City of Ten Thousand Buddhas, the headquarters of their order just outside of Ukiah, California. Heng Sure maintained a vow of silence the entire way, and both monks performed a prostration every three steps. Dedicating their pilgrimage to peace for the entire world, the monks took two years and nine months to complete their journey.[13]

BUDDHISM AND ART

Buddhism has a deep aesthetic dimension. Siddhartha excelled in the arts of writing and music, and the Dharma itself is said to be "lovely in its beginning, lovely in its continuation, lovely in its ending."[14] For centuries devout Buddhists have created great paintings and statues (practices that at times have been regarded as forms of meditation), and the artworks themselves are often the focus of cultic worship. The spread of Buddhism has been greatly facilitated by Buddhist artworks that have evoked tremendous wonder and admiration from foreign peoples.

For the first few centuries after his passing, the Buddha was never actually depicted in artworks. Instead, his presence was signified by a "trace" (a footprint, an empty seat, a parasol). By the early common era, however, many Buddha images depicted Siddhartha in human form, clad in monastic robes. These early images differ in detail but generally share two distinct features: a cranial bump and a curl of hair on the Buddha's forehead (both signs of his cosmic wisdom and supernatural status). Over time two major styles of Buddha images developed. One style, originating in Gandhara (north Pakistan and Afghanistan), betrayed strong Hellenistic influence, with youthful, realistic figures shown with wavy hair and tuniclike robes. The other style arose in Mathura, a city along the Ganges, and reflected more indigenous Indian sentiments, with figures having rounder, heavier proportions. From the fourth to the sixth century, an ideal image of the Buddha was created, establishing a set formula following specific proportions and always including certain distinguishing marks such as a downward glance, a distinct spiritual aura (often shown by a background halo or nimbus), and hair meticulously arranged in tiny curls. To a large extent, this "ideal Buddha" became the model for all later Buddhist artists.

The rise of Mahayana tradition led to a veritable explosion of Buddhist deities whose images became central to popular devotion. Much Mahayana art depicted compassionate savior figures such as Amitabha and Maitreya in their glorious heavenly abodes. In conjunction with these celestial Buddhas and *bodhisattvas,* Buddhist artworks featured a host of protective deities, often with fearsome appearances. These deities, often originally local gods and spirits, grew to have major roles in the Tantric styles of Buddhism that came to dominate Tibet and its environs. As Buddhist Tantra evolved, such images became the focus of intricate rituals involving colorful costumes, music and elaborate *mandalas.* These various sensual dimensions fused together, lending Tantric rituals great aesthetic and psychological power.

Chinese Buddhist art combined foreign and indigenous styles, often absorbing waves of influence from India, Central Asia, and Tibet. The typical Indian styles featuring sensuously modeled human forms became married to the more linear depictions favored by the Chinese. Chinese Buddhist artworks depicted deities similar to those in India but with some changes. Perhaps the biggest change was the portrayal of Avalokiteshvara in female form (Guanyin), the *bodhisattva* of compassion. Chinese artists also depicted the Pure Land in loving detail, borrowing from indigenous Chinese views of the heavenly realms as well as accounts of the lavish furnishings found in the imperial court. The traditional Chinese love of nature so ex-

Calligraphy master Shiryu Norita. Courtesy of Ronald Y. Nakasone.

emplified in Daoism also melded with Buddhist views, finding expression in the great landscape paintings produced during the Middle Ages.

It is probably in Japan, however, that Buddhist art reached its height. Japan has a highly developed aesthetic that has always been intertwined with religion. Buddhism came to Japan heavily imbued with Chinese and Korean influences that the Japanese seized upon and modified to suit their own tastes. At first, Buddhism was confined to the elite classes, who sought to imitate the high culture of China and Korea. Their Buddhism was thus aristocratic in nature, marked by a sense of elegance and refinement. By the twelfth and thirteenth centuries, though, Buddhism had spread to the common people. With such popularization, there was a sharp rise in devotional imagery, particularly depictions of Pure Lands and visual narratives of the lives of saints. At the same time, the school of Zen was also being established. Zen art was stark and disciplined, reflecting a warrior mentality very much in keeping with the rising power of the samurai warriors. This Zen aesthetic is best shown in monochrome ink paintings and calligraphy. These works, with their bold black-on-white lines, directly expressed the artists' spirit and are even said to have provoked students' experiences of *satori*. The Zen focus on enabling the Pure Mind to flash suddenly into view and integrating such insight into ordinary life also influenced the development of the *Noh* style of drama as well as the tea ceremony, or *chado* (the Way of Tea). Zen Buddhists regularly engage in other arts such as composing *haiku*, flower-arranging, and gardening.

Zen garden, Kyoto, Japan. Courtesy of the author.

BUDDHISM AND THE MARTIAL ARTS

Buddhism seeks peace but also has a more martial side. The Buddha himself came from the warrior caste and as a youth was trained in the arts of war (wrestling, archery, etc.). Buddhist monastic training is rigorous, with distinct parallels with military life, and Buddhist texts often use martial imagery. Many famous Buddhists have also been warriors. According to legend, when the legendary Indian monk Bodhidharma (sixth century?) brought Chan teachings to China, he founded the famous Shaolin monastery where he taught a method of fighting that monks could use to defend the people against bandits and other evildoers.

Buddhist martial arts have mainly evolved in East Asia (particularly Japan) but have spread elsewhere. Some of the best known styles include *gongfu* ("powerful ability," a Chinese form that uses indigenous Chinese breathing exercises and may include the use of weapons), *karate* ("empty hands," a Japanese style that eschews the use of weapons), *judo* ("the soft way," another Japanese style that teaches yielding to an opponent so that his own force works against him), *kendo* ("the way of the sword," Japanese fencing, the specialty of the samurai), and *kyudo* ("the way of the bow," Japanese archery). Whatever the form, all Buddhist martial arts help practitioners develop "no thought," a nonreflective, spontaneous way of being.

Martial arts training has often been used as a form of "moving meditation," especially by practitioners of Chan/Zen. Like other types of meditation, martial arts require rigorous mental and physical discipline as a way of integrating mind and body. In theory at least, these arts are purely defensive and cannot be used for aggressive purposes. Martial arts promote health and may open a way of spiritual cultivation for those of a more athletic or violent temperament. They have also helped spread Buddhist teachings throughout much of the world.

CURRENT OVERVIEW OF BUDDHISM

At the beginning of the twentieth century, virtually all of Asia was Buddhist, thus accounting for around 30 percent of the world's population.[15] However, the percentage of Buddhists around the world has declined precipitously since then. This decline is largely the result of the political and economic rise of the West and the corresponding retreat of traditional societies worldwide. Together, these circumstances have sparked a complex series of social changes propelled by science, technology, and the spread of

capitalism, all of which have fostered an increasingly secular and material-
ist worldview among many of the world's people.

It is notoriously difficult to get accurate demographic information on
any religion, especially in parts of Asia, Africa, and Latin America. Current
estimates for the number of Buddhists in the world run anywhere from
230 to 500 million, with most agreeing that the number stands around 350
million. This would make approximately 6 percent of the world's population Buddhist.[16] South and East Asia have the highest concentration of
Buddhists, but Buddhists also reside in Latin America, Europe, and North
America as well as the former Soviet Republics. Generally speaking, there
are few Buddhists in Africa and Oceania (the islands of the central and
South Pacific). Such numbers, however, tell us very little about how Buddhism has fared in recent years. For that we need to look at specific individual regions.

India

One of the great ironies of history is the fact that Buddhism was almost
wiped out in India, its land of origin. As Islam began to expand, Muslim
merchants came to dominate the Silk Road trade once controlled by Buddhists. Islamic armies followed, and by 1200 they had conquered north
India and destroyed many monasteries. This same period also saw the
great rise of popular Hindu movements (often borrowing Buddhist ideas
and practices) that brought about a severe decline in Buddhism's popular
base. Lacking financial and state support, monks fled and many of the great
Buddhist centers in the Ganges region were left in ruins. Some monks journeyed to surrounding regions in Nepal and central Asia, where Buddhism
remained relatively strong.

From 1200 on Buddhism dwindled in India until the late nineteenth and
early twentieth centuries when various revival movements began, in part
encouraged by the policy of religious tolerance under British rule. Most of
these revivals began in other Asian countries and succeeded in reestablishing Buddhism on Indian soil. The largest Buddhist revival movement was
the Maha Bodhi Society, led by Sri Lankans intent on bringing the Dharma
back to its homeland. The European "discovery" of Buddhism also revived
interest in the religion, particularly among the educated classes. In 1956,
Dr. B. R. Ambedkar (1891–1956), a high-ranking member of the Indian
government who hailed from the "untouchable" class (the lowest of India's
castes), led more than 500,000 other untouchables in a mass conversion to

Buddhism, which he saw as the one religion capable of morally reforming the individual and society.

Today Buddhism remains a small but vital tradition in India, claiming some seven million followers. Many of these new Indian Buddhists come from the ranks of the untouchables (sometimes called "Ambedkar Buddhists") and follow the example of Christian missionaries by engaging in charitable work. Since 1959, Tibetan exiles fleeing the Chinese takeover of their homeland have established major centers in both the north (Dharamsala, headquarters of the Dalai Lama) and the south (Mysore). Buddhist sites, particularly Bodh Gaya, continue to attract pilgrims from all over the world. In recent years monasteries have been established at Bodh Gaya by Buddhists from Tibet, Japan, Burma, and China. There is even a Buddhist school for children there, and some signs indicate that local villagers are converting.

From the time of Emperor Ashoka (third century B.C.E.) on, Buddhism spread through most areas of central Asia, largely as the result of Indian patronage. Various regions in what are now Pakistan, Afghanistan, and

Colossal Buddha of Bamiyan, before destruction by the Taliban, Afghanistan. Courtesy of the American Institute of Indian Studies.

other countries in western Central Asia became major Buddhist strong-holds. Although eventually Buddhist influence in these areas waned in the face of Islamic pressure, Buddhism left a lasting mark on these societies. Many Buddhist sites continued to attract pilgrims throughout the centuries. Among the most famous of these were the ruins at Bamiyan with their spectacular Buddhist statues. When the Taliban seized control of Afghanistan in the 1990s, it imposed a very strict Islamic rule and systematically began a campaign to stamp out all vestiges of pre-Islamic culture. In 1998 Taliban forces singled out the Bamiyan Buddhas for destruction, demolishing them completely in May of 2001. News of their destruction provoked a major outcry from people the world over, both Buddhist and non-Buddhist, and late in 2001 a Swiss firm announced plans to rebuild the statues with the help of the international community. As of yet, however, such reconstruction has not begun.

Southeast Asia (Sri Lanka, Cambodia, Laos, Burma, and Thailand)

Much of Southeast Asia came under European control during the seventeenth and eighteenth centuries, a process that had enormous repercussions for the indigenous cultures. Nonetheless, Buddhism remains the dominant religion throughout the region with the exception of Indonesia, where Islam has displaced it. In Sri Lanka Buddhism was already on a decline because of pressure from Hindus on the Indian mainland. The decline continued as Western powers (Portuguese, Dutch, and British) lay claim to the island and, in the sixteenth century, persecution by a Hindu king stamped out the ordination line for monks. The line was reintroduced in 1753 from Thailand, but pressure from European missionaries continued. However, there was a surprising resurgence of Buddhism in the nineteenth century. In the late 1800s, members of the Theosophical Society, an American spiritualist group, came to Sri Lanka, where they led a Buddhist backlash against Christian oppression, giving rise to what is sometimes called "Protestant Buddhism." As with its Christian namesake, Protestant Buddhism was led by lay members who portrayed their faith as scientific and rational (as opposed to "superstitious religions") and it became the basis of a major reformation in the Sri Lankan *sangha*. It also spearheaded various Buddhist movements directed against European rule.

Since the country attained its independence from Britain in 1948, Sri Lankan monks have become increasingly active in politics, thus stirring much controversy. Sporadic armed conflict between the indigenous Sinhalese (mainly Buddhists) and the Tamil Hindu population has sometimes given popular Sir Lankan Buddhism a militant tinge. Another major development in recent decades has been the rise of lay-led movements such as Sarvodaya Sramadana (Donating Energy for the Awakening of All), a charitable organization promoting rural development that, in turn, has sparked a growing desire for Buddhism to permeate all aspects of Sri Lankan life. Currently, there are some 12,500,000 Buddhists in Sri Lanka, roughly 70 percent of the population. Buddhism is almost an unofficial state religion in Sri Lanka. In recent decades the government has sponsored the updating of the Pali Great Commentary, and in 2004 Sri Lanka's Supreme Court issued a verdict banning all swimwear depicting Buddhist imagery.

Beginning in 1893, the territories of modern Cambodia, Laos, and Vietnam were united as Indochina under French rule, which only ended after World War II. Buddhism in Cambodia came under severe attack in the Vietnam War and during the aftermath of the Khmer Rouge terror (1975–78), when thousands of monks were massacred or defrocked. By the time a more tolerant government was established in 1981, it was estimated that only six hundred monks remained and two-thirds of Buddhist temples had been destroyed. Various attempts at revival met with stiff government resistance at first, but since the 1980s things have improved. A major Buddhist resurgence has led to increased *sangha* membership. At present approximately 90 percent of Cambodia's population (more than nine million people) identify themselves as Buddhist.

In Laos, the situation has been similar. Most Laotian monks supported the Communist government that came to power in 1975, but many high-ranking monks fled across the Mekong River to Thailand. Despite guarantees of religious freedom, Buddhism exists in Laos under tight state control and lacks the political and financial support it once enjoyed. As a result local temples function only at the barest subsistence level. Lately, however, the Laotian *sangha* has forged ties to Laotian refugee communities in other countries, and there are movements to make Buddhism the official state religion. Recent estimates say that 60 percent of Laotians are Buddhists.

For centuries Buddhism enjoyed strong patronage in Burma under rulers such as King Mindon (r. 1853–78), who presided over the fifth Great Buddhist Council in 1868. The *sangha* flourished and colossal representations of the Buddha abounded, attracting throngs of devotees. A common saying went, "To be Burmese is to be Buddhist." However, British colonial rule led to a general weakening of Buddhism, much as it did in other areas of Southeast Asia. When Burma won its independence in 1948, Buddhism

Colossal statue of Buddha reclining as he is about to enter his "final nirvana," Pegu, Burma (Myanmar). © Getty Images/32104.

came to fore again with the encouragement of Prime Minister U Nu, who promoted a form of socialism as a means of establishing a peaceful and just Buddhist society. U Nu also presided over the sixth Great Council (1954–56), in which monks from all over Southeast Asia took part.

In 1962, a coup ushered in a Marxist government whose militant and dictatorial activities have led to almost constant civil war. By maintaining rather strict isolationist policies, this government has helped preserve traditional Buddhism, but social discontent has mounted. During the 1990s Burma officially changed its name to Myanmar, and opposition to military rule increased. The most prominent protest leader is Aung San Suu Kyi (1945–), a devout lay Buddhist who was awarded the Nobel Peace Prize in 1991 for her peaceful activities. Presently there are more than 41 million Buddhists in Myanmar, about 88 percent of the overall population.

Unlike many of its neighbors, Thailand avoided European colonization, in large part thanks to skillful rulers such as King Rama IV (r. 1851–68).[17] It has still come under great Western influence, however. Since 1932 the country has been a constitutional monarchy, and royalty continue to be respected and devout Buddhist patrons. In fact, Thailand remains (apart from the small Himalayan state of Bhutan) the last nation on earth to have a Buddhist king and Buddhism as the official state religion. High-ranking monks serve on the Supreme Buddhist Council, an official government body, and are supported by the government's Religious Affairs Department. These bodies have sometimes acted to squelch religious and political reform movements. Currently there are more than 55 million Thai Buddhists accounting for 95 percent of the population, making Thailand the most Buddhist nation in the world.

As in other South Asian countries, monks in Thailand have become increasingly involved in politics. There has also been renewed interest in meditation among the urban educated classes, many of whom have joined lay-based organizations such as Dhammakaya, which holds meditation programs at universities all over Thailand. One of the most prominent Thai monks in recent decades was Buddhadasa (1906–93), who sought to apply Buddhist ideas to social and economic issues. Operating outside the official state-sponsored hierarchy, Buddhadasa founded a forest retreat in 1932 and slowly began attracting both lay and monastic followers. His most prominent student, Sulak Sivaraska, is a leader of Engaged Buddhism and an outspoken critic of harmful national and international economic policies.

Vietnam

For centuries Vietnam was a thriving area for Mahayana Buddhism. Often under the influence of China, Vietnam adopted much of Chinese culture and religion while maintaining its indigenous heritage. From the sixteenth century on, Catholic missionaries from Spain and France began to appear and had some success at making conversions in the south. As Vietnam came under French rule, Catholicism made greater and greater inroads into Vietnamese society and Buddhism waned, although it experienced a brief revival during the eighteenth century.

With the end of French colonial dominance after World War II, Vietnam gained its independence but was soon plunged into civil war between the Communist north and the anti-Communist south. The war proved particularly devastating to Vietnamese Buddhists, who were often persecuted by both Communists and Catholics. Many monks such as Thich Nhat Hanh (1926–) engaged in welfare and peace work, drawing the ire of both sides, while other monks staged public protests during which some burned themselves to death to call attention to their country's plight. These acts, although not officially sanctioned by any Buddhist group, provoked the United Nations to investigate the Vietnamese government's role in religious persecution.

Since 1975 Buddhism has been in sharp decline in Vietnam, with many temples and monasteries being closed and various prominent monks being harassed by the government. The state founded the Vietnamese Buddhist

Church, but many Buddhist organizations have resisted such government control. The most prominent resistance movement is the United Buddhist Church of Vietnam (UBCV), which includes both Theravada and Mahayana members. The UBCV was officially banned in 1981 but has gained international support in pressuring the Communist government to desist in its persecutions.

At present there are almost 50 million Buddhists in Vietnam, accounting for 55 percent of the country's population. Nonetheless, despite recent signs of liberalization, the future of Buddhism in Vietnam remains uncertain. In 2004 a dissident monk from the UBCV, Thich Tri Luc, was granted United Nations refugee status after fleeing to Cambodia to avoid imprisonment for practicing his religion. Both Amnesty International and Human Rights Watch issued statements condemning the Vietnamese government's actions, but the government denies any wrongdoing.[18]

China and Taiwan

After the Tang dynasty (618–907) Buddhism began to decline in China as Confucianism gained increasing prominence. However, Buddhism continued to have a place in Chinese culture and enjoyed a brief renaissance during the Yuan dynasty (1269–1367), when China was under Mongol rule. With the founding of the Ming dynasty (1368–1644), Confucianism once more became the official state ideology, but Buddhism thrived at the popular level. During this time there was a strong move toward religious syncretism, blending Buddhism with Confucianism and Daoism, and many Chinese proclaimed the "unity of the Three Teachings," a practice that continued into the twentieth century.

With the Communist takeover in 1949, the fate of Chinese Buddhism appeared to be sealed. For years, the government actively suppressed the religion, particularly during the Cultural Revolution (1966–76). As a result, many monks and nuns fled to Hong Kong and Taiwan. In recent years, however, the government has eased restrictions, in part motivated by the desire to increase promotion of international tourism.

Currently Buddhism in China is thriving to a limited extent. There are more than 100 million Buddhists in China, about 10 percent of the total population. Along with Daoism, Protestantism, Chinese Catholicism, and Islam, Buddhism is one of the five officially recognized religions, all of which operate under the auspices of the government's Religious Affairs Bureau. Such official state recognition would have been unthinkable during the Cultural Revolution. It appears that the Chinese government will continue to allow limited freedom for Buddhism so long as it remains part of "true religion" rather than "popular superstition."

A major test of China's tolerance of Buddhism has come in the form of a new religious movement, Falun Gong (Dharma Wheel Power). Founded in 1992, Falun Gong, like many Chinese religions, combines Buddhist, Daoist, and Confucian teachings. By following the practices of Falun Gong practitioners claim to produce in their abdomens protective energies that promote harmony and health in the individual and society, and will lead to enlightenment. This movement self-consciously identifies itself as Buddhist, and its leader is often depicted in typical Buddhist posture, sitting on a lotus. Falun Gong has attracted numerous followers (their Web site at one time boasted of having more than one hundred million members) and has met with severe oppression from the Chinese government. After a large protest in April of 1999, during which thousands of members surrounded the compound of high-ranking Communist officials, the authorities condemned the group as "antigovernment." A major crackdown followed in which leaders were arrested, property was confiscated, and millions of publications were destroyed. Li Hongzhi, the founder of Falun Gong, now lives in exile in New York, but the movement still commands an international following.

Taiwan presents a peculiar case with regard to Buddhism, largely because of its problematic relationship with the People's Republic. Buddhism originally was brought to Taiwan in the seventeenth century by Chinese immigrants. There it was able to avoid some of the decline Buddhism suffered on the mainland. With the founding of the Nationalist Chinese government after the Communist revolution, there was a concerted attempt to revive ancient Chinese culture as a way of establishing a "real Chinese" identity. Buddhism benefited greatly from these efforts, as new temples and monasteries were built and study and meditation groups arose on various university campuses. Currently Taiwan has a more than nine million Buddhists, making up about 43 percent of the island's population. Such numbers are somewhat suspect, however, since most Taiwanese do not identify exclusively with any one religion.

Unlike in other Asian countries, women take active roles in the Taiwanese *sangha,* where they account for more than 80 percent of the members of monastic orders. Fo Kuang Shan, a major Taiwanese Buddhist organization, has sponsored the full ordination of Buddhist nuns in many areas around the world, including Sri Lanka and Tibet. One of the most prominent Buddhist movements in Taiwan is Ciji (the Buddhist Compassion Relief Association), a nongovernmental organization founded in 1966 by a Buddhist nun. Ciji is renowned for its work in administering medical and social aid (it has the third-largest bone marrow register in the world and runs medical missions in many countries). Ciji volunteers were among the first to provide relief after the earthquake that devastated parts of Taiwan in 1999. Members of Ciji view their work not just as giving aid to the poor and the sick but also as opportunities for their own spiritual growth.

Korea

For centuries Korea was essentially a Buddhist country. Just as in China, however, the situation changed drastically over time. During the Yi dynasty (1392–1910), Buddhism suffered a stunning reversal of fortune. Chinese Neo-Confucianism was adopted as the state ideology, and as a result, the government confiscated monastery lands and reduced the number of Buddhist schools. By the sixteenth century monks could no longer enter the capital, and the children of aristocrats were forbidden from being ordained. In response, many monks retreated to monasteries deep in the mountains. Despite government suppression, though, Buddhism continued as a popular religion among the masses.

From 1910 to 1945, when Korea was under Japanese occupation, Buddhism enjoyed something of a revival, although this has been eclipsed in the north since the Korean War (1950–53). In the south Buddhism remains the largest religious community, with some 16 different sects, and it continues to thrive under strict government regulations. Little is known about the state of Buddhism in North Korea except that it exists under tight control by the Communist government and that it lacks its former political, financial, and educational support.

Several lay-centered Buddhist movements have arisen in Korea, including a network of Sunday schools for children modeled on Christian examples. Won Buddhism, founded in 1916, gained enormous popularity in the 1960s and 1970s, attracting more than a million members. Won's leaders do not take monastic vows but female leaders tend to be celibate. The 1960s also saw the establishment of a Korean form of Tiantai (originally a Chinese school) that has attracted more than a million lay members as well. Both of these movements encourage followers to combine traditional Buddhist teachings and meditations with service to the greater society.

Just as in Taiwan, women play a large role in the running of the Korean *sangha*, promoting renewed interest in Buddhism among the laity and monastic involvement in social services. Since the late 1970s, the South Korean government has been actively promoting Buddhism as an expression of Korean national identity. This nationalistic movement has lent Buddhism a high profile but has also led to charges of monastic corruption because of political patronage. Today South Korea is home to approximately 11 million Buddhists, although they face stiff competition from Christian denominations such as the Presbyterians.

Japan

The Tokugawa era (1600–1867) was a time of sweeping changes in Japanese society, characterized by major drives toward centralization and modernization. Although Buddhism was officially encouraged, the government began to exert direct control over the *sangha* by requiring all families to register as members of Buddhist temples. Moreover, Chinese Neo-Confucianism exercised increasing influence on state policy, in large part because of what was perceived as Buddhist-inspired disunity in earlier times. In addition, a new movement began to develop, claiming that Shinto was the "true religion" of the Japanese, not the "foreign creed" of Buddhism. Such trends culminated in a coup in 1868 in which the Tokugawa shogun was defeated and the Meiji emperor was installed on the throne.

The period from 1868 on was a tumultuous time in Japanese history with far-reaching consequences for Japanese Buddhism. The new government declared Shinto the official state religion and began a series of persecutions against Buddhism, in which all Buddhist temples were converted into Shinto shrines. During the late nineteenth and early twentieth century, Japan followed an aggressive militaristic policy that led it into a series of wars culminating in World War II. This militant imperialism was justified by state Shinto, which taught the natural and cultural superiority of the Japanese race. Under the pervasive influence of this Shintoist doctrine, a new generation of thinkers reinterpreted Buddhism in the service of Japanese nationalism. These thinkers gravitated toward Zen, whose long association with the warrior class made it an ideal instrument for promoting the war effort. Many monks of the Rinzai school in particular were called upon to help train soldiers to face death in battle.

Japan's defeat in World War II and the subsequent restructuring of Japanese society dealt a severe blow to the Japanese Buddhist establishment. The rapid modernization leading up to the war and the rise of state Shinto had caused a decline in the influence of traditional Buddhism on Japanese society. These trends, coupled with the Allied occupation and creation of a secular government, resulted in the loss of much village-level Buddhism. Buddhism was reduced to a cultural relic, a marker of Japanese identity but hardly a living, vibrant faith.[19] The most conspicuous aspect of Japanese religion in the latter half of the twentieth century was the phenomenal growth of the so-called New Religions, many of which flourish at Buddhism's expense. Ironically, a number of New Religions incorporate folk Buddhist teachings and practices. The most successful of them, Soka Gakkai (Society for the Creation of Values), draws on the Nichiren sect's practice of chanting and aims at decidedly this-worldly goals (wealth, career success, family harmony). Soka Gakkai is an aggressively proselytizing movement, both in Japan and the West, and it retains great influence on the Japanese government through its political party, Komeito.

It is extremely difficult to get an accurate count of Buddhists in Japan. Buddhism has so long been part of traditional Japanese culture that many Japanese do not consider themselves "Buddhist" even when engaging in Buddhist practices. Moreover, the Japanese (like the Chinese) do not view religion in exclusive terms and often practice different religions. Recent counts have more than 89 million Japanese Buddhists, about 50 percent of the current population.

Tibet

With the rise of the Gelugpa order in 1641, Tibet became the only nation in the world ruled by Buddhist monks. Tibet continued to exist in relative isolation from the rest of the world except on a few occasions. The Gelugpa government formed a brief alliance with China's Manchu rulers in the nineteenth century, but it diminished as China grew progressively weaker. In the early twentieth century, the 13th Dalai Lama began an effort of modernization in hopes of protecting Tibet from British, Russian, and Chinese invasion. In 1903 a British force marched into Lhasa, the capital city, and forced the country to open trade relations with India. Tibet, however, remained essentially isolated save for occasional contact with Western explorers, whose wondrous tales of this "Land of the Snows" became the basis for the mythical kingdom of Shangri-La.

In 1950, however, the Communist Chinese set their sights on Tibet in hope of gaining a strategic hold in central Asia. Refused aid from the United Nations, Tibet was overrun in 1951 by the Chinese, who claimed it as "recovered" territory. The newly enthroned 14th Dalai Lama sought peaceful coexistence, but in 1959 the Chinese imposed a harsh system of colonial rule. The Dalai Lama and his direct followers fled in disguise to India, while the Chinese began a systematic crackdown on the Tibetan people and their culture. It is estimated that 6,000 monasteries were destroyed along with their collections of art and manuscripts, while some one million Tibetans have died, either from violence and torture or from famine and disease.

Conditions in Tibet have improved since 1980, with several monasteries being rebuilt and ordination of monks and nuns increasing. There is a limited amount of religious expression now, but any demonstration for Tibetan nationalism or human rights meets with prompt repression. Moreover, traditional Tibetan culture has been diluted by Chinese settlers (who make up 20 percent of the total population now) bringing their state-run education system and consumerism. Despite all this, most Tibetans retain a strong devotion to Buddhism and the Dalai Lama, even in the absence of a viable monastic order. At present, about 65 percent of Tibet's population is Buddhist. Tibet was opened to tourists in 1984, and although this helps Tibetans to draw attention to their oppression, greater contact with the outside world is also leading to further cultural erosion.

Europe and North America

Although there are hints of Buddhist influence in the West in ancient and medieval times, sustained contact with the Buddhist world did not begin until the Renaissance. By the sixteenth century, Europe had entered the Age of Exploration, and vast areas of the globe were opened up to commercial interests. Often, missionaries intent on converting the "heathens" to Christianity accompanied explorers and merchants. The Jesuits were particularly zealous in their efforts in Asia, and their writings contained some of the first detailed descriptions of Buddhist belief and practice. Throughout the eighteenth and nineteenth centuries, European nations took over major portions of the world, in the process bringing many indigenous populations under colonial rule. Control of various parts of Asia, particularly India, led to a more sound knowledge of Asian religions, although European overlords often took little more than passing interest in the "exotic" ways of the native peoples.

At the same time, during the eighteenth century Europe saw the rise of Enlightenment thinkers such as Voltaire and Rousseau, who stressed the use of reason as the way to throw off the intellectual shackles of the past.

Many Enlightenment thinkers questioned church dominance in European society and subjected Christian doctrine and practice to critical scrutiny. The Enlightenment critique of religion and its role in European society led many intellectuals to the critical study of other religions. Asian traditions, especially Buddhism, held a special fascination for many European thinkers. Some viewed Buddhism as a "rational religion" that did not rely on faith in God or priests, and hence more compatible with the findings of science than Christianity. These developments had a major role in making the Western world aware of Buddhism and its place in Asian history, and paved the way for the small but significant influence Buddhism has exerted on Western philosophy and religion.[20]

Buddhism appeared in the Americas later than in Europe. For much of the nineteenth century it had a limited presence in the United States because of strict immigration laws. Except for sporadic reference in the writings of Ralph Waldo Emerson and Henry David Thoreau, Buddhism was mainly confined to small communities of immigrant Chinese and Japanese on the West Coast. This situation changed, however, with the 1893 World's Parliament of Religions held in Chicago. One of the "stars" of the parliament was Shaku Soen, a Rinzai Zen monk who was invited back to the United States in 1905 to teach Zen. He and his disciples (including D. T. Suzuki, the foremost early interpreter of Buddhism to an American audience) became the first of a series of Buddhist missionaries to West. Other well known Buddhist missionaries during the twentieth century were Shunryu Suzuki-roshi, a Soto Zen priest who founded the San Francisco Zen Center, and Chogyam Trungpa, a Tibetan lama who founded the Naropa Institute in Boulder, Colorado.

One result of such missionary work was the growth of Buddhism as a religion for Westerners, especially after World War II. During the 1950s and 1960s, Buddhism became something of a fad among members of the counterculture (beats and hippies). At the same time, the relaxing of immigration laws resulted in increasing numbers of Asians settling in America, bringing their Buddhist beliefs and practices with them. Buddhist centers were founded in the United States and other Western countries during the latter half of the twentieth century, and their growing numbers of followers have led to major changes as Buddhism adapts to a Western cultural setting. Some of these reforms parallel trends in Christianity, such as a greater focus on the role of the laity and the opening of leadership to women. Another interesting development in Western Buddhism is its eclecticism, with leaders and followers freely mixing practices and teachings from a wide range of Buddhist traditions.

Whatever the ultimate result of Buddhism's Western spread, it is clear that it enjoys an increasingly higher profile in popular culture. Whereas the number of Buddhists in Europe remains small (anywhere from 750,000 to 1.5 million), it is larger in North America. Recent estimates run anywhere from 1.3 to 3 million Buddhists there, not quite 1 percent of the total population. What is more remarkable, however, is the fact that in North America Buddhism is growing three times as fast as Christianity.

An interesting feature of Western Buddhism (particularly in the United States) is the division between immigrant practitioners from Buddhist countries and Western converts. The former follow the traditional ways of their homelands: their Buddhism is faith based, centering on temple worship and major festivals. Buddhist immigrants also make a sharp distinction between monks and laity. Western converts, in contrast, follow a more or less "Protestant model" of religion: individualistic and lay focused, with women having greater roles. Typical Western Buddhists practice meditation, regularly attending meditation centers for instruction and retreats. They may have home altars but tend to downplay traditional devotional practices and often continue observing Western holidays such as Christmas. There have been some steps at bringing these two divisions in the Western *sangha* together but they often do not see eye-to-eye.

Decline or Renewal?

There is no doubt that Buddhism has suffered major setbacks during the past few centuries. In India, Buddhism lost out to Hinduism and Islam for popular support. Throughout much of Southeast Asia Buddhism was weakened by European colonialism with its attendant Christian missionaries and Western values. Moreover, as traditional monarchies in Asian countries have been replaced by other forms of government, Buddhism has lost much of its former political support. The rise of modern urban societies has also severely curtailed the traditional role of Buddhist monks, who are no longer the main educators, social workers, and advisers of the common people. Increasingly, monks and nuns must settle for relatively minor roles as ritual specialists and religious teachers.

Interestingly, Buddhism has long held that such declines are to be expected as part of the cosmic process. The Dharma, it is said, inevitably goes into a period of decline several centuries after the appearance of a Buddha. In our era, Shakyamuni recovered the eternal teachings and set the Wheel of Dharma in motion again. Having been reestablished, the Dharma has spread, but just as all things decay, so, too, will the Dharma. However, even when the Wheel of Dharma ceases to turn in the distant future, it will not be destroyed. At that point the next Buddha, Maitreya, will appear on earth and set the Wheel of Dharma in motion once again.

This notion of the Dharma's decline, although rooted in traditional Buddhist texts, has not led to an overall sense of pessimism. Rather, there is a renewed sense of mission among many Buddhists, evident in the growth of volunteer associations promoting Buddhist solutions to problems such as environmental degradation, economic development, political oppression, and health care. In the West in particular there is a strong sense that Buddhism can be a resource for combating contemporary social ills that result from stress, rampant materialism, and the self-centered individualism that modern society often encourages.

IMPORTANT RECENT DEVELOPMENTS

Societies have never been static, but lately the pace of change has accelerated at an unprecedented rate. Many of these changes are part of the globalization process that has drawn the world's diverse cultures together through trade, communications, and large-scale population movements resulting from immigration as well as political and social instability. Interestingly, Buddhism has been very involved in these global changes—something perhaps only to be expected of a tradition that has stressed change since its founding. Several recent developments in Buddhism are making an increasing impact on the larger world community.

Engaged Buddhism

Many modern Buddhists have begun to express their ideals of compassion and equality and press for political reforms around the world. This socially active Buddhism is called "Engaged Buddhism," a term coined by the Vietnamese monk Thich Nhat Hanh. Although such Buddhist activism resembles many secular liberal movements, Engaged Buddhism is set apart with its emphasis on mindfulness, interdependence, and the linking of outward reform to inner transformation.

Engaged Buddhism is not just a Western movement but can be found all over the world. Engaged Buddhists see their work as part and parcel of their spiritual practice. Typically they address issues such as racial and ethnic oppression, women's rights, policies that promote economic and social inequality, and environmental degradation. In keeping with Buddhist principles, Engaged Buddhists stage peaceful protests and campaigns, always seeking to reach mutual understanding to enact political and social reforms. Although they draw on traditional Buddhist ideas and practices, Engaged Buddhists also model their work on non-Buddhists such as Mahatma Gandhi and the Rev. Martin Luther King Jr. In addition to Thich Nhat Hanh and Sulak Sivaraksa, prominent Engaged Buddhists include A.T. Ariyaratne (1931–), leader of Sri Lanka's Sarvodaya movement; Joanna Macy (1929–), "eco-philosopher" and teacher; and the Pulitzer Prize–winning poet and ecologist Gary Snyder (1930–).

There are various international organizations of Engaged Buddhists, one of the most successful being the Buddhist Peace Fellowship (BPF). Founded in 1978 in Berkeley, California, the BPF seeks to bring a Buddhist perspective to the peace movement. The BPF has chapters all over the world and sponsors political protests, environmentalist projects, prison outreach work, and seminars and workshops on a multitude of issues of interest to social activists. It also publishes the quarterly *Turning Wheel: The Journal of Socially Engaged Buddhists.*

The Elevation of Women

Female Buddhists have long been subordinate to men and have even been denied full access to monastic training. This situation is changing, however. Much of the impetus toward such changes comes from the West, where Buddhism and feminism began to intersect during the 1970s. The rise of Buddhist feminism is largely the result of the work of scholars such as I. B. Horner and Diana Paul. Rita Gross, a practitioner of Tibetan Buddhism, has found that her meditation practice gives her calm and compassion to help her work to challenge the male-dominated *sangha.* Her book *Buddhism After Patriarchy: A Feminist History, Analysis, and Reconstruction of Buddhism,* published in 1993, is a landmark work in promoting female Buddhist leadership.

The West has been at the forefront in seeking to elevate women, mainly because there are fewer cultural constraints on female advancement than in many Asian societies. Nonetheless, movements for elevating women's status have made remarkable strides in traditionally Buddhist countries. In both Taiwan and Korea, women have prominent leadership roles in the *sangha,* and more than 80 percent of the members of Ciji, the Taiwanese Buddhist relief organization, are lay women. Women have also led the way in reestablishing ordination lineages for nuns. In 1971 Voramai Shatsena (1908–) went from Thailand to Taiwan to be ordained as a nun and has since been working to reestablish a Thai nuns' lineage. Karma Lekshe Tsomo, an American nun, began to work in 1982 to establish full female monasticism in the Tibetan tradition, founding her own nunnery in 1985. In 1991 the Tibetan Nuns' Project and the Dalai Lama also set up the Dolma Ling Training Institute for Tibetan Nuns. Such events mark historic changes for Buddhism as it enters the twenty-first century.

Ecumenism

As Buddhism has attained a more self-conscious global identity, there has been greater cooperation among Buddhists of different traditions and cultural backgrounds—a trend that has distinct parallels with the Christian ecumenical movement. Buddhists increasingly view themselves as Buddhists first rather than "Zen Buddhists" or "Theravada Buddhists." Even Buddhists who do not regularly go to temple or attend meditation centers still think of themselves as Buddhists and live according to Buddhist teachings and values. The role of the Dalai Lama as an international Buddhist spokesman has certainly contributed to this sense of shared religious identity. In his many travels he has spoken to large crowds and had audiences with numerous politicians, scholars, business leaders, and celebrities. Invariably, he has been well received and his personal presence—marked by a mixture of sincerity, modesty and self-deprecating humor—has served as an excellent example of what a "real Buddhist" is like.

Beyond the role of the Dalai Lama and other international Buddhist figures, the growth of Buddhist ecumenism is a direct response to the setbacks Buddhism has suffered over the last few centuries. This ecumenical trend may be responsible for stemming the tide of decline, as Buddhists from different countries have banded together to help reintroduce Buddhism in areas when it was in danger of dying out. Buddhist ecumenism has also increased thanks to the work of networks and organizations of Engaged Buddhists. Moreover, the increasingly ecumenical character of Buddhism has been encouraged by the growth of various interfaith movements. Of these, the Buddhist-Christian dialogue is one of the best known.

It has brought together dozens of scholars and practitioners of both faiths, and has sponsored numerous conferences and publications, including the academic journal *Buddhist-Christian Studies.*

The "Cyber-Sangha"

The explosion of information technology has had a profound impact on Buddhism, leading to what might be called a "cyber-*sangha*." The rapid spread of electronic communications has enabled a far closer integration of the international Buddhist community than at any time before. The growth of this "cyber-*sangha*" offers a new illustration of Buddhist teachings on interdependence and Dependent Origination. It is interesting to note that large numbers of information technology professionals are drawn to Buddhism, perhaps indicating an affinity between their work and Buddhist ideas. Certainly, the vision of networks of Buddhists connected across space and time via glowing computer screens provides an intriguing contemporary update of the traditional image of Indra's jeweled net.[21]

The emergence of the "cyber-*sangha*" is directly related to the rise of Buddhist ecumenism and Engaged Buddhism, both of which have fostered several international associations. New communities have sprung up online, thus extending the reach of Buddhism and giving the tradition a new life. Currently there are myriad Buddhist Web sites and discussion rooms. Meditation centers regularly post information about Dharma talks and retreats on their Web sites, and the Internet attracts various organizations peddling Buddhist products ranging from incense and meditation cushions to guided pilgrimages to Bodh Gaya and other Buddhist places.

Electronic media are increasingly being used to store and disseminate Buddhist texts (often in their original languages). Several online Buddhist publications have also appeared, the *Journal of Buddhist Ethics* being the most prominent. Although it is doubtful it will replace the direct face-to-face contact that has been so important in the transmission of the Dharma, the "cyber-*sangha*" promises to be part of Buddhism for a long time to come.

NOTES

1. Scholars refer to religions that stress practice (such as Islam, Hinduism and Buddhism) as *orthoprax* (right practice) versus traditions that stress belief (such as Christianity), which are called *orthodox* (right belief). The difference

between orthoprax and orthodox traditions, however, is more a matter of degree than kind.

2. The automobile manufacturer Mitsubishi takes its name from the Japanese rendering of the Three Jewels (*mitsu* = "three," *bishi* = "jewels"). It was founded as an enterprise firmly based on Buddhist principles.

3. The *bodhisattva* path is described in more detail in the section on Mahayana Buddhism in Chapter 3.

4. Monks are allowed eight possessions: three robes, a water strainer, a needle, a begging bowl, a razor, and a belt.

5. The Buddha certainly believed that women could attain *arhat* status and may have hesitated to ordain women merely to avoid problems that could arise when housing celibate men and women together.

6. Before the Chinese invasion of Tibet, the great monastery of Drepung housed some 10,000 monks. In ancient times such large monasteries were found throughout Asia. According to some sources, the Abhayagiri monastery at Anuradhapura in Sri Lanka was home to more than 5,000 monks.

7. Jetavana (Forest of Jeta) was a park owned by Prince Jeta. He was persuaded to offer it to the Buddha and his followers by a merchant who bought it by covering its grounds with coins. The Buddha spent 19 rainy seasons there and the monastery continued to be a major Buddhist center for centuries. Since then, most monasteries have been founded through the cooperation of wealthy merchants and powerful rulers.

8. The typical Theravada monastic routine is outlined in the section on Theravada Buddhism in Chapter 3.

9. Theravada includes 16 different types of breathing practice, involving extending or shortening the breath or focusing on the breath's location in the body. In Chan/Zen, the most common practice is breath counting, in which the practitioner silently counts each exhalation until reaching the number 10, at which point he starts over at 1.

10. The Buddhist practice of using beads as an aid to chanting was borrowed by Muslims when they took over Buddhist lands. Eventually this practice made its way into Christianity, where it became the rosary.

11. Digha-nikaya, II, 142. Quoted in Mitchell, *Buddhism: Introducing the Buddhist Experience*, 31.

12. Jizo gives comfort to the parents of stillborn children and dead infants. In recent years he has taken a central role in rituals devoted to helping dead children (and aborted fetuses) attain a happy rebirth.

13. The experience of the entire pilgrimage is detailed in Heng Sure et al., *With One Heart Bowing to the City of 10,000 Buddhas*, 9 vols. (Burlingame, CA: Dharma Realm Buddhist Association, 1977–83).

14. The Vinaya Pitaka, 1: 21. Quoted in Corless, *The Vision of Buddhism,* 66.

15. Masao Abe, "Buddhism," in *Our Religions,* ed. Arvind Sharma (New York: HarperCollins, 1993), 83.

16. These figures and all others cited in this section come from http://www.adherents.com/Religions_By_Adherents.html#Buddhism.

17. Rama IV, like many Thai kings, was an ordained monk for many years before ascending the throne. A skilled diplomat and reformer, he was a promoter of modernization while seeking to maintain traditional ways. He served as the real-life model for the ruler in the musical *The King and I.*

18. "Monk Given Asylum," *Washington Post,* 26 June 2004, B7.

19. Some Japanese refer to the traditional forms of Buddhism as "funeral Buddhism" because of the ritual role to which many priests have been confined in recent years.

20. Arthur Schopenhauer (1788–1860) was the first Western thinker to proclaim an affinity with Buddhism, and his work in turn influenced the composer Richard Wagner, who attempted to write an opera on the life of the Buddha. Carl Gustav Jung (1875–1961), the Swiss analytic psychologist, drew heavily on Buddhist ideas in formulating his theories of the archetypes of the collective unconscious. Since the 1960s several prominent Roman Catholic priests such as Thomas Merton (1915–68) have explored using Buddhist meditation as part of Christian contemplative life.

21. Indra's net is a traditional Buddhist image that likens all phenomena in the cosmos to a net of jewels, each reflecting all the others much like the mirrors in a fun house.

5

RITUALS AND HOLIDAYS

Buddhism, like other religious traditions, marks time with an array of festivals, holidays, and other observances. Many of these celebrations commemorate historical events in the life of the Buddha or in the lives of "wisdom beings," (*bodhisattvas*, devout Buddhists who postpone their own enlightenment to aid other beings), renowned saints, and other great religious figures. There are also seasonal observances in various Asian societies in which Buddhism has a large role. In addition, there are numerous regional festivals throughout the Buddhist world that, although originally expressions of indigenous peoples' cultures, have taken on Buddhist aspects over time. Many of these regional celebrations differ considerably from region to region. In addition to these regularly scheduled observances, there are also various important Buddhist rituals and ceremonies such as funerals and weddings that, although not tied to specific dates or historic events, are held when the need arises and may often have a holiday atmosphere. Examining some of these observances provides a fuller understanding of popular Buddhist practice and a greater appreciation for how Buddhism shapes the lives of its followers.

PAN-BUDDHIST CELEBRATIONS

Festivals observed by all Buddhists are some of the most joyous religious events in the world. There is no single standardized calendar in Buddhism (although Buddhism originally seems to have closely followed the Hindu calendar), so the exact dates of most Buddhist celebrations differ from region to region and tradition to tradition. There are, however, certain Buddhist festivals that Buddhists of all cultural backgrounds observe, and they remain important markers of Buddhist identity.[1] It is thus appropriate to refer to them as "pan-Buddhist celebrations." The three most important pan-Buddhist celebrations commemorate the date of Buddha's birth, the day he attained Enlightenment (*bodhi*), and the day when he made his final entry into the state beyond suffering *(nirvana)* and passed from this world.

One of the most significant features of pan-Buddhist celebrations is that they are all synchronized with the phases of the moon. In part this is because most traditional societies in Asia and elsewhere follow a lunar calendar (an association evident in the word *month,* which comes from *moon.*) Certainly, both the sun and the moon have played significant roles in the religions of various peoples. More to the point, the new, half, and full moons were considered powerful, even ominous times in ancient India, and were often marked by fasts and special rites. The full moon was the ritual high point of the month, and its significance is attested far back in Sanskrit literature. The moon is continually dying and being reborn—a powerful symbol of the cyclical spinning of the wheel of life and death (*samsara*). When the moon is full, however, it imitates the fullness of the sun, the giver of warmth, light, and life. Thus, even in the midst of continuous change, the full moon provides a vivid example of the eternal light and power of the cosmos, the changelessness that lies at the very heart of existence.

Buddha's Birthday

As in the case of Jesus Christ, it is almost impossible to determine the exact date of the historical Buddha's birth. Most Buddhists hold that Siddhartha Gautama, their founder, was born in 563 B.C.E. in Lumbini, in what is now Nepal. A sizeable minority, however, argue that he was born in 623 B.C.E. Such disputes may never be finally resolved to everyone's satisfaction, and they have not prevented Buddhists from commemorating his birth.

Followers of Theravada, the most conservative branch of Buddhism and the one that dominates Southeast Asia, maintain that the Buddha was born on Full Moon Day (Vesak), which falls somewhere in April or May, depending upon the year.[2] It is a public holiday in many Asian countries. This is perhaps the most important Theravadin festival, because it also commemorates the Buddha's Enlightenment and his final entry into *nirvana,* all of which, according to Theravada tradition, occurred on the same day of the year although many years apart. In Theravadin countries such as Sri Lanka, people decorate their houses with paper lanterns and flowers and often illuminate driveways and temple courtyards with lamps. Pavilions and stalls displaying paintings of the Buddha's life and offering free food are set up along roadsides. Burmese Buddhists mark this day by watering *bodhi* trees like the one under which the Buddha became enlightened with scented water. In other Theravadin countries, such as Thailand and Laos, monks lead the laity in circumambulating a temple, relic mound *(stupa)*, or Buddha image. Typically, lay Buddhists bring offerings of flowers to temples, sing devotional songs, and listen to sermons on the Buddha's life, some of which may last all night. Vesak always takes place during the full moon, a highly auspicious time in Buddhism when monks and nuns will gather to chant the Code of Discipline and renew their monastic vows. Some dedicated lay people spend all day at the temple, taking additional vows and seeking to deepen their faith and devotion.[3]

Celebrations of Buddha's birthday differ somewhat in Mahayana, the more liberal and lay-oriented branch of Buddhism that dominates East Asia, although here, too, the day of the festival is determined by the moon. Chinese and Korean Buddhists, following the lunar calendar, commemorate the Buddha's birth in early May, while Japanese Buddhists celebrate it on April 8th. The principal rite involves placing small statues of the infant Buddha in bowls and ladling scented water or tea over them, recalling the legend that the newborn Shakyamuni was bathed by waters sent from the gods' heavenly abodes. Chinese Buddhists may also mark the day by releasing living beings (birds, fish) into the air or water. In Korea, temples are illuminated with paper lanterns. Some of the most colorful observances of this day occur in Japan, where the day is also known as the Flower Festival (Hanamatsuri) in remembrance of the showers of blossoms that were said to have rained down from the sky to herald the great teacher's birth.[4] Devout Buddhists will set up flower shrines in temples in front of the main shrines where people worship. Often they also enshrine a small statue of the infant Buddha among the flowers.

Despite the differences between the time and styles of observance, it is interesting to note certain commonalities between Theravada and Mahayana celebrations of Buddha's birth. One of the most obvious is the fact that these commemorations take place during a specific season, a feature common to celebrations of the birth of other religious figures the world over. In particular, the Buddha's birthday comes in early spring, a time of natural re-birth and flowering. It is also a time of increasing light and warmth, herald-ing the abundance of summer and the harvests that will follow. This sense of cosmic renewal fits well with the idea that the Buddha's birth marks a period of universal joy and celebration, similar to Easter and other spring celebrations. By being situated within this large cyclic pattern, the celebra-tion of the Buddha's birthday underscores the basic Buddhist teachings of impermanence and the fact that human beings, like all beings, are situated within the great round of birth and death *(samsara)*.

In accordance with the Buddha's own instructions, Buddhists often cel-ebrate his birthday by making pilgrimages to Lumbini, the legendary site of his birth. Each year thousands of pilgrims descend upon the site and per-form a series of devotional rites. These typically include circumambulating the major temple there and watching priests and monks dance around the temple precincts to the accompaniment of traditional music. Some of the temples rare treasures—geometric depictions of various Buddhas in their realms *(mandalas)* and colorful paintings of Buddhas and *bodhisattvas*—are typically put on display.

Bodhi Day

Bodhi Day commemorates the Buddha's Enlightenment. This is primar-ily a Mahayana festival, since Theravadins celebrate the Buddha's birth, Enlightenment, and passing all during Vesak. Traditionally observed on December 8th, Bodhi Day recalls the moment when, after sitting in medi-tation through all three watches of the night, Siddhartha observed the first faint glow of dawn in the eastern sky and suddenly attained *nirvana.* It was at this moment that he became Buddha, the "Awakened One."

Bodhi Day is a very joyous occasion somewhat reminiscent of the Bud-dha's birthday (one could argue that it is the *real* birthday of the Buddha, since before his Enlightenment he was technically a "Buddha-to-be," or *bo-dhisattva*). Lay people go to temples to make offerings and pay homage to Buddhist images and listen to Dharma talks. At night temples and shrines are often colorfully illuminated by candlelit processions of the faithful. At this time Bodh Gaya, India, the traditional site of the Buddha's Enlighten-ment, becomes host to thousands of pilgrims from all over the world. Major celebrations take place at the site, many of which center on the Bodhi tree and the "diamond seat" beside it where Siddhartha "woke up." Various Bud-dhist communities mark this day with their own distinctive celebrations.

Chan/Zen communities, for instance, observe this day with the beginning of an arduous, weeklong meditation retreat.[5]

Tibetan Buddhists, who mainly follow Vajrayana tradition, celebrate the Buddha's Enlightenment and earthly death on the 15th day of the fourth lunar month. On this day, sacred verses *(sutras)* are recited in every monastery and spectacular dances are performed. Tibetan tradition hold that any good deed performed on this occasion rebounds 300-fold upon the doer. As a result, this is a major time for donations, and beggars will often throng Tibetan monasteries to benefit from the increased generosity.

Nirvana Day

Like Bodhi Day, Nirvana Day is primarily a Mahayana celebration. Nirvana Day is generally observed on February 15th and commemorates the occasion of the Buddha's final entry into *nirvana* and his earthly death. According to traditional accounts, after wandering the Ganges region for some 45 years, preaching the Dharma and acquiring thousands of followers, the Buddha succumbed to illness (perhaps dysentery or food poisoning). After calmly addressing the community *(sangha)* one last time, reminding them that all things were impermanent and that they should continue to follow the path with great diligence, he passed out of existence. His remains were cremated and the relics distributed across the region, eventually being enshrined in memorial mounds *(stupas)* that became important sites of pilgrimage.

Like the Buddha's birthday and Bodhi Day, Nirvana Day is a festive occasion. Although it marks the Buddha's passing from this world, it is not a time of sadness but a reminder of the Buddha's continuing presence among his followers. Like the other two pan-Buddhist celebrations, Nirvana Day is a time when devout Buddhists flock to temples and shrines to make offerings and receive further religious instruction. Kushingara, the traditional site of the Buddha's earthly death, becomes a major destination for pilgrims on this day, as do other *stupas* throughout the Buddhist world.

THERAVADIN CELEBRATIONS AND RITUALS

In addition to these pan-Buddhist celebrations, there are various festivals and rituals found in each of the major branches of Buddhism. Theravada tradition includes many such celebrations, some of the more important of which are discussed here.

Poson

Primarily a Sri Lankan festival, Poson is celebrated on the full moon in June, one month following Vesak. This holiday commemorates the beginnings of the proclamation of the Dharma to foreign countries, specifically its spread to Sri Lanka under the patronage of Emperor Ashoka. During this festival, paintings of the venerable Mahinda, Ashoka's son and the first missionary to Sri Lanka, are paraded through the streets, accompanied by singing and drumming. Thousands of pilgrims also journey to Anuradhapura, the ancient capital, where Mahinda met and converted Sri Lanka's king. This festival is an important reminder of Buddhism's long history of missionary activity.

One of the most important sites visited during Poson is a mountaintop at nearby Mihintale, where Mahinda delivered his first sermon to the king and which, according to legend, was visited by the Buddha himself. Excavations at the site have uncovered numerous *stupas* and the ruins of a large monastic complex. This festival is usually coupled with Sanghamitta Day, a day honoring Princess Sanghamitta (Mahinda's sister and fellow missionary), who is said to have presented the king of Sri Lanka with a cutting from the original *bodhi* tree. The tree was planted in Anuradhapura, where it took root and still thrives (making it one of the oldest living trees in the world). Devout pilgrims come from miles around to the ancient temple, where they pay homage to this living symbol of their faith. In recent decades, Poson has attracted a great deal of media attention and has been used by politicians to infuse Sinhalese nationalism with popular Buddhist devotional sentiments.

Dharma Day

This festival takes place on the full moon day of the eighth month (usually July). It commemorates the Buddha's renunciation (when he left his palace home to become a wandering ascetic) and his first sermon (when he began "turning the Wheel of Dharma") to the five ascetics in the deer park at Sarnath. According to Buddhist tradition, it was on this occasion that the most senior of the ascetics achieved the first stage of enlightenment. Symbolically speaking, Dharma Day is among the most significant Buddhist holidays because it honors the Buddha's teaching and the first instance of it being received and understood. In some traditions this occasion also marks the beginning of the annual three-month "rains retreat," the period corresponding to the monsoon season in Asia, which the Buddha set aside as a time of intense meditation training for the *sangha*. During the rains retreat, members of monastic orders are confined to monastery grounds, although lay Buddhists may visit them to make offerings and receive special blessings.

Sangha Day

Also known as "Four Miracles Assembly" or Magha Puja, this festival is usually held in March and commemorates a meeting between the Buddha and 1,250 of his followers in Rajagriha, India, that was marked by four miracles:

1. All the assembled disciples became enlightened.
2. The meeting occurred spontaneously (it was not planned beforehand).
3. All of the disciples arrived independently and seemingly by coincidence.
4. The official monastic brotherhood was established.

It was at this meeting that the Buddha is said to have first proclaimed the Code of Discipline with its 227 rules regulating monastic life.

Sangha Day is celebrated with devotees bringing offerings (candles, incense, and lotus flowers) to temples by the light of the full moon. There they engage in chanting, listen to Dharma talks, and sometimes free living creatures (birds or fish) from captivity. At sundown on this day, monks lead the laity in circumambulating temple grounds, each person carrying lighted incense or candles and flowers.

Loi Krathong

Originally having little to do with Buddhism (it appears to have borrowed heavily from the Hindu Devali, the Festival of Lights), Loi Krathong (the Festival of Floating Bowls) has now become one of the most popular Theravadin festivals, especially in Thailand. It takes place after the Presentation of New Robes (Kathina Ceremony) usually on the night of the full moon in the 12th lunar month (November). By this time, the rains have ended and rice crops have been planted yet there still are some weeks before the harvest. Although there are conflicting stories concerning the festival's origins, it has become customary on this night for Buddhist monks to preach the story of Prince Vessantara, the Buddha's last lifetime before being reborn as Siddhartha Gautama.

Loi Krathong is one of the most picturesque of Buddhist festivals. People fashion small boats from banana stalks or leaves and float them on rivers and lakes. The boats contain flowers, coins, lighted candles, and incense. As they float away on the waters, the small boats carry away bad luck. According to some traditional explanations, the offerings are meant to pay homage to the holy footprint of the Buddha on the sandy shore of the Namada River in India.

Festivals Surrounding the "Rains Retreat"

There are a series of ritual observances surrounding the traditional three-month "rains retreat" (Vassa) held during the monsoon season. This practice usually begins in late July and goes back to the Buddha and his first followers, who spent their days wandering from community to community until the annual rains made travel almost impossible. The retreat is a time of increased discipline for the monks, who must remain in their monasteries while devout laity bring them offerings of food and other permitted gifts. Some scholars have suggested that this period of confinement may also serve the practical purpose of preventing the monks from trampling villagers' young rice plants, which are particularly vulnerable in the early stages of development. The retreat is a time of general restraint and abstinence in Theravadin society, similar to the Christian observance of Lent. Weddings are not held, and people avoid beginning new ventures. Some laity may become monks for the three-month period, and so there are often many ordination ceremonies at this time.[6] There is also a marked increase in temple attendance.

The end of the retreat (usually in October) is a joyful time. Lamps remain lit in homes and temples and on altars for three days, and every evening there are long processions to temples and *stupas*. At the full moon marking the retreat's official conclusion, the monks perform the Pavarana ("purification"), a ceremony from which the laity gain "merit." While the monks chant and meditate, a burning candle drips wax into a bowl of water, symbolically gathering some of the "merit" the monks have built up over the previous three months. The water is then sprinkled on the laity to give them extra blessings.

The festivities conclude with the Presentation of New Robes (Kathina Ceremony), one of the popular occasions for "merit making." The whole community takes part (including anonymous donors) in gathering together gifts of food, toiletries, writing materials, and so forth. Large numbers of women are involved in spinning and weaving the new robes for the monks. The actual presentation of the offerings occurs in the evening. A large procession of laity (often in traditional costumes) winds through streets of village or town, accompanied by traditional and modern music. Dancers and other entertainers may also be part of the parade as it makes its way to the monastery. There, participants file into the main assembly hall with their gifts, and together recite the Five Precepts. Afterward, a community leader ritually presents the gifts to the monastic assembly, and the abbot accepts them. The chief donor will then officially present the first set of robes, offering them first to the large Buddha image. The monks and novices then receive their new robes and chant a blessing in return.[7]

Paritta Ceremonies

Among the most common and interesting of Theravadin observances are "protection" *(paritta)* ceremonies. These rituals, as their name implies, offer protection from evil spirits, disease, bad luck, and so forth. They have long been an important part of village Buddhism in Theravadin societies and have spread in modified form to other Buddhist societies, where they may appear as ceremonies seeking protection for the nation as a whole.

The core of a *paritta* ceremony is the chanting of a special text, usually a passage from a Pali *sutra*. *Parittas* may be used for general protection but may also be directed toward specific dangers such as snakebite, illness, to ward off attacks, or to drive away evil spirits. They may also be used to attain a good harvest, bless a new house, or simply to gain merit. Monks are usually hired to do the chanting, as they are thought to be the purest and most devout members of the *sangha*, although laity may recite as well. The actual ceremonies may last all night or up to seven days, with reciters working in shifts. Especially elaborate *paritta* ceremonies may require the construction of a special pavilion where the monks sit while chanting and the use of a special string and vases of water that are thought to absorb the chanted words' sacred power. During the ceremony, one end of the string may be tied to a Buddha image, and the monks will hold it while they chant. After the ceremony, the string and water vases may be used to make amulets. *Parittas* are generally considered very powerful and have a decided soothing effect on those present. As a general rule, however, they cannot erase bad *karma* and will only help virtuous, faithful people.

Other Theravadin Festivals

There are a number of other festivals commonly celebrated in Theravadin lands. The New Year has a mixture of religious and secular features and is typically celebrated for three days during the full moon in April. Images of the Buddha are bathed in water and people playfully splash each other.[8] In May, when the moon is half full, followers of Theravada celebrate the Plowing Festival, during which two white oxen pull a golden plow followed by four girls dressed in white who scatter seeds from silver and golden baskets. This is done to commemorate the Buddha's first glimpse of enlightenment, said to have occurred when he was seven years old and watching a field being plowed.

In addition to these, there are a host of other festivals in specific Theravadin countries. Burmese Buddhists observe Abhidharma Day on the full moon day of October, in honor of the occasion when the Buddha is said to have ascended to the lower heavens to teach his deceased mother the Abhidharma ("further teachings," extended philosophical explanations of Buddhist teachings).[9] On November 19th, the Burmese also have a holiday in honor of the robes that the Buddha's mother wove for him. Typically young girls enter weaving competitions to make entire robes. When they are finished, they present the new robes to the monks. In Thailand, the third Saturday in November is marked by the Elephant Festival, which was inspired by the Buddha teaching that new converts to Buddhism should form a special friendship with a senior Buddhist, just as a wild elephant is tamed by being harnessed to a tame one. The city of Kandy in Sri Lanka is the setting of one of the most colorful of all Theravadin festivals, the Festival of the Tooth. Each year in August a tooth said to have belonged to the Buddha is brought out of its temple residence and paraded through the streets. This celebration can last as long as 10 days and appears to date back to the fourth century C.E.[10]

MAHAYANA CELEBRATIONS AND RITUALS

Mahayana tradition also includes numerous popular festivals. Because Mahayana remains the dominant form of Buddhism in East Asia (China, Japan, and Korea), most examples come from these countries. The majority of these celebrations have been colored by Chinese culture in particular, which has long exerted tremendous influence in this region of the world. Nonetheless, the examples we will look at have distinctly *Buddhist* features.

Japanese New Year

Officially Japan follows the Western (solar) calendar, so unlike other people in East Asia, the Japanese generally celebrate the New Year (Oshogatsu) at the beginning of January. Known as the "festival of festivals," this is a national holiday lasting from January 1st to 3rd and, like many observances, mixes indigenous Japanese and Buddhist elements. It is a happy occasion for most Japanese. Preparations begin in December, when streets throughout Japan are decorated with the branches of pine and plum trees, as well as stalks of bamboo and ropes decorated with white paper. People clean their houses, pay off debts, and exchange gifts as a way of saying good-bye to the old year and welcoming the new.

On New Year's Eve, people often don traditional kimonos and visit local shrines. At the stroke of midnight, the great bells in Buddhist temples toll 108 times (to remind people of the 108 human frailties) to drive away the previous year's impurities and ward off evil spirits. New Year's Day celebrations begin as early as 4:00 A.M., following the example of the emperor, who in ancient times would offer prayers in all four directions for peace and prosperity for the nation. During the day, families gather together to offer prayers at household shrines and to eat special foods (steamed rice cakes, black beans, and shrimp).

Chinese (Lunar) New Year

This is probably the best-known Asian festival and it is celebrated in most East Asian countries. Officially it begins on the first day of the full moon of the first lunar month (usually between January 21st and February 19th).[11] This festival combines family rituals, ancestor veneration, and high celebrations, and actually lasts for 14 days, each of which has a special significance. On the first day family members offer good wishes for each other and prayers of gratitude to the ancestors. During this day the youngest child in the family may wear a special cap embroidered with depictions of 18 Buddhist saints. On the second day, families visit their neighbors to wish them well for the coming year. The next several days are spent visiting other friends, feasting, exchanging gifts, and so forth.

The celebrations culminate on the 14th day, sometimes known as the "Lantern Festival." The legend of its origins concerns a contest staged long ago by the emperor to determine once and for all the true "Way." He ordered three altars set up (one for the Buddhist scriptures, one for the Daoist scriptures, and one for the local gods) and then had them set on fire. As the story goes, only the Buddhist scriptures did not burn. In response, the emperor ordered that from then on that day was to be commemorated by the lighting of lanterns throughout the land to symbolize the light of Buddhism. Regardless of the historical truth of this legend, on this day homes and streets are colorfully decorated with lanterns and red banners. People dress up in costumes to perform traditional plays, and firecrackers are set off to frighten away evil spirits. The highlight of the day is a large parade through the streets of town featuring celebrants dressed as folk heroes, Buddhist saints, lions, and dragons. Chinese New Year parades are becoming increasingly popular in cities in the United States with large Chinese populations, such as San Francisco and New York.

Birthday of Guanyin

There are a number of Mahayana festivals celebrating important events in the lives of major *bodhisattvas.* Of these, the most widely observed revolve around the figure of Guanyin, the female version of Avalokiteshvara, who is far and away the most popular Buddhist deity and the one who, in many respects, best represents the Mahayana ideal of combining wisdom and compassion.[12] Although there are festivals commemorating Guanyin's Enlightenment and worldly death, the most joyous celebrations mark her birthday. They are usually observed in February or March.

Fire and Water Festival

Dating back some 1,200 years, this festival takes place in the first two weeks of March in Japan at Todaiji (Great Eastern Temple) in Nara, the ancient capital. The exact origins of this festival are unclear, but it appears to have derived from pre-Buddhist rites of cleansing and purification that preceded the annual spring rice planting. It now includes an entire series of rituals focusing on the temple's Buddha image, the largest Buddha statue in all of Japan. Over the course of two weeks, monks make special offerings, confess their shortcomings, and pray for prosperity for the coming year. During this festival many devotees gather at the temple to recite *sutras* and blow conch shells..

For the first two weeks, monks carrying pine torches assemble every evening in the temple gallery for the first watch of the night. This series of evening vigils climaxes with the Fire Ceremony on the night of March 12th.

The monks assemble as usual in the temple gallery with their torches, but then run around circumambulating the sacred area, waving their torches and wooden swords to drive off evil influences. In the course of this vigorous exorcism, the monks shake off burning embers to the participants waiting below who try to catch them for good luck. This is followed by the Water-Drawing Festival, which begins at 2:00 A.M. on March 13th. At this time the monks carry buckets to the temple well and draw up perfumed water. This sacred water, which is believed to have healing and rejuvenating powers, is given to the people and offered before the statues of the Great Buddha and other religious figures. The Water-Drawing Festival has a very meditative atmosphere, perhaps because of the centrality of water, which in addition to its purifying powers often symbolizes the clear, still Buddha Mind. The ceremony closes with a dramatic fire dance accompanied by the vigorous beating of drums.

Ohigan

Primarily a Japanese observance, Ohigan is celebrated twice yearly around the spring and autumn equinoxes. The term means "other shore," and refers to the common belief in Buddhism that the spirits of the dead reach *nirvana* by crossing the river of existence. The idea of "crossing over" also serves as a metaphor for the spiritual move from suffering to enlightenment. Ohigan is a day for remembering the dead, particularly the family ancestors. Families celebrate it by visiting graves, cleaning and decorating them, and reciting prayers and *sutras.* Most likely it is a Buddhist adaptation of ancient ancestral rites, as it bears a strong resemblance to annual ancestral observances in Chinese culture such as Clear and Bright Festival *(qing ming),* which is also held during the third lunar month near the spring equinox.

Airing the Scriptures

This celebration, which is especially observed by Chinese Buddhists, takes place in June or early July. It commemorates a legendary event in ancient India when a boat carrying various Buddhist *sutras* capsized in a river. The texts were rescued and spread out along the shores to dry. In honor of this event, Buddhist monasteries bring out the books from their libraries and inspect them for damage. This is an important day that serves several functions for Buddhists. Practically, it is a way for monks to help preserve their most valuable texts by preventing the buildup of mold and insect damage (both quite common in warm climates). It may also encourage scholarship by letting monks become acquainted with their monastic holdings. Spiritually, it serves to broadcast the great power of the Dharma and provides an opportunity for the laity, who generally do not read or even look at their scriptures, to see them and bask in their aura.

Festival of the Hungry Ghosts

Probably the single most widely observed festival in Mahayana traditions is the Festival of Hungry Ghosts. Known in Sanskrit as *Ullambana,* it has become such a large part of East Asian society that it is even celebrated by many non-Buddhists as a demonstration of filial devotion to their family ancestors. During this time it is thought that the ancestors are reborn in this world as ghosts to wander the earth as a potential source of danger and misfortune. Monks and nuns will typically transfer the merit they have accrued from observing their summer retreats, put out food, and chant *sutras* to help the spirits attain a better rebirth. Laity sponsor these rites and may also participate by burning paper boats or lanterns to help ferry the ghosts to a better world, similar to the Thai festival of Loi Krathong. Often, celebrants will perform rituals before two altars—one for offerings to feed the ancestral spirits and one for offerings to feed "hungry ghosts," spirits of people who died in violent or untimely fashion, or who do not receive homage from their descendents. There are many parallels between the Festival of the Hungry Ghosts and the Western Hallowe'en as well as the Day of the Dead (Dia de Los Muertos) observances in Mexico and other areas of Latin America.

There are several stories explaining the origins of the Festival of the Hungry Ghosts. The most famous is that of Mulian, a great disciple of the Buddha. After his mother died, Mulian was distressed to discover that she had been reborn in one of the "hell realms," or, in some versions of the story, as a hungry ghost condemned to wander the world without rest. Mulian consulted the Buddha, who, gratified at the young monk's deep filiality, directed him to perform the rituals of merit-transfer so that his mother would attain a better rebirth. Because of its overriding familial themes, this story and its accompanying festival quickly caught on in China and other areas of East Asia.

In Japan this festival is known as *Obon,* the Feast of the Dead, and is celebrated in either July or August, depending on the region.[13] The entire celebration usually lasts from the 13th to the 15th of the month and it is a time when most Japanese return to the home in which they grew up. Graves are tended, often being sprinkled with water by each family member, and offerings of flowers, herbs, and incense are placed on the ancestral altar. Candles are lit to welcome the ancestral spirits home to partake of the offerings, and a Buddhist priest may be invited to chant a *sutra* before the altar. In the evenings most temples put on lavish performances of dances and plays. The climax of Obon comes on the evening of the 15th, when bonfires are lit to usher the spirits back to their realm. The festivities in Kyoto are especially colorful, with crowds of people dressing in traditional kimonos and flocking to local rivers and parks for evening picnics. At nightfall large bonfires in the shape of Chinese letters light up the surrounding mountainsides.

On August 15th at the conclusion of Obon there is a special observance among the Japanese who live in Hawaii. Held in Honolulu, this is the Floating Lantern Ceremony, which commemorates the end of World War II. In many respects this is an American adaptation of traditional Japanese observances in that small lanterns are lit and floated on rivers and streams. They are said to symbolize the spirits of the deceased as they cross the river of existence.

Other Mahayana Celebrations

Each school of Mahayana Buddhism also has its own festivals and celebrations. For example, Chan/Zen tradition observes Bodhidharma Day every October 5th in honor of the legendary patriarch who is said to have brought Chan teachings from India to China. Chan/Zen monasteries mark this day with daylong meditation retreats. In addition to these celebrations, which are mainly observed annually in Mahayana countries, there are also more regular observances in certain traditions. For example, on the 15th of every month followers of Pure Land honor Amitabha, the Buddha of Infinite Light who has established his western paradise where the faithful will be reborn. Meanwhile many Japanese Buddhists set aside the 24th of each month to express devotion to Jizo (Earth-store), the *bodhisattva* who is the special guardian of travelers and children, and takes it upon himself to be reborn in the "hell realms" to ease the sufferings of the beings there.

VAJRAYANA CELEBRATIONS AND RITUALS

Vajrayana is overwhelming associated with Tibet, but it also dominates the entire Himalayan region, including Bhutan, Ladkh, and much

Tibetan mountain pass decorated with prayer flags to ensure blessings.
Courtesy of John C. George.

of Nepal.[14] Festivals and celebrations in Vajrayana Buddhism more or less
coincide with those in Theravada or Mahayana with minor variations. As
with the other two branches of Buddhism, Vajrayana celebrations tend
to be colored by their cultural setting and yet retain distinctly Buddhist
features. Over time Vajrayana has fused with indigenous traditions, particularly the practices and rites associated with Bon, the indigenous religious tradition of the Tibetan region. As a result, Vajrayana festivals often
center on rituals featuring dramatic dances and are accompanied by loud
music and chanting.

Tibetan New Year

The Tibetan New Year (Losar) celebration covers three days and is usually held in February, the exact date being determined by astrologers. Its
festivities closely resemble those of the Chinese New Year. Preparations
begin in the weeks leading up to the observance, with people buying new
clothes and gathering special food and drink for the major feast that will
be held. Some of the special foods prepared beforehand include various
dishes of sweet rice mixed with raisins, fruit, potatoes, meat, and other
treats. The day before New Year's Eve families gather to eat a special dump-
ling soup. They then exorcise any lingering evil spirits of the old year by
parading around a doll that represents a fierce Tibetan deity and setting
off fireworks. In some areas monks don bright robes and grotesque masks
and wigs to perform a dance dramatizing the struggle between good and
evil. New Year's Eve continues this "cleansing" routine with people cleaning
and whitewashing their homes in anticipation of the next day. Sometimes

a handful of dirt is saved so that it may be sprinkled at crossroads where spirits are believed to dwell.

On the first day of the New Year, people place dishes of water or beer and other offerings at the shrines of their household deities. They also offer thanks to the dragon-spirits who oversee their water supply. Most of the day is spent feasting and drinking with family and neighbors. Overall it is a time of great merrymaking, with lots of gambling as well as traditional music and dancing. It is still observed, albeit in somewhat subdued fashion, in Tibet and among Tibetan exiles.

The New Year has long been a time of pilgrimage during which devotees would prostrate themselves for hundreds of miles as they made their way to the capital city of Lhasa, the site of Jokhang, Tibet's most sacred temple.. In recent decades many exiled Tibetans have made their pilgrimage to Dharamsala, the site in India where the Dalai Lama now lives in exile. On the second day of the festivities, the Dalai Lama himself blesses those assembled by touching their heads and giving them a piece of red and white string that the faithful often wear around their necks for good luck and protection. Another popular site of pilgrimage is Katmandu, Nepal, where crowds of Tibetan refugees visit a large *stupa* to see the priests perform traditional ceremonies. Long copper horns are blown, and the pilgrims enjoy masked dances and can catch a glimpse of a large portrait of the Dalai Lama that has been put on display.

Tibetan monks making music, Drepung monastery, Tibet.
Courtesy of John C. George.

The Prayer Festival

From the 4th to the 25th day of the first lunar month (usually February), Tibetan monks perform the ceremonies of the Prayer Festival or Festival of the Great Vow (Monlam). This is a major Tibetan holiday dating back to the fifteenth century when it was instituted by the great monastic reformer Tsongkhapa (1357–1419). The center of this festival is the five-day celebration of one of the Buddha's great miracles, the "marvel of the pairs" at Sravasti, India. According to legend, the Buddha was challenged by some rivals to demonstrate his psychic powers in hopes that he would abstain and so appear to lack such abilities. The Buddha, who usually declined such shows as pointless or even dangerous, responded by saying he would meet the challenge at a later date, when he rose in the air and miraculously produced both fire and water from his body. Immediately afterward, he ascended to the heavens to preach the Abhidharma to his mother. Since this occasion marks the Buddha's triumph over rival teachers, it has come to be associated with Buddhism's victory over Bon as well as a symbol for the overcoming of evil forces.

This festival, like many in various societies around the world, aims at ensuring success and prosperity for the coming year. On the 13th day, dancers portray Buddhism's fierce protector deities ("Dharma protectors") in their struggles against the demons of ignorance. The demons of ignorance are represented by a small human figure that is ritually "killed" as a symbol of Buddhism's victory over evil. This period is marked by other celebrations such as horse races and archery contests, both of which reflect the ancient roots of Tibetan culture.

Traditionally, the Prayer Festival was also a time when crowds of pilgrims would flock to Jokhang monastery in Lhasa. There, they would view the great images of Buddhist figures that the monks had sculpted from butter, some towering as high as 10 meters (35 feet). The Dalai Lama would journey to Jokhang monastery where great debates were held in his honor. The high point of the festivities was a large procession around the old city carrying a statue of Maitreya, the future Buddha. These observances ceased with the Chinese takeover of Tibet in 1959 but were revived on a more modest scale in 1986, only to be officially prohibited again in 1990. Some of the traditional festivities, however, are observed in Dharamsala.

Hemis Festival

Centered at the Hemis monastery in Ladkh, this festival takes place in June or July and celebrates the birthday of Padmasambhava, the legendary teacher credited with bringing Vajrayana teachings to Tibet in the eighth century. This is a colorful and dramatic event in which dancers in elaborate robes and masks twirl to the music of drums, cymbals, and pipes. Various companies of monks act out morality plays and perform mock exorcisms. Major fairs are held in temple precincts for local artisans to peddle their wares.

The climax of the Hemis Festival is the Devil Dance. In preparation for this performance, a select group of monks dresses as monsters, skeletons, and wild beasts while another group portrays famous Buddhist saints wearing opulent silk robes and carrying pastoral staffs. To the accompaniment of loud music (including blasts from the traditional 10-foot-long Himalayan trumpets) a dramatic battle ensues, at the end of which the "good monks" drive off the "evil creatures." In addition to reenacting the myths of how Buddhism spread through the Tibetan region, the dance also symbolizes how the Dharma can help avert the evils that beset ordinary people.

The Dalai Lama's Birthday

As the spiritual and political leader of the Tibetan people, the Dalai Lama (traditionally regarded as an incarnation of the great *bodhisattva* Avalokiteshvara) is the focus of tremendous adoration. His birthday, July 6th, is an occasion of great festivity and has become a marker of Tibetan national identity. The present Dalai Lama, Tenzin Gyatso, was enthroned in 1940 at the age of five and is the 14th Dalai Lama in a line stretching back to the fourteenth century. Each Dalai Lama is thought to be a reincarnation of the previous one.

Celebrations of the Dalai Lama's birthday are extremely popular among Tibetan laity, who regard it as an especially auspicious day. They mark the day by burning incense to appease local spirits and make offerings before altars bearing portraits of the Dalai Lama.. Much of the day is spent on family picnics, doing traditional dances, and singing. This day is not officially recognized in Tibetan regions now occupied by the Chinese.

Marya

This Nepalese celebration, held in July or August, honors the Buddha's victory over Mara, the tempter, while he sat under the *bodhi* tree. In the town of Patan a major procession of some 3,000 worshippers journey from shrine to shrine, offering butter lamps (dishes of clarified butter, or *ghee*, with wicks floating in them) to the Buddha. Celebrants may wear masks and costumes and play traditional Nepalese instruments as they make their way through the streets of town. During this parade, those dressed as Mara and his minions may jump out to scare the children, who line the streets as the procession goes by.

Festival of Lights

Held sometime from late November to December, this celebration honors the birth and death of Tsongkhapa, the great Tibetan scholar and adept who founded the Gelugpa order and founded the annual Prayer Festival (Monlam). The occasion is celebrated by the lighting of thousands of butter lamps that are then placed on windowsills, roofs, and temple altars. Many people visit temples to pray, make special offerings, and receive additional religious instruction.

Other Tibetan Celebrations

One minor celebration is the Yogurt Festival, held at the conclusion of the monks' intensive summer retreat. As a symbol of the monks' breaking of their fast, they are served bowls of fresh yogurt. It is also a time of competitive performances of Tibetan Opera. Almost every temple in Tibet and the surrounding regions has its own celebrations of its founding as well as the birthdays of its most important patriarchs. As in other countries, there are a great number of other indigenous festivals in the Tibetan region that, although originally not Buddhist, have taken on certain Buddhist aspects. These may include various horse-racing festivals in spring and autumn, as well as the harvest and bathing festivals. A recent addition to the roster of Tibetan holidays is Tibetan Uprising Day, held on March 10th in commemoration of the large-scale uprisings against the Chinese that began on March 10, 1959. Tibetan refugees round the world mark this day with demonstrations and Buddhist memorial services. Every year on this day the Dalai Lama also issues a statement calling for world peace.

Tantric Initiations

Tantric rituals and ceremonies are a major part of Vajrayana Buddhism. To study with a Tantric master, a disciple must undergo an initiation in which the teacher passes on basic details of the practices, transfers the blessings of the relevant deities, and bestows protection from the powerful spiritual and emotional forces to which the disciple will be exposed. Rites of initiation begin with the master undergoing a complex series of visualizations. In these meditations he visualizes himself as the focal deity, sees the ritual objects to be used (bells, *vajras*) as instruments of enlightenment, and views an image of the deity as being suffused with the divinity's presence. The master offers the initiate water that has been blessed for use in purification and asks the student to repeat the *bodhisattva* vows stating he will devote himself to the welfare of all beings. The disciple must then seal the vow by ringing a bronze bell and displaying the *vajra*, the "diamond scepter." The master then touches a sculpture of the deity to the student's head and then visualizes the deity's image merging with the student's body.

Next, various symbols of the deity are touched to the disciple's body at specific sites where centers of energy (*chakras*, literally "wheels") are located. Master and disciple both then take hold of a rosary and the master begins chanting the deity's "heart *mantra*" (a secret chant that elicits the deity's compassion) as he visualizes the *mantra* emanating from his heart into that of his disciple. A series of other offerings and ritual gestures *(mudras)* then seal the transmission, permanently binding student, master, and deity together. Some initiations include vows to practice this rite every day for the rest of the initiate's life.

Fire Sacrifice

Fire ceremonies form the centerpiece of almost all Vajrayana rituals. These fire rituals, known as *homa,* appear to have been adopted from the ancient Vedic rites that were first observed more than 3,500 years ago and formed the foundation of early Indian society. A typical fire ceremony requires the construction of a special altar in the shape of a *mandala* following time-honored procedures. During the ceremony itself, a senior monk will invoke the presence of certain deities and offer grains, clarified butter, and other foods into the fire, all the while chanting *mantras.* Other monks may assist in the ceremony by chanting *sutras* and beating on drums to accompanying the senior monk's ritual offerings. The various offerings placed in the fire symbolize the individual's mental and spiritual afflictions (attachments and ignorance), while the flame (symbolizing wisdom) is understood as consuming any and all obstacles to enlightenment. Vajrayana masters throughout Tibet, Nepal, and Japan regularly perform such fire sacrifices for the benefit of all beings.

Rites of Tulku Succession

Tibetan monastic orders are led by reincarnated teachers *(tulkus)* who are regarded as great *bodhisattvas. Tulkus* are thought to take repeated birth in a human body to aid humanity through teaching, healing, and spreading the Dharma. Thousands of *tulkus* have been recognized in Tibet over the centuries and almost all of them have been men. The birth of a *tulku* is a great honor for a family, and certain aristocratic families have become famous for producing many *tulkus.* Because *tulkus* wield a great deal of political power and may own large amounts of property and wealth to support themselves along with their regents and teachers before they come of age, disputes often arise over the recognition of a new incarnation.

There are a number of steps involved in *tulku* succession and they are fairly consistent across Tibetan schools. Typically a *tulku* will give clues (often in writing) about the direction in which his next birth will occur as he nears the end of his life. After his death, his senior students follow these signs, perhaps consulting a medium or another *tulku* for more specific instructions. Parties from the monastery may disguise themselves as laity and seek out families with children of suitable age. When a likely candidate is found, the delegates will carefully examine the child for auspicious marks and ask him questions to discern his wisdom and character. Next, they present the child with an array of items, ranging from liturgical objects such as *vajras,* bells, and rosaries to personal objects such as mirrors, glasses, or teacups. The child must then correctly and repeatedly choose those belonging to and used by the former *tulku.* If the child passes these tests, he is officially acknowledged as the new *tulku* and is paraded back to the monastery with great fanfare, often accompanied by his parents and other family members. From then on the new *tulku* lives at the monastery and embarks on his monastic studies.

BUDDHIST FUNERALS

Although it may seem morbid to contemporary Westerners (who tend to avoid or deny death), Buddhism faces death head on. Buddhist teachings stress the inherently fragile and impermanent nature of existence and try to promote acceptance and understanding so that we may transcend the suffering that comes with life and its inevitable end.[15] One of the four sights that prompted Siddhartha to embark on his religious quest was a corpse, and Buddhist monastics often meditate on corpses in various states of decay to gain insight into the nature of reality. One reason Buddhism was able to spread to so many cultures is that it has had more to say about death and the hereafter than most indigenous traditions. Over the years Buddhism has developed a number of ways of handling death, often devising special rituals to both aid the deceased and comfort the bereaved.

Buddhism teaches that death must be prepared for. As it approaches, friends and relatives join to help the dying person have a "good death" and so ease the transition from this life to the next. Often monks will be called in and fed on the dying person's behalf, and in return the monks will chant passages from *sutras* or other ritual texts. The ideal death, for a Buddhist, is to pass on in a calm, even joyful state, recollecting one's blessings and good deeds to insure the best possible rebirth. Most Buddhist funerals involve cremation, reflecting the religion's Indian roots. It is common in Buddhist societies to hold a memorial service in honor of the deceased shortly after the funeral (usually 49 days, the period traditionally thought to exist between a person's lives) and each year on the anniversary of the person's death.

Among Theravadin Buddhists, funerals often have a festive atmosphere except in extraordinary circumstances, and grief is rarely displayed. Most of the rites involve sharing merit with the deceased. This is typically done by pouring water into a bowl until it overflows, while monks chant verses stating that, just as water flows downward, so may the merit offered by those assembled reach the departed.

In the Mahayana traditions of East Asia, the dying person may hold a string attached to hands of an image of Amitabha Buddha. This not only comforts the dying person and the assembled family members, it reminds them of Amitabha's promise that they will be reborn in his Pure Land. Chinese Buddhists make special donations in honor of the deceased and may have monks perform rites for the dead a number of times during the 49-day between-life period. Monks repeatedly chant the name of the Buddha or certain *sutras* and then transfer the merit from such services to the deceased. Monks also make special requests on behalf of the living that heavenly *bodhisattvas* and Buddhas remember the departed with compassion and aid in transferring any merit given on his or her behalf.

In Vajrayana tradition, a dying or deceased person has the Liberation through Hearing in the Bardo (Bardo Thol Dro, commonly translated as The Tibetan Book of the Dead) read to him to guide him through the 49-day period between lives *(bardo)*. Such readings are intended to help the deceased overcome attachments to his body or family, gain further insight into reality, or provide clarity through the series of visions the deceased is thought to experience based upon his *karma*. Particularly advanced yogins may become enlightened during this stage, but more often, the deceased will be drawn to a new rebirth. It is possible, however, that through insight gained in previous lives or through the aid of others, the deceased can progress along the *bodhisattva* path or attain rebirth in a Pure Land. After death, the corpse is usually cremated, but it may alternatively be dismembered and fed to vultures so that they might benefit.

It may seem that all of this focus on funerals and death gives Buddhism a gloomy air. Moreover, there is some concern among Japanese Buddhists, for instance, of their religion being reduced to "funeral Buddhism" as their society becomes increasingly secularized. Nonetheless, facing death is an important aspect of Buddhism. After all, the Buddha taught that one overcomes suffering by understanding and acceptance rather than avoidance. By and large, cultures where Buddhism has flourished are resigned to death, regarding it as the basic accompaniment to life. Funerals are a regular part of the Buddhist life cycle. Moreover, because life is a constant process of change, grief, too, shall pass. Buddhist teachings and practices, by helping promote understanding, attest to one of life's great paradoxes: that joy can be found even in the midst of suffering.

NOTES

1. Differences in the dates of these Buddhist holidays are comparable to discrepancies regarding the dates of some Christian holidays. For example, Western (Roman Catholic and Protestant) churches and Eastern Orthodox (Greek, Russian, etc.) churches use different liturgical calendars and usually celebrate Easter at different times.

2. The word *Vesak* comes from the name of the month according to the traditional Indian calendar that is still used in some Buddhist countries.

3. For details on these lay observances, see the section "Devotion" in Chapter 4.

4. Some scholars suggest that this festival retains elements of pre-Buddhist celebrations when villagers would venture out to gather wild mountain flowers as a way of bringing home protective deities to guard their rice fields.

5. This day also reveals Buddhism's darker side, as it was on December 8, 1941 (December 7th in the United States) that the Japanese chose to bomb Pearl Harbor. This event demonstrates how Buddhism was pressed into the service of Japanese nationalism in the early half of the twentieth century.

Similar examples of other religions being co-opted for national and/or military ventures are quite common in world history.

6. The Burmese have a special holiday (usually on or around September 2nd) for young boys, during which they throw a special family feast for their sons, who wear colorful robes and headdresses. Afterward they are taken to the temple where their heads are shaved and they enter monastic life for a short period (anywhere from three days to three months). This is a major way for entire families to earn great merit.

7. In Laos, the retreat occurs later than in other countries, usually in September. Laotian parents may give their children candy and toys during this period, which typically ends in joyous celebrations marked by boat races on Laos's major rivers.

8. The splashing and general horseplay lends a distinct carnival atmosphere to the New Year celebrations. Many scholars think it may derive from the Hindu festival of Holi, which has similar features. It is interesting, however, that the elderly continue to be treated with respect: the young sprinkle their elders' hands and feet with water as a sign of honor rather than splash them.

9. According to traditional accounts, this event was immediately preceded by the Buddha's triumph over several rival teachers by performing the "marvel of the pairs." For details see the section on the Prayer Festival.

10. The Buddhist pilgrim Faxian witnessed this festival on his visit to Sri Lanka in 413 C.E. Similar processions of Buddhist relics have occurred throughout history. One such procession in China during the eighth century so incensed a Confucian critic of Buddhism that he sent the emperor an essay denouncing such foreign practices.

11. In Vietnam, the Lunar New Year celebration is known as *Tet* and begins when the moon enters the constellation of Capricorn in late December.

12. As noted earlier, Guanyin (*Kannon* in Japan) is the East Asian form of the Indian *bodhisattva* Avalokiteshvara (The Lord Who Looks Down [from Above]). Although usually represented as a male figure in India, Avalokiteshvara takes on female form in Central and East Asia, where she has a role analogous to Mary in Christianity.

13. August is the most common time and, in fact, is known colloquially in Japan as "Ghost Month."

14. The Japanese Buddhist school Shingon is also a form of Vajrayana, although it tends to be relatively close both ritually and culturally to other Japanese schools, which are predominantly Mahayana.

15. Death is still regarded as an inauspicious, even "polluting" event at the popular level in many Buddhist societies. However, Buddhist teachings stress that death is neutral, neither inherently bad nor inherently good.

6

MAJOR FIGURES

Buddhism's spread across the globe required the efforts of innumerable people. Most of these devotees are not noted in any traditional histories and chronicles. However, a number of people have made such important contributions to Buddhism that their memories have been preserved. The following is a sampling of some these eminent Buddhists, selected from a wide variety of traditions to convey the richness of Buddhist history. The survey concludes with several figures whose influence is particularly apparent in contemporary Buddhism.

EARLY FIGURES

The Buddha's Disciples

During his life the Buddha attracted many talented disciples, several of whom attained Enlightenment. Buddhists around the world continue to venerate their examples. These early figures include the five ascetics with whom Siddhartha practiced austerities before his Enlightenment and who formed the audience for the Buddha's his first sermon at the deer park in Sarvasti. Despite their initial resistance, all five were won over. One of them, Kaundinya, attained the first level of Awakening after hearing the first sermon. Within a week all five reached the state beyond life and death *(nirvana)*. They thus achieved the status of "saints" *(arhats)*. Together with the Buddha they formed the nucleus of the monastic order.

Another important early disciple was Ananda, the Buddha's cousin and constant attendant for the last 20 years of his life. Ananda figures prominently in stories of the Buddha's passing, weeping uncontrollably at the prospect of losing his beloved teacher since he alone among the great disciples had not reached *nirvana.* The Buddha consoled him, singling him out for his kindness and assuring him that he would become enlightened as long as he continued on the path. Ananda was originally to be excluded from the First Great Council (following Siddhartha's death, the meeting of five hundred monks during which the authoritative canon was established) but he attained *nirvana* the night before the council was to convene, just as the Buddha promised. Ananda's prodigious memory enabled him to recite all of the Buddha's sermons before the assembly. Eventually these became the entire "basket" of Sutras.

Perhaps the most philosophically astute of the Buddha's disciples was Shariputra. Often regarded as the Buddha's chief disciple, Shariputra had originally followed a rival teacher. After hearing the Buddha preach, however, Shariputra and his friend Maudgalyayana (famed for his great psychic powers) converted. Shariputra achieved wide renown for his wisdom and became a great teacher of the Abhidharma (Further Teachings), the collection of texts that elaborate on the more technical aspects of Buddhist metaphysics. He died before the Buddha but his relics are enshrined in the great memorial mound *(stupa)* at Sanchi, India, an important ancient Buddhist site.

One of the most enigmatic of the Buddha's disciples was Mahakashyapa (Great Kashyapa). Renowned for his asceticism and mastery of meditation, it was Kashyapa who received the legendary Flower Sermon, inaugurating the famous "separate transmission outside the scriptures, not relying on words and letters" that has come to be associated with Chan/Zen, the great meditation school. Traditionally Buddhists have maintained that it was also Kashyapa who called the First Council after the Buddha's passing to establish an accepted body of authentic teachings and discipline.

Several nuns have made lasting contributions to Buddhism, and many of their teachings and experiences are recorded in the Songs of the Female Elders, a Pali (the sacred language in which the Theravadin canon is written) text that provides an important window on early monastic life. Perhaps the foremost nun was Mahapajapati (Great Pajapati), Siddhartha's foster mother. Traditional accounts state that unlike other members of his family, Pajapati was accepting of Siddhartha's transformation and quickly converted after hearing him preach. It was she who, along with five hundred other laywomen, entreated the Buddha to accept women into monastic life, eventually prevailing with the help of Ananda. As the first nun, Pajapati was also the first female Dharma teacher and had many disciples. Her death at the age of 120 was marked by numerous miracles, another indication of her great holiness. Another prominent nun was Patachara. In lay life, Patachara was an independent-minded woman who often defied the conventions of Indian society. After a series of accidents, she lost her entire family and went mad with grief. For years she wandered, feared and hated by local people, until she met the Buddha and he convinced her to join his order. She thrived in monastic life and eventually attained *nirvana*. Later, she became a great teacher with some 30 nuns as her disciples. The examples of both Mahapajapati and Patachara show that women were a powerful presence in the community *(sangha)* from early on.

Buddhist tradition also remembers several important early laypeople. Among them are Sujata, a young woman who gave Siddhartha a meal of milk rice when he was on the point of starvation, and two merchants named Trapusha and Bhallika, who offered the Buddha food seven weeks after his Enlightenment. These men formally "took refuge" in the Buddha and the teachings (Dharma), becoming his first lay followers and foreshadowing the establishment of the *sangha*. Some accounts state that as they were departing they asked the Buddha for something of his to venerate. He gave them a few hairs from his head that they later enshrined in a *stupa,* thus instituting the basic form of worship still in use. Other important lay disciples include Yasa, the son of a wealthy merchant from Benares (present-day Varanasi) who went on to become a monk, and his father, mother and wife, who retained their lay status.

Emperor Ashoka (r. 274–36 B.C.E.)

Ashoka has a special place of honor in Buddhism as its greatest imperial patron. As with many ancient rulers, Ashoka's life has become the stuff of legend over the course of the centuries. He ruled over India's first large empire, which was centered on the Ganges plain, extending eastward to the Bay of Bengal and southward into what is now central India. Upon assuming the throne, Ashoka began a campaign of consolidating his frontier regions and extending them by military force. In particular, Ashoka focused his armies on Kalinga, a southeast coastal region. The ensuing war caused such horrific destruction and bloodshed that despite his victory, Ashoka felt deep remorse. Just at that time, Ashoka encountered a charismatic Buddhist monk whose teachings convinced him to convert. From that point on, Ashoka was a devout Buddhist layman, particularly concerned with promoting an ethic of "nonharming" *(ahimsa).* Ashoka sent envoys and missionaries to explain the Dharma throughout his realm and to regions beyond his borders.

Much of the evidence of Ashoka's life comes from a series of edicts he issued, which he had inscribed on pillars posted throughout his domain.[1] These are widely spread across India and Pakistan (areas that lay within his empire), with one inscription being found as far away as Kandahar in modern Afghanistan. Ashoka's great concern was to spread Dharma, a term with numerous meanings and associations in India, many not necessarily Buddhist. Perhaps the best translation is "goodness" or "rightness," an ideal shared by all ancient Indian traditions. Ashoka posted basic principles supporting Dharma in many public places and sought to administer his empire in accordance with Dharma. Since rule by Dharma meant encouraging the public good, Ashoka embarked on a widespread campaign of planting trees and digging wells along major thoroughfares, and ordered the construction of numerous clinics and rest houses for the common people. He also discouraged animal sacrifice and hunting and outlawed wasteful ceremonies. In addition, Ashoka took steps to ensure that justice was administered fairly in his realm and that prisoners were well treated.

Although scholars have looked for ulterior motives, Ashoka's devotion appears to have been genuine. He supported all religious sects and encouraged his subjects to do so as well, but he himself went on pilgrimages to the sites associated with the Buddha's life. He unearthed numerous relics associated with the Buddha and his disciples and had them enshrined in thousands of new relic mounds *(stupas)* across his realm. Ashoka supported Buddhist missionaries in their journeys to spread the Dharma and is even alleged to have presided over the Council of Pataliputra (a council called to settle ongoing debates concerning monastic discipline) held in 250 B.C.E.[2] Traditional accounts state that his son Mahinda and daughter Sanghamitta, both members of the Buddhist monastic order, headed up his official mission to Sri Lanka where they succeeded in converting the entire island to Buddhism.

For centuries Ashoka has been the model of Buddhist leadership. His concern for justice, charity, and the common good, along with his generosity to the *sangha* set the standards by which all Buddhist rulers have been judged.[3] Ashoka is the ideal "Wheel Turning Monarch," one who orders the state and protects the people yet exemplifies purity, self-discipline, and devotion. Since his time, Buddhists have consistently relied on rulers to help establish a moral and spiritual civilization in which the Dharma can flourish. Ashoka's missionary zeal helped spread Buddhism throughout the world, including such faraway regions as China, Southeast Asia, and areas of the Mediterranean. Because of his patronage, Buddhist monasteries and shrines sprang up along all the major trade routes of Asia, spreading into nearly every Asian society.

SOUTHEAST ASIAN BUDDHISTS

Buddhaghosha (Fourth-Fifth Centuries c.e.)

The early common era was a period of great change in Buddhism, when various new movements (Mahayana, Tantra) were beginning to spread. Although many embraced these innovations, some sectors frowned on such things as departing from the Buddha's teachings. Sri Lanka in particular developed a reputation for conservatism, as the monks there intentionally sought to maintain what they saw as the purity of the Buddha's original teachings. This reputation for strict adherence to Dharma attracted many devout monks from the Indian mainland. One of these Indian monks was named Buddhaghosha (Speech of the Buddha).

Buddhaghosha was born near Bodh Gaya, the site of the Buddha's Awakening, into a non-Buddhist family that followed the Brahmanical teachings of early Hinduism. Buddhaghosha was trained as a high-caste *(brahmin)* priest but he converted to Buddhism, eventually making his way to the ancient Sri Lankan capital of Anuradapura, where the first great monastery on the island had been established. Buddhaghosha asked permission to translate the great body of Sinhalese (language of the indigenous Sri Lankan people) commentaries into Pali, thus making them accessible to an international Buddhist audience. The Sri Lankan monks, wary of the foreigner, decided to test his understanding of the Dharma by asking him to compose a treatise on Buddhist practice based on two lines from one of the Buddha's sermons. The result was the massive Path of Purity, a veritable encyclopedia outlining the way to *nirvana*.[4] So impressed were the monks that they willingly provided Buddhaghosha with all their old commentaries as well as scribes and other materials he would need. Buddhaghosha then dedicated himself to collating all the existing Sinhalese commentaries, translating them, and composing extensive Pali commentaries on most of the texts from the Tripitaka (Three Baskets), the official collection of sacred Buddhist writings.

Despite their conservative reputation, Buddhaghosha's works, especially *The Path of Purity*, mark a major innovation in Buddhist history. In places they actually depart from earlier Buddhist teachings on certain points, possibly showing the influence of Vedic (early Hindu, brahmanical) beliefs or even indigenous, pre-Buddhist ideas. For example, Buddhaghosha extols the supernatural qualities of the Buddha, revering him essentially as a god. He also speaks of certain "secret teachings" that the elder monks should reserve for only a select few of their disciples, seemingly in direct contradiction to the Buddha's claim that he always taught "with an open hand."[5] Buddhaghosha also stresses certain techniques of meditation *(dhyana)* that had received only peripheral treatment in the actual scriptures. Among these is the use of circular devices of various colors (blue, yellow, red, etc.) that the practitioner constructs to serve as a focal point for developing concentration. Gradually, the practitioner learns to deepen his concentration by constructing these aids solely with his mind, going on to achieve states of trance *(samadhi)* beyond sensory perception. In so doing, Buddhaghosha essentially redefines meditation in terms of these trance states rather than other practices such as mindfulness of the breath. This privileging of trance over calm, mindful awareness in the path of mental cultivation is still a source of controversy in Theravadin circles.

Buddhaghosha's contributions to Theravada tradition cannot be overemphasized. It was directly through his editorial efforts that the various vernacular commentaries to the scriptures were translated into Pali, thereby establishing the mainstream Theravada interpretation of the canon. One legend even states that the Sri Lankan monks were so impressed with his work after it was completed that they burned their original commentaries. *The Path of Purity*, his signature composition, continues to be a source for study and a guide to meditative practice. Indeed, Buddhaghosha's work is so revered that in Sri Lanka and Burma it is regarded as more authoritative than the scriptures themselves.

King Rama I (r. 1782–1801)

Traditionally Buddhism has emphasized cooperation between worldly and spiritual powers to establish a firm basis for the Dharma. In this regard, Emperor Ashoka has been the prime example of how a worldly ruler can employ Dharma as an effective instrument of his rule. One of the most notable rulers in recent centuries to follow his lead was the Thai King Rama I. Rama was a great protector of the Dharma and a major reformer of the *sangha,* citing the examples of previous rulers who exercised the king's duty to correct the *sangha* when they saw the need.

From 1782 to 1801, Rama issued a series of 10 edicts concerning monastic life. Collectively these essentially command the monks to adhere to the rules outlined in the Code of Discipline and to preach the Dharma with all faith and zeal. Several edicts specifically call for all monks to carry official identification papers, while others enumerate additional penalties for monks committing offenses that require being disrobed. Rama's 10th edict describes how the king had more than one hundred monks who had been found guilty of major offenses disrobed and sentenced to hard labor. In 1788 Rama called a great council (designating it the ninth such council after the Buddha's passing) of Thai monks to revise and collate the official collection of Pali scriptures. Rama, however, was not merely interested in extending state control over the *sangha.* Following the example of other Theravadin rulers, he regularly solicited the advice of various senior monks and abbots on certain aspects of royal policy.

Rama I's insistence on taking an active interest in the affairs of the *sangha* and in consulting elder monks on matters of civil administration was continued by his successors. The practices that he inaugurated during his reign exemplify the close connection between throne and *sangha* that has been so characteristic of Theravada Buddhism. He remains a lasting influence on Thai society, in particular, despite recent decades of Westernization.

CHINESE BUDDHISTS

Fotudeng (Fourth Century c.e.)

One of the more remarkable figures in early Chinese Buddhism was a monk named Fotudeng (also known as Buddha Matanga, an epithet connoting his "barbarian" origins) who was famed for his wondrous abilities. A native of the distant western regions, Fotudeng visited various Buddhist centers in Kashmir and central Asia, developing the passion and canniness of a true missionary. He arrived in northern China in 310 and quickly established a close relationship the Shi family, a clan of "barbarian" military leaders who ruled the region, a relationship that he maintained for more than 37 years.

Fotudeng's genius was in understanding what his patrons were looking for and presenting Buddhism as the solution. Most often this involved use of Buddhism's magical "fetish" power to bring about large harvests, success in war, cure diseases, and bring order to the ever-treacherous royal court. Fotudeng could supposedly summon rain, make spirits do his bidding, bring the ill back from the brink of death, and foretell events when he heard the tolling of bells. Among his most remarkable powers was his ability to see events at a great distance by smearing magical potions on his palm. Fotudeng's great success in all these areas won over the Shi rulers and he became their court chaplain and closest adviser.

Although Fotudeng was a man of great intelligence, he owed much of his success to his shamanistic powers. Tales of such things may strike contemporary people as incredible, but these sorts of skills have been valued at the popular level in nearly every religious tradition.[6] Buddhism is no exception. Such miraculous powers were thought to be directly related to a monk's own understanding of Dharma and his meditative abilities. The purpose of monastic training was never to acquire such abilities, but monks who did put them to good use in their ministries, using such "magic" powers to heal, protect, bring comfort ,and reinforce basic Buddhist teachings. Fotudeng was but one of many such Buddhist "wonder workers" who played a major role in China, Japan, and other Buddhist countries in the past and still do today.

In addition to his magical gifts, Fotudeng was a shrewd administrator who finagled state support for the *sangha*, something that enabled Buddhism to become a truly popular religion in the northern regions of China. He began a program of widespread temple building with state sponsorship, and, perhaps, more importantly, convinced his ruler to issue an edict officially tolerating the Buddhist monastic order as an institution virtually outside of government control. He was particularly fortunate to attract a group of talented disciples (among them several nuns) who, following the lead of their master, furthered the establishment of Buddhism in China.

Kumarajiva (Fifth Century C.E.)

Few figures in Buddhist history led as colorful a life as Kumarajiva, a brilliant monk who spent much of his life as a living "war trophy." Originally from the Silk Road city-state of Kucha, Kumarajiva at a young age traveled to India and Kashgar (an ancient Silk Road town located in what is now extreme western China), where he mastered the intricacies of Abhidharma philosophy before converting to Mahayana, the more "liberal" branch of Buddhism. During adulthood, he was greatly revered by the ruler of Kucha and was visited by pilgrims from all over Asia. Eventually his fame reached

Chang'an, the capital of northern China. Wishing to increase his prestige and consolidate his power, the king of Chang'an dispatched an army led by his most trusted general to capture Kumarajiva and bring him back. On the return journey, however, the general learned that his king had been overthrown and a new king installed. Incensed, the general halted his army and set up his own mini-kingdom in western China, where he kept Kumarajiva for 17 years. After various diplomatic requests failed, the new rulers of Chang'an sent another army to defeat the rebellious general, bringing Kumarajiva back as their prize.

In Chang'an Kumarajiva was both prisoner and royal adviser. He was appointed head of the *sangha,* an important official government post. The emperor of Chang'an valued Kumarajiva so highly that he resolved a plan in which the monk would sire a line of sages to serve as royal advisers in perpetuity. Thus the monk was given his own harem of Chinese maidens, provoking him at one point to describe himself as a lotus that blossoms in the air and sun yet remains rooted in the mud. Through it all he impressed his followers with his charisma and air of detachment and tranquility, serving as a prime example of the Buddhist holy man.

Although not an innovative thinker in his own right, Kumarajiva was a master preacher who gave the Chinese their first systematic exposition of Buddhist doctrine. Before then, the Dharma had been transmitted to China in a piecemeal fashion, with various texts being translated and taught more on the whims of missionaries and their patrons than with any regard for a coherent presentation. The "Buddhism" that emerged from this morass of texts and teachings was often puzzling and even contradictory, which made it virtually impossible to understand. Kumarajiva was able to present the entire range of Buddhist teachings as a coherent whole, mainly from a Mahayana perspective chiefly informed by the Madhyamika school.[7] From this point on, the Chinese could build on a solid understanding of how different Buddhist teachings were related and form their own distinctive schools of Buddhist thought and practice.

Kumarajiva made his greatest contributions to Buddhism through his translation activities. As head of the *sangha* he also was in charge of the imperial translation bureau, a major government institution employing numerous monks and scribes dedicated solely to producing official translations of any and all Buddhist texts. Although the extent of his command of Chinese remains unknown, Kumarajiva, with his vast knowledge of Buddhist doctrine, as well as Sanskrit and other central Asian languages, was a veritable fountain of Dharma. Assisted by a team of disciples that included many of the leading scholar-monks of the day, Kumarajiva translated many Buddhist texts into Chinese, including Perfection of Wisdom texts (notably the Heart and Diamond Sutras), the Lotus Sutra, the Vimalakirti, and even some Pure Land texts. His translations, often highly polished and poetic in style, are still prized by the Chinese, many of whom prefer them to the more technically accurate translations done by later scholars.

Zhiyi (538–97)

One of the most influential teachers in all of East Asia was a monk named Zhiyi, who taught in a mountain monastery that eventually gave Zhiyi's school its name: Tiantai (Heavenly Terrace). Zhiyi was a creative thinker devoted to intellectual pursuits and meditation practice. At this time, Chinese Buddhism was made up of two distinct movements—a more philosophically oriented style centered in the south, and a more devotional and disciplined style in the north. Zhiyi conceived these two approaches to be complementary, like the two wings of a bird. He thus set about combining both styles, forming a school renowned for its philosophic content and strong emphasis on meditative practice.

Zhiyi was a great scholar of Buddhism who understood the Lotus Sutra as the final expression of the Buddha's Awakening. In fact, he viewed the teaching of the Lotus as an expanded version of the Buddha's teaching of Dependent Origination, the basic Buddhist doctrine that all reality is a grand, interdependent, and ongoing process. According to the Lotus, the Buddhist universe is actually a "pluriverse" made up of 10 realms of existence, each of which is interwoven with and inseparable from the others. These realms, in turn, share in each other's various characteristics and dimensions to such an extent that they can only be understood from multiple perspectives, each of which can also be considered its own distinct dimension of reality. Experienced reality, thus, is a diverse array of multiple realms, distinct yet interdependent. Because of such thorough interdependence between these various realms, they may be considered to be "immanent in a single instant of thought." That is, all possible worlds are involved in each minute moment in any single realm. Ultimate Truth, here, is not some separate sphere but available right here and now. When it is realized, one has merely awakened to the Buddha-nature within us all.

Despite such a rarified metaphysics, Tiantai teachings are not just abstruse philosophy. Rather, they make up a systematic laying-out of the path to *nirvana,* just as all schools of Buddhism claim. As a means of attaining

this full Awakening, Tiantai particularly stresses "calming and contemplation" (the Chinese understanding of the basic twofold practice of "calm"
and "insight") to perceive the ultimate truth as it manifests in the everyday.
To facilitate such meditative training, Zhiyi wrote The Great Calming and
Contemplation, a treatise outlining methods for attaining full realization.
This manual has been studied and commented on by many Buddhist masters and is still in use today.

Viewing the cosmic teachings of the Lotus Sutra as the most complete
of all Buddhist teachings, Zhiyi was able to rank the other major teachings
according to a scheme of five periods. The first four are the teachings of
various Buddhist schools and are basically provisional, a means of leading
a disciple up through progressively more comprehensive doctrines until he
reaches the fifth period, the final synthesis of all previous levels as found
in the great Lotus Sutra itself. The Tiantai doctrinal scheme thus, while
favoring the Lotus teachings, is all-inclusive and promotes the message of
universal salvation that is a hallmark of the Mahayana.

Xuanzang (596–664)

The Tang dynasty (618–906) was the era when Buddhism was at its height
of cultural influence. Many of the great lights of Chinese history lived during this period and they made lasting contributions to the Dharma. One of
the first of these was the pilgrim-monk Xuanzang, who illegally left China
to journey to India to retrieve the original teachings of the Buddha. His pilgrimage lasted 17 years and took him all over central Asia via the Silk Road,
eventually landing him at Bodh Gaya, Nalanda, and other great Buddhist
centers in India. He returned to Chang'an in 645, bringing a vast collection
of ancient texts and fabulous artifacts that stunned the populace with their
beauty. Xuanzang received a hero's welcome and was granted a series of
imperial interviews to detail his journeys to distant lands. Eventually he
even succeeded in converting the emperor to Buddhism.

Taking advantage of his imperial connections, Xuanzang gained support
for a new translation team to begin translating the vast collection of texts
he had brought from India. Xuanzang himself had thorough knowledge
of Sanskrit and had mastered the entire body of Buddhist philosophical
teachings. He assembled a talented translation team, and together they developed a revised, more accurate vocabulary for rendering Buddhist terms
into Chinese. Xuanzang's translations, although never as popular as Kumarajiva's, are thus technically superior from a doctrinal standpoint. His

translation team was disbanded before he could translate the full assortment of texts he had brought.

Xuanzang is also credited with founding the Yogachara (Practice of Yoga) school in China through his translations of treatises by Vasubandhu and Asanga, the two Indian thinkers most associated with Yogachara teachings. Xuanzang's school, however, lasted scarcely a century before dying out because of pressure from other doctrinal schools competing for imperial patronage. As a doctrinal school, it was assimilated by the other major schools such as Tiantai and Huayan, and it continued as a distinct philosophical tradition in both Korea and Japan.

As an individual, however, Xuanzang had a lasting influence on East Asian popular culture. His adventures so fired the imagination of his contemporaries that stories about him spread throughout China. These stories were told and retold, receiving various embellishments along the way and enjoying great popularity. Eventually these folk tales were compiled and used as the basis of the novel *Journey to the West* (better known in the West as *Monkey*), one of the classics of Chinese literature that has inspired countless plays, movies, and television shows. Moreover, Xuanzang was honored in his day with the construction of the Great Wild Goose Pagoda that served as the library to store his texts and artifacts. The pagoda still stands in Xian (the modern name for Chang'an) and is a major tourist attraction.

Statue of Xuanzang with the Great Wild Goose Pagoda in the background, Xian, China. Courtesy of the author.

Tanluan (476–542)

Pure Land Buddhism has long enjoyed immense popularity in China. The first acknowledged patriarch of this school was a northern Buddhist named Tanluan. Tanluan supposedly received a vision of a heavenly paradise when he was recovering from a serious illness. Convinced of his religious vocation, he explored Daoist techniques of immortality before being converted to Buddhism by an Indian missionary. This missionary taught Tanluan that the way to everlasting life lay in devotion to Amitabha Buddha, the Celestial Buddha who established a paradise in the western regions, where those who have faith will be reborn after they die.

Tanluan borrowed from Indian teachings concerning the use of ritual chants *(mantras)* but developed his own techniques for meditation that he called "remembering the Buddha" *(nianfo)*. Differing from traditional Buddhist techniques of mental concentration, "remembering the Buddha" came to have more of a sense of vocal recitation as a means of focusing the mind. Reciting the Buddha's name increased mindfulness and faith by helping to orient the practitioner toward the Buddha himself. The power of this simple technique proved irresistible to many commoners who could not master complex methods of concentration.

Tanluan had great success spreading the Pure Land cult, especially in organizing societies dedicated to reciting Amitabha's name. He worked out some of the most important aspects of Pure Land doctrine, including the idea that anyone, even evildoers, may be reborn in the western paradise if they repent and have sincere faith in Amitabha. This sense of universal salvation may have been encouraged by Tanluan's conviction that all beings possess the Buddha-nature, the capacity for Awakening. Over time he came to believe that one depended upon "other power" for salvation, maintaining that even the merit one earns through devout practice of *nianfo* is aided by Amitabha's vows. Ultimately, rebirth in the Pure Land and attaining Buddhahood are the result of Amitabha's compassionate power, not an individual's own efforts. By developing the basic technique of recitation *(nianfo)* as well as preaching total reliance on Amitabha and the view that even sinners were included within Amitabha's embrace, Tanluan established the major features of Pure Land Buddhism that continue to attract support from the common people.

Huineng (638–713)

Chan (in Japanese, *Zen*) masters are often legendary figures whose exploits and eccentricities always arouse interest among students of Buddhism. Although each of the great Chan masters—Mazu (709–88), Linji (d. 867), Dongshan (807–69), and others—is a truly memorable character, none of them is more important than Huineng, the legendary Sixth Patriarch.[8] Modern scholarship has made it clear that many of the traditional stories surrounding early Chan in general and Huineng in particular are more or less mythical reconstructions and elaborations of later Chan writers. Nonetheless, this pious Chan mythology reveals a lot about how Chan/Zen conceives itself as a "separate transmission outside the scriptures" in which Dharma comes directly to the student from the master, "transmitted from mind to mind." Certainly Huineng's association with the notion of "sudden enlightenment" remains a decisive component of Chan/Zen teachings.

Most of the information we have on Huineng comes from the famous Platform Sutra, a complicated text that may bear little resemblance to actual historical events. Purporting to be a sermon delivered by Huineng from a high seat in the lecture hall of a great temple (hence the "platform" alluded to in the title), the *sutra* gives intriguing details of Huineng's biography. According this *sutra*, Huineng was an illiterate peasant boy who became instantly enlightened upon hearing a phrase from the Diamond Sutra. When he revealed his realization through the composition of a poem, the current master (the Fifth Patriarch) recognized the truth. However, he also knew that passing on his robe (the official symbol of Dharma transmission) to an uncouth peasant would provoke disruption among the monastic hierarchy. Therefore he summoned Huineng for a secret audience in which he gave him further teachings. Passing on his robe, the master admonished him to flee for his life, predicting, however, that eventually he would transmit the teachings. With that, Huineng fled southward. After some months, Huineng was traced to a mountain by a band of pursuers intent on killing him and stealing the robe. Most of the pursuers turned back after climbing only halfway, but one reached him on the summit. There, rather than slay the young master, he received the teaching and became enlightened. Thus being officially recognized, Huineng dispatched his new disciple to the north to convert the people.

Although Huineng's life is exciting, much of the Platform Sutra is actually an extended Dharma talk, a sermon on realization in which Huineng presents some decidedly puzzling advice on Chan cultivation. Much like the great *bodhisattvas* in the Perfection of Wisdom texts, Huineng spoke from the standpoint of Ultimate Truth, the nondual reality lying beyond our everyday unenlightened experience of separation and division. To awaken to this Truth, Huineng emphasized "nonclinging" to any verbal teachings, which only present obstacles to True Awakening. Instead, Huineng stressed the perspectives of "no-thought," an open, nonconceptual state of mind that allows one to experience reality directly, as it truly is. As he stated, "No thought is not to think even when involved in thought.... To be unstained in all environments is called no-thought. If on the basis of your own thoughts you separate from environment, then, in regard to things, thoughts are not produced. If you stop thinking of the myriad things, and cast aside all thoughts, as soon as one instant of thought is cut off, you will be reborn in another realm."[9] Huineng's presentation pioneered Chan's distinctive teaching style that makes use of paradox and cryptic statements aimed at jolting students out of their habitual discursive reasoning. The Platform Sutra became wildly popular in China, perhaps because of its paradoxical air, and a great number of copies circulated. The traditional version, printed some five hundred years after the oldest original text, is almost twice the size of the original because of later additions and expansions.

The portrait of Huineng that emerges from the Platform Sutra is quite compelling. The master is portrayed as brilliant despite (or perhaps because of) his humble beginnings and takes on almost a heroic stature through his trials and eventual triumph. In his direct statements, Huineng comes across as immensely charismatic. He is by turns insightful, iconoclastic, and humorous. Throughout his discourse he challenges his audience to leave behind intellectual preconceptions while undercutting all attempts to grasp his meaning by rational means. Ironically, during this lengthy verbal discourse he proclaimed, "the practice of self-awakening does not lie in verbal arguments"[10]—and this despite offering long harangues against Chan practitioners who have "false views." In many respects Huineng is the archetypal Chan master, a stock figure who serves as the model for all later Chan/Zen practitioners. Traces of Huineng can even be seen in the character of Yoda, the great Jedi master from the *Star Wars* series.

JAPANESE BUDDHISTS

Prince Shotoku (573–672)

Few people have such an honored position in Japanese history as Prince Shotoku. The second son of Emperor Yomei, he served as regent during much of the reign of his aunt, Empress Suiko. Shotoku was born at a time when Japan was struggling to become a united country and looking to Chinese culture for models to imitate. Shotoku himself is often regarded as the founder of Japanese Buddhism and appears to have had faith in Buddhism as a way of life that could transform the populace and bring order to his troubled land. To help spread the faith, he ordered the construction of various temples, among them the Horyuji, a large temple complex at Nara housing many Buddhist texts and works of art. Shotoku was also a gifted student, schooled in Chinese culture and knowledge, who sent the first official Japanese envoys to visit the Chinese imperial court. He even lectured and wrote commentaries on Buddhist texts such as the Lotus Sutra.

Shotoku's main claim to fame, however, is his authoring of Japan's first "constitution." This document (actually a set of 17 principles for ordering the nation) is notable for the prominent place it affords Buddhism. For example, the second article reads, "Sincerely reverence the Three Treasures [Jewels]. The Buddha, the Law [Dharma], and the religious orders [*Sangha*] are the final refuge of all beings and the supreme objects of reverence in all countries."[11] Many historians have argued that Shotoku actually made greater use of Confucianism than Buddhism in drawing up his "constitution" (something not altogether surprising, given the long-standing emphasis in Confucianism on maintaining a harmonious social order). However, by this time there was no clear distinction between these two religious and philosophical traditions even in China, let alone Japan. Certainly both traditions were regarded as hallmarks of Chinese civilization, the manifestly dominant culture in East Asia at the time and thus the most appropriate model on which to base Japan's budding form of government. The "constitution" is Japan's first written moral code, and in presenting Buddhism as a major component of Japanese government, Shotoku officially recognized it as having an important message for the Japanese people. He thereby set the precedent for Buddhism's use as a rationale for the state.

After his death, a huge body of myth and legend grew up around Shotoku's life. He is alleged, for example, to have been born in a stable (like Jesus) and to have been able to speak from birth (like the Buddha). Over the years he also is said to have given special revelations to Shinran, a great proponent of Japanese Pure Land. During the Middle Ages Shotoku became the focus of a popular cult and was even revered as a manifestation of the Buddha himself.

Saicho (762–822) and Kukai (774–835)

One of the great figures in early Japanese Buddhism was a monk named Saicho (762–822), who founded the Tendai school (the Japanese version of

Path on Mount Hiei, where Saicho established the
head temple of the Tendai school, Kyoto, Japan. Courtesy of the author.

the Chinese Tiantai) and, like Zhiyi, proclaimed the Lotus Sutra to be the
Buddha's essential teachings. Keenly aware that the various schools that
had been established at Nara, the old capital, had become corrupt and lax
through close relationships with Nara's aristocracy, Saicho founded a new
monastery in the mountains northeast of Kyoto, which became Japan's new
capital. This monastery, located on Mount Hiei, went on to become one of
the great centers of Japanese Buddhism, and Tendai produced many of the
most important Buddhist leaders in Japanese history.

Having received proper ordination and training during his stay in China,
Saicho was concerned that Japanese Buddhism be fully orthodox in matters
of ordination, scriptures, doctrine, and practice. In direct contrast to what
he perceived as the lack of discipline and training among the Nara schools,
Saicho prescribed an intense 12-year period of training for monks on
Mount Hiei. This was essentially an extended retreat, during which monks
were not allowed to leave the mountain. He also required long periods of
meditation (probably a form of Chinese *chan*) and encouraged devotion to
Amida Buddha. This emphasis on devotion to Amida eventually gave rise
to the practices used in Japanese Pure Land sects.

Despite his great accomplishments, however, Saicho was eclipsed by
Kukai, another monk who was his great rival for imperial patronage.[12]
Kukai was a truly illustrious figure who founded Shingon, the Japanese
form of Tantric (Vajrayana) Buddhism, created the Japanese phonetic system of writing *(hiragana),* and made numerous pilgrimages to holy places
throughout Japan. Kukai journeyed to China in 804 where he remained

for two years, learning all he could about Buddhist philosophy and ritual, particularly of the more spectacular and wondrous kind, since these were in such high demand in Japan. He returned to Japan with a thorough training as well as a treasure trove of Buddhist scriptures, instruction manuals for performing liturgical rites, and Tantric ritual paraphernalia (*mandalas, vajras*, etc.).

Soon after his return, Kukai cleverly separated himself from the old Buddhism of Nara and the newer forms such as Tendai that were flourishing at Kyoto. Instead, he ventured into the mountains to found a monastery on Koyosan, not far from present day Osaka. In so doing he was imitating the Chinese tradition of mountain monasteries as well as invoking the indigenous Japanese association of mountains with supernatural power. Yet despite his seclusion, Kukai maintained close contact with the imperial court and used it to his advantage. He even was granted approval to establish a branch monastery just outside the city precincts. This monastery, Toji (Eastern Temple), guarded one of the main entrances to the capital and its towering pagoda is a major symbol of Kyoto to this day.

In his retreat at Koyosan, Kukai concentrated on the mystical and esoteric teachings he had obtained, seeking to develop Shingon as a systematic way to translate the secret knowledge he had attained and apply it to the basic predicament of human life. In the Shingon view, ordinary life is beset by suffering because of the inherent instability and ever-present divisions of existence. However, the Ultimate Truth lies in the higher unity of all things, the Transcendent Sun Buddha from whom the cosmos emanates. This great unity lies within all beings as their Buddha-nature and, when fully realized, marks an end to suffering. According to Shingon, such realization can come in this very lifetime through proper training and ritual performance.

Kukai and his disciples were major advocates of secret cosmic rites such as the powerful Fire Ceremony *(goma)*. Within a few years after establishing his monastic base at Koyosan, Kukai and his followers were in great demand at court, especially for performing rituals to aid healing and childbirth. As a way of gaining and using supernatural power to solve immediate problems, Shingon held great attraction for many people. The magical formulas, colorful imagery, and dramatic rites employed by Kukai and his followers inspired great awe among the imperial court and nobility as well as the common people. Soon they were borrowed by other Buddhist sects and became a mainstay of popular Japanese Buddhism.[13]

Eisai (1141–1215) and Dogen (1300–53)

Zen, probably the best-known but least understood school of Japanese Buddhism, is the direct result of borrowing Chinese Chan teachings and practices (especially meditation) and then lending them a distinct Japanese quality. Although basic Chan practices were brought to Japan by Saicho and continued to form part of Tendai training, the establishing of a separate meditation school was the result of the efforts of Eisai, a Tendai monk. During the period following Saicho's death, discipline in Tendai had declined. Eisai was alarmed at the laxity he observed among the monks on Mount Hiei and longed to go to India to find true Buddhism. In the end, however, he only got as far as China, but he was particularly impressed with disciplined life among the Chan monks.[14] He was converted to the Linji tradition of Chan (*Rinzai Zen* in Japanese), eventually receiving full ordination and bringing the teachings back to Japan.

Eisai encountered many obstacles in establishing Zen around Kyoto because of the influence of older sects. However, he found a more receptive audience among the military leaders several hundred miles away in Kamakura, the base of the various feudal groups led by the shogun (military dictator). The Kamakura warlords were drawn to Rinzai's regimented lifestyle and its focus on "sudden enlightenment" that could be attained in the course of everyday activities rather than through study of abstruse doctrines or by practicing secret rituals. No doubt the warlords were also attracted to the manner in which the concentration promoted in Zen training was particularly useful for samurai warriors facing death in battle. Eisai is also credited with introducing tea to Japan, which was a handy antidote to the lethargy often brought on by long hours of meditation. Drinking tea quickly became a mainstay of Japanese culture.

Eisai's greatest student was another former Tendai monk who came to him after finding little but disappointment during his studies on Mount Hiei. This young monk, Dogen, eventually followed his master's example and went to China, where, unlike Eisei, he received training in the Caotong (Soto) school. After attaining enlightenment under a Chinese master, Dogen returned to Japan but did not seek to reform the Buddhism of his day. Rather, he formed a small monastery on the outskirts of Kyoto, eventually moving far into the mountains in what is now Fukui Prefecture. Although Dogen died in relative obscurity, the Soto school of Zen grew, eventually becoming a major influence on Japanese religious life.

Dogen has often been considered one of Japan's most creative thinkers, and Soto (unlike Rinzai) gives some weight to the study of Buddhist scriptures. There is a certain irony here, in that for Dogen the heart of Zen is an experience of intuition beyond the reach of reason. Such realization cannot arise from discursive reasoning but rather manifests in "sitting meditation" (Chinese *suochan*, Japanese *zazen*), a practice involving both body and mind. He was highly critical of Rinzai training, which he saw as placing too much emphasis on the study of the puzzling riddles (Chinese *gongan*, Japanese *koans*) often used by Chan/Zen masters to provoke awakening. Instead, Dogen stressed *zazen*. In fact, rather than seeing *zazen* as the way to attain enlightenment (a seemingly commonsensical view of Zen as a path leading to a goal) Dogen maintained the unity of *zazen* and enlightenment. In Dogen's eyes, the relation between *zazen* and enlightenment was intertwined with another more existential problem that had long vexed him: the relation between "original enlightenment" and "attained enlightenment." Why is it that people, who are essentially Buddha (have Buddha-nature), must struggle so much to become enlightened? Should it not it be easy to be what one always already is? Dogen's solution was informed by his own experiences of realization. Essentially, the apparent divorce between "original enlightenment" and "attained enlightenment" stems from a practical, even "ethical" failure. People get caught up in *thinking* about enlightenment rather than *practicing*. In *zazen* body and mind as separate entities disappear; one realizes that enlightenment and *zazen* are one and the same. Thus, for Dogen, *zazen* is the True Reality, the very fullness of life.

Honen (1133–1212) and Shinran (1173–1263)

In Japan, faith in the saving grace of Amida (Amitabha) Buddha, the cosmic Buddha who established the Western Pure Land, has always been more popular than all the other Buddhist movements combined. Many monks during Japan's medieval period promoted faith in Amida, but one of the most famous was Honen, a Tendai monk who is remembered as the founder of Pure Land as a formal Japanese sect. Honen began his career as a great scholar, only to grow frustrated with complex doctrines. He just did not see how the elaborate philosophical teachings of Tendai and Shingon were of much use to ordinary people, who could not master such schemes or devote themselves to intricate ritual practices in what Honen saw as an increasingly degenerate world. He concluded that there had to be another path.

Byodoin Temple, said to resemble Amida (Amitabha)
Buddha's Palace in the Pure Land, Uji, Japan. Courtesy
of the author.

For Honen, earlier Buddhist teachings were well suited for previous eras
in history but were not appropriate in his era, which he viewed as the third
and final age in the Buddhist cosmic scheme. In an age of increasing corruption and chaos, it was too much to expect people to achieve enlightenment through their own efforts. Their only real hope was for rebirth in
the Pure Land through the practice of reciting Amida's name. Much like
Christian writers such as Saint Paul (first century C.E.) or Augustine of
Hippo (354–430), Honen taught that people needed to acknowledge their
imperfection and throw themselves on the mercy of a higher power, Amida
Buddha. Honen's school became known as the "Pure Land School."

Honen attracted many followers who expounded upon different aspects
of Pure Land teachings. None of them was more zealous than Shinran, another disillusioned Tendai monk. Shinran came under Honen's influence
and, like his master, was convinced that promoting Pure Land teachings
and practices was the appropriate form of Buddhism in his troubled times.
Yet Shinran went to even greater extremes, advocating *faith* in Amida
above all else. In fact, according to Shinran faith is more important than the
practice of *nembutsu* (Japanese translation of Chinese *nianfo*)—so much
so that even one sincere "calling" on Amida was enough for salvation. This
decidedly radical view became the basis for Shinran and his followers establishing a separate movement, the True Pure Land School, which is now
the largest Japanese Buddhist sect.

One of Shinran's lasting contributions to Japanese Buddhism was a major
reform he instigated in the priestly lifestyle. Until his day, religious profes-

sionals in Buddhism were essentially all monks and nuns who led celibate lifestyles dedicated to disciplined ritual and meditation practice. However, this presupposed that monastics could attain salvation through their own efforts, something Shinran and other Pure Land proponents denied. Moreover, monastic life also implied a lack of faith in Amida's grace. In contrast, Shinran believed that even an ordinary householder could lead a good Buddhist life. To demonstrate his view, he married and had a family.[15] Some scholars doubt the truth of this story, but Shinran is popularly venerated for introducing the practice of a married priesthood, one of the unique features of all Japanese Buddhist schools. In light of his insistence on faith alone and the introduction of marriage into Buddhism, Shinran is sometimes compared with the Christian reformer Martin Luther (1483–1546), whose efforts contributed so much to the rise of Protestantism in late medieval Europe.

Nichiren (1221–82)

Nichiren has the distinction of being one of the most powerful personalities in Japanese history. Passionately despised by some, almost worshiped by others, he began his career as a Tendai monk on Mount Hiei. There he became engrossed in the Lotus Sutra, which Tendai regarded as the ultimate teaching of the Buddha. Nichiren, however, was convinced that he alone realized the true significance of the Lotus, and he set out to return Tendai to the original ways intended by Saicho. Eventually his views led to the founding of an entirely new sect of Buddhism.

The Lotus Sutra exerted an incredible power over Nichiren, prompting him to agree that it was the true vessel of the Dharma. Moreover, he became entranced at the *sutra's* depiction of the Buddha as manifesting in three bodies: historical (Shakyamuni), Cosmic (the universe itself), and Bliss (the transcendent, godlike form). For Nichiren, the truth of such teachings meant that the Lotus Sutra itself should be the true focus of devotion. To this end, he even devised a new sacred diagram of the cosmos *(mandala),* based on the title of the *sutra* that was to be used in worship. He also encouraged his followers to chant the name of the *sutra* as an expression of devotion: *Namu myoho renge kyo* (Hail the Scripture of the Lotus of the Perfect Truth). Such chanting is still practiced by followers of the Lotus sect. Nichiren agreed with many of his contemporaries that they were living in a degenerate age, but he taught that the proper response was for human beings to actively change their situation and return all of Japan to pure faith in the Lotus Sutra.

Nichiren was deeply critical of other forms of Buddhism in his day, as he saw them ignoring the threefold nature of the Buddha and promoting pointless practices. He ridiculed Shingon, for example, claiming that its esoteric teachings and attendant ritualism was little more than foolish superstition. As for the Pure Land schools, Nichiren viewed their stress on faith in Amida as removing any reason for human initiative. Some priests thought that the way to combat the growing degeneration of the age was to return to the strict following of Buddhist monastic rules. Again, Nichiren dismissed such views with contempt. During his time Zen was becoming more influential as well, but Nichiren saw no use for sitting meditation *(zazen)* or talk about "sudden awakening." Everything needed, in Nichiren's view, could be found in the Lotus Sutra, which held the key to enlightenment and prosperity. His vehement outspokenness aroused the ire of many prominent people, and he was actively persecuted, almost being executed several times.

As a militant crusader for his faith, Nichiren advocated the forceful conversion of all other Buddhist sects to the religion of the Lotus Sutra. Such religious exclusivism has rarely been found in Japanese history. He also saw his Lotus sect as intimately bound up with the fate of the Japanese nation. In his patriotic zeal, Nichiren saw all the persecution he suffered as just the price for his devotion to his country. He predicted that the Mongols would attempt to invade Japan (which they did, albeit unsuccessfully, in 1274 and 1281) as a divine punishment for the failures of Japanese Buddhism and further evidence of the continued decay. Nichiren's sect remains one of the most active in Japan and, although by no means the largest, it has had great influence. Certainly it helped feed Japanese nationalistic movements leading up to World War II and gave rise to Soka Gakkai, one of the most prominent religious movements in Japan today.

TIBETAN BUDDHISTS

Padmasambhava

Buddhism came to Tibet surprisingly late considering the region's proximity to India. In the late eighth century, however, a Buddhist king in Tibet was anxious to establish a native monastery in his realm. He invited Shantirakshita, a renowned scholar-monk from the great Buddhist university at Nalanda, to come and preach the Dharma. However, a series of natural disasters occurred that were interpreted as evidence of Tibet's indigenous deities' displeasure over the introduction of the new faith. Shantirakshita therefore recommended Padmasambhava, a Tantric adept, as more suited to Tibet's wild and magical landscape. This "wonder worker" apparently was an ideal candidate, and there are numerous accounts of his exploits in taming the local gods and demons and forcing them to pledge their protection for the Dharma.

History provides little definitive information about Padmasambhava after the consecration of Sam-ye monastery. He certainly does not seem to have left his mark on the Sam-ye monastic establishment, since soon after the monastery's consecration the king formed a council of senior monks charged with translating Buddhist scriptures into Tibetan. In part this policy was aimed at containing the potentially dangerous effects of rendering the Tantras into a form accessible to a wider audience. The policy was ineffective. In a relatively short time numerous Tantras were translated into Tibetan, although this was usually thanks to individual efforts rather than royal sponsorship.

Despite the relative silence of historical records, Padmasambhava went on to become a truly legendary figure in Tibetan lore. He is said to have spent decades in the mountains, traveling throughout the country and subduing all manner of demonic forces as he spread the Dharma. So great was his name that in some Tibetan circles he has become a second Buddha, virtually overshadowing the historical Buddha, Shakyamuni.

Padmasambhava's greatest claim to fame, though, is as the founder of the Nyingma order, often regarded as the oldest of Tibet's various Buddhist schools. Later Nyingma tradition views Padmasambhava as the source of the key meditation practice of the Nyingma school, *dzogchen.* According to Nyingma tradition, Padmasambhava hid certain secret texts underground or underwater that were rediscovered centuries later by other spiritual adepts. Although some Tibetans have disputed the truth of such tales, the tradition of "rediscovered hidden texts" became a standard means of transmission in Tibetan Buddhism.

Atisha (982–1054)

Soon after Buddhism was first introduced into Tibet, its various Tantric strains mixed with the indigenous shamanism and thus drifted away from orthodox Buddhist teachings. Several regional rulers viewed such developments with alarm as evidence of moral decay among their subjects. In response, they began a Buddhist revival, often called the "Second Propagation of the Dharma." Tibetan rulers were particularly concerned with promoting only those teachings and practices that were attested in Indian Buddhist texts. To aid them they invited Atisha, a great Indian scholar who also had Tantric training. Atisha is noteworthy not just for his own contributions but for how he was able to combine both scholarly pursuits and Tantric expertise, thus becoming a powerful example of Tibetan Buddhism.

In Tibet Atisha promoted Madhyamika (Middle Way) interpretations of Buddhist teachings. The Madhyamika school stresses the inherent emptiness of all phenomena, and the necessity of surrendering all attachments to dogmatic views of reality, even our attachments to Emptiness itself. Ever since Atisha, Madhyamika has been the dominant school in Tibetan intellectual life. He also, however, had received special instruction from the Indian Tantric adept Naropa (1016–1100) and is remembered for establishing several initiation lineages. Atisha's form of Tantric yoga, though, was tamed for a monastic setting; the ritualized sexual yoga was recreated *internally,* within the practitioner, as a way of arousing male and female energies without the use of an actual partner. This meant that even celibate monks or nuns could engage in the practice without violating their vows, although such innovations sparked a controversy over whether the imagined rite was as effective as its physical performance.

Atisha's invitation to Tibet also reveals interesting developments in institutional practices in Buddhist universities at the time. Originally the Tibetan king paid his university a vast sum of gold for Atisha to stay for three years. When the three years were up, however, political difficulties prevented his return to India. Atisha agreed to remain in Tibet, provided the king would make additional payments to his university. This suggests that by the eleventh century, Buddhists had departed from the original practice of offering teachings for free. In any event, from this point on it became standard practice for Tibetans to charge for their teachings.

Among Atisha's other great accomplishments was the founding (with the help of his chief Tibetan disciple) of the Kadam monastic order, which eventually became famous for its strict adherence to the Code of Discipline and its high levels of scholarship. Tibetan tradition also maintains that Atisha imported the worship of Tara, the goddess of mercy, to Tibet, which has since become the region's dominant *bodhisattva* cult. According to tradition, Tara was born from a tear shed by Avalokiteshvara, the great *bodhisattva* of compassion.

Milarepa (1040–1123) and Ma-cig (1055–1145)

Vajrayana, the "diamond vehicle" stressing secret texts and the acquisition of magical powers, has long been the dominant form of Buddhism in Tibet. The stereotypical representative of this branch of Buddhism is the adept meditator *(siddha)* who possesses miraculous abilities as a result of his wisdom and ascetic training. There are no better examples of Tibetan *siddhas* than Milarepa (Cotton-clad Mila) and his contemporary, Ma-cig.

The details of Milarepa's life are extraordinary. As a youth he learned black magic to exact revenge on his evil uncle, who had abused his widowed mother. After destroying his uncle, Milarepa spent years trying to expunge his bad *karma* and find liberation. Finally, he became a student of the great Marpa (1012–96), a noted layman who revealed his Tantric prowess only to a select few. Marpa subjected him to harsh ordeals, including the Herculean task of constructing several towers all by himself. At the end of six years, Milarepa received the special initiation he so coveted, and then he spent the rest of his life meditating in caves and wandering in the Himalayas. His reputation spread, and over the course of several decades he taught many disciples and performed many wonders to aid ordinary Tibetans. Milarepa's "autobiography," a highly fictionalized account of his life written long after his death, is a classic of Tibetan literature.

Milarepa is but one example of Tibet's many great adepts. Quite a few Tibetan *siddhas* were known for their wondrous powers, but some obtained them through the yogic practices associated with Tantra. One of his contemporaries was a nun named Ma-cig. Ma-cig was drawn to illicit Tantric rites, eventually renouncing her monastic vows after engaging in sexual intercourse. She married her partner but he died. After his death, Ma-cig suffered various illnesses because of her indiscriminate practice of Tantra with various untrained partners. Finally she met a practitioner who had trained at Nalanda, and he became her principle partner. He arranged for her to undergo a special ceremony of atonement, after which she was cured. From that point on, Ma-cig's powers increased, and she earned wide renown. To this day many Tibetans regard her as an incarnation of Tara.

Tsongkhapa (1357–1419)

As Buddhism took hold in Tibet, the Tibetans were faced with the daunting problem of how to make sense of the bewildering array of texts, practices, and teachings that they had inherited. Clearly, some sort of systematic order was needed, and many scholar-monks threw themselves into the task. However, it was only in the fifteenth century that a young monk from northeastern Tibet, Tsongkhapa, was able to develop a doctrinal system that could resolve the inconsistencies among various schools of Buddhist thought while maintaining strict adherence to Buddhist teachings on morality.

Tsongkhapa wrote more than two hundred works on all aspects of Buddhist thought and, like many Tibetans, advocated the compatibility of Tantric practice and Mahayana thought. One of his primary accomplishments was a system of ranking the various Buddhist schools, similar to earlier schemes devised in the Chinese doctrinal schools of Tiantai and Huayan. For Tsongkhapa this system was based on the different schools' views of Emptiness, with the higher schools showing a more perfect understanding. It was natural, thus, that his scheme placed the Madhyamika school as the highest.

In 1409 Tsongkhapa founded a new monastic university just outside of Lhasa as an institution where his doctrinal system served as the basis for a full curriculum of Buddhist studies. The curriculum, which eventually was adopted by most Tibetan universities, was based on Indian models. A key feature involved dividing the students into two teams that would argue against their opponents' positions. After many years of intense study, a student could advance to the final level of debate, which ultimately became a celebrated national event. University students followed a program of preliminary Tantric practices. Only after completing this program could they

Relic mound *(stupa)* at Kumbum, Tsongkhapa's home monastery, Tibet. Courtesy of John C. George.

advance to higher practices requiring periods of retreat. Tsongkhapa always insisted, though, that the monks abide by strict monastic discipline.

Tsongkhapa's program of study proved so impressive and influential that it led to the founding of an entirely new branch of Tibetan Buddhism, the Gelugpa school, which is also the order to which the Dalai Lamas belong. Over time the Gelugpas came to dominate Tibetan thought, essentially replacing the Kadam school founded by Atisha. The Gelugpa curriculum remained virtually unchanged until Chinese conquered Lhasa in the 1950s. Tsongkhapa's curriculum is still followed, however, in Gelugpa monasteries that have been established among exiled Tibetan communities scattered throughout the world.

RECENT AND CONTEMPORARY BUDDHISTS

14th Dalai Lama (1935 –)

There is probably no Buddhist in the entire world as famous as Tenzin Gyatso, the 14th (and current) Dalai Lama. The subject of a major Hollywood film, *Kundun* (1997), His Holiness is a prominent spokesman for world peace and was awarded the Nobel Peace Prize in 1989. He is the official political and spiritual leader of the Tibetan Buddhist community in exile, and his current headquarters is in Dharamsala, located in northern India. He rarely stays there very long, however, as he is constantly traveling around the world to give Dharma talks, meet with world leaders, and address various audiences on issues of global concern.

His life story is interesting. Born in 1935, he was recognized as a *tulku*, the reincarnation of the previous Dalai Lama, and eventually ascended the Tibetan throne in 1950. Like his immediate predecessor, he sought to reform Tibetan culture to bring the benefits of modern Western learning and technology to his people without destroying their traditional way of life. His rule, however, was immediately interrupted by the Chinese Communist invasion of Tibet, officially described as an effort to "reassert" ancient claims over Chinese territory. The uneasy situation continued until a popular uprising against the Chinese occupation in 1959 was violently quashed and direct colonial rule was imposed. As the Chinese Red Guard began to systematically destroy all aspects of Tibet's Buddhist culture, the Dalai Lama and his immediate followers fled across the Himalayas to India, where he was given asylum. He quickly established an administrative center at Dharamsala, where an estimated 50,000 Tibetan refuges have also settled.

Dalai Lama. Courtesy of Photofest.

Over the years His Holiness has proven to be a tireless advocate of human rights, and, as an immensely charismatic speaker, he receives countless invitations to give talks and presentations from leaders all over the world. He has written numerous books, is deeply involved in interfaith projects and ecological movements, and has expressed interest in the work of various scientists exploring the boundaries of science and religion. Although officially a member of the Gelugpa order, the dominant Buddhist school in Tibet since the fifteenth century, the Dalai Lama promotes mutual cooperation among all schools of Buddhism, seeking to encourage unity in the face of the common tragedy that the Tibetan people face. He also refuses to countenance the use of violence against the Chinese, always preferring peaceful negotiations in true Buddhist fashion. Through his efforts he has won some concessions that have allowed Buddhism to be practiced again in Tibet, albeit under the watchful eyes of Beijing.

Through all of his efforts, the Dalai Lama remains the focus of intense love and devotion from Buddhists of all backgrounds. One of the Dalai Lama's most compelling character traits is his ability to make connections with people from all walks of life—something perhaps only to be expected from a reputed incarnation of Avalokiteshvara, the *bodhisattva* of compassion. In large part this is aided by his disarming personality, a remarkable

combination of compassion and self-deprecating humor with which he in-
fuses his message of peace and interreligious cooperation. He counts many
"celebrity Buddhists" among his friends and followers, including actor
Richard Gere and Adam Yaunch, leader of the rap group the Beastie Boys.

Thich Nhat Hanh (1926–)

Perhaps the foremost spokesman for Engaged Buddhism, Thich Nhat
Hanh is an international celebrity. Born in central Vietnam in 1926, he was
ordained as a Thien (Zen) monk in 1942. In 1950 he helped found one of
the leading centers for Buddhist studies in South Vietnam. He came to
the United States in 1961 to study but returned to help his country when
the Vietnam War broke out. He and many of his fellow monks became
actively involved in helping war victims and speaking out for peace. Their
movement, based on Gandhian principles of nonviolent resistance, caught
international attention. In 1966 he was invited by the Fellowship of Rec-
onciliation to tour the United States and publicize the plight of the Vietnamese people. He gave hundreds of talks and met with various figures,
including Secretary of Defense Robert McNamara, Senator Robert F. Ken-
nedy, and Dr. Martin Luther King Jr. King was so impressed with him that
he publicly came out against the war and nominated Nhat Hanh for the
1967 Nobel Peace Prize. Nhat Hanh went on to meet with Thomas Merton,
the famous Trappist monk and writer, and traveled to Europe for an audience with Pope Paul IV. Because of his outspoken opposition to the war, he
was threatened with arrest should he return to his homeland.

In 1969 he formed the Buddhist Peace Delegation that journeyed to Paris
to participate in the Peace Talks. With the end of the war, Nhat Hanh and
his colleagues from the Vietnamese Buddhist Peace Delegation founded a
small retreat southwest of Paris that they called "Sweet Potato," where they
lived while seeking ways to send money to aid Vietnamese children and
other war victims. From 1976 to 1977, he led an operation to rescue various groups of Vietnamese "boat people" in the Gulf of Siam, only to meet
hostile opposition from the governments of Thailand and Singapore. This
opposition forced him to discontinue, and he and his colleagues retreated
to Sweet Potato. He emerged in 1982 when he founded a larger retreat center, Plum Village, and returned to New York to begin lecturing once more
on how to apply Buddhist teachings and principles in daily life.

Nhat Hanh still officially lives in exile in Plum Village. However, much of
his time is spent traveling, giving lectures, and leading meditation retreats

throughout Europe and the United States. He has written more than 75 books in English, French, and Vietnamese (among them the best-selling *Being Peace* [1987] and *Peace Is Every Step* [1991]). Although officially banned, his books circulate widely in Vietnam. Many of his students and colleagues have spread his message throughout the world through work in support of the displaced, hungry, and imprisoned. In the spring of 2005, the Vietnamese government finally allowed Thich Nhat Hanh to return to his homeland and permitted several of his books to be published. His two-month-long visit, featuring stops at numerous pagodas and holy sites, drew enormous press coverage and may signal a moderating of the current regime's attitudes toward the monk-activist.

Over the years Nhat Hanh has expanded his work on behalf of the Vietnamese people to address the plight of refugee communities in Thailand, Malaysia, Hong Kong, and other areas of the world. He has also turned his attention to global issues of human rights, environmental degradation, rampant consumerism, and the increasingly frenzied quality of life in industrialized nations such as the United States, which he sees as a subtle form of violence that only increases suffering. He has also continued to espouse interreligious cooperation in addressing the moral, social, and politi-

Thich Nhat Hanh. Courtesy of Plum Village Practice Center, France.

cal issues confronting humanity. Charismatic and very unassuming, Thich Nhat Hanh has been hailed as a modern day *bodhisattva* for his work and inspiration.

B. R. Ambedkar (1891–1956)

One of the primary architects of the modern nation of India was also in large part responsible for the modest revival of Buddhism in its ancestral homeland. Bhimrao Ramji Ambedkar was born an "untouchable" (member of the lowest caste) and thus encountered discrimination and hostility throughout his life. Despite such obstacles, he attained a doctorate degree and became a prominent figure in Indian politics. Aghast at what he saw as the insidious nature of India's caste system, Ambedkar burned sections of ancient Hindu texts mandating the caste system, and spearheaded the movement to insure legal safeguards for India's marginalized population. It was during this time that Ambedkar increasingly turned to Buddhist teachings for political guidance and inspiration. He chaired the committee that drafted India's constitution and served as a cabinet member under India's first prime minister, Jawarhalal Nehru, where he worked to establish India's official policy of nondiscrimination on caste grounds. It was Ambedkar who proposed that the Buddhist "Wheel of Dharma" appear on the Indian flag as a potent symbol of Indian nationalism.

Ambedkar's personal journey to Buddhism was a long one. As early as 1935 he declared that to overcome the caste system he would convert from Hinduism to another religion. Immediately, various religious leaders began courting him. He rejected Christianity and Islam (primarily for their non-Indian origins) but was drawn to Sikhism, a mystical devotional movement that draws on both Hindu and Muslim teachings and practices. In 1950, he officially chose Buddhism for what he saw as its rationality and egalitarianism. However. Ambedkar wanted to avoid the traditional "merit-making" focus of lay Buddhism, preferring to view Buddhism as a sort of "social gospel" whose monks and nuns would help teach the Dharma as a way to transform society. Ambedkar marked this shift away from traditional Buddhist practices by referring to himself as a "neo-Buddhist."

Ambedkar's espousal of Buddhist teachings culminated in 1956, when he publicly converted to Buddhism along with some 500,000 other "untouchables" at a mass "consecration" ceremony. This event was followed by various other mass conversions, which have continued into the present. What has come to be known as "Ambedkar Buddhism" follows the example of its leader by focusing on moral reform of the individual and society. The stress tends to be on devotion and action, not meditation. Moreover, Ambedkar himself is taken as the fourth "refuge" (in addition to the traditional "three refuges"—the Buddha, Dharma, and *sangha*) with many converts regarding him as a *bodhisattva*.

It is difficult to assess Ambedkar's Buddhist legacy. He is directly responsible for India having far more Buddhists than before, but it appears many "Ambedkar Buddhists" may be Buddhist more in name than practice. The explicitly political motivation for the movement's founding has raised many eyebrows, as does the fact that many converts take their late leader as an additional "refuge." Some scholars have noted that few of the converts probably knew much of their new faith except that it did not recognize caste distinctions. Ambedkar's movement has also led some Indians to view Buddhism as "the religion of the untouchables," a notion that does not encourage conversion from other castes. Nonetheless, this new Buddhist movement has established several temples throughout the country and, although standards of discipline are generally low, there is a concerted effort at educational advancement. Most leaders have been laypeople, but there are a growing number of monks as well. Many of these native Buddhists engage in charitable work, modeling their efforts on Christian communities.

Buddhadasa Bhikku (1906–93)

The Theravadin monastic community has long been marked by a major division between popular or "village Buddhism" and "forest Buddhism." Monks from the former tend to have more direct contact with the laity, serving as ritual officiates for everyday needs, while monks from the latter tend to be more engaged in spiritual cultivation and meditation. Ironically, because of their reputation for purity and otherworldliness, forest monks have been sought out by ordinary people in times of crisis and have actually had a major impact on postcolonial Buddhist society. One of the best examples is Buddhadasa Bhikku, a monk who became a great critic of the effects of modernization on Thailand. He entered a small monastery at the age of 10, where he gained a basic education in Buddhist teachings and ritual. After full ordination, he went to Bangkok for more advanced studies. Soon after the fall of the absolute Thai monarchy in 1932, Buddhadasa quit his studies, returning to his hometown in southern Thailand. He brought with him a complete copy of the Pali Canon and settled on the grounds of an old abandoned monastery.

For three months Buddhadasa lived in seclusion in absolute silence, studying and meditating much in the vein of the celebrated forest monks of old. During this time he developed a balanced way of monastic life that combined both study and practice. After five years, three other monks joined him, drawn by rumors of this forest holy man. Soon he began to publish books and give Dharma talks to spread his ideas of reform. He became a major public advocate of Buddhist meditation, teaching that monks and laity alike should meditate regularly to reduce the basic self-ishness resulting from the arising of our sense of "I." He also founded Suan Mokh (Garden of Liberation), a meditation hermitage. His various books and collected sermons continue to enjoy wide circulation in Thailand and abroad.

One of Buddhadasa's realizations was that popular forms of Buddhism in Thailand needed major reform. In particular he was highly critical of what he perceived to be the corruption of the Dharma through superstition and the influence of folk beliefs. Rather, he espoused a rationalist approach to traditional Buddhist teachings. For instance, Buddhadasa maintained that *karma* bears fruit immediately rather than over time, and that rebirth really refers to the continuous arising of our sense of "self." Moreover, he also taught that the notion of rebirth after death was irrelevant to the Buddha's true teachings. Buddhadasa was very outspoken about the necessity of putting Buddhist teachings into practice in social life. For him, personal and social transformation tended to reinforce each other. For instance, he insisted that no one can truly understand the Buddhist teaching of "no-self" without dedication to a life of social service aimed at returning society to the moral principles that lie at the heart of nature.

Buddhadasa was critical of capitalism, which he saw as being predicated on selfishness and therefore only leading to more personal and social suffering. In addition, capitalism encourages competition, pitting person against person and thus ignoring Buddhist teachings of interdependence and selflessness. Buddhadasa attracted many disciples from Thailand's more educated and progressive classes, including Sulak Sivaraksa, a leading figure in Engaged Buddhism. Building upon his master's teachings, Sulak has highlighted the way national and international economic interests have reshaped Thai society by creating a market economy. One effect has been to drive farmers and fishermen from their villages to cities, where they live in slums. Another result has been the systematic deforestation of much of

Thailand for international trade. The effects on the Thai countryside have been devastating.

D. T. Suzuki (1870–1966)

Few individuals have shaped Western understandings of Buddhism as much as Daisetz Teitaro Suzuki, a great popularizer of Buddhism in general and Zen in particular. Although never a monk, Suzuki's presentation of Zen proved to be a major catalyst for the growth of Buddhism in American society. Suzuki himself was a product of a late-nineteenth-century movement in Japan called "New Buddhism" that insisted that Zen, stripped of its institutionalized forms, was the essence of Buddhism. Moreover, they also taught that the Rinzai Zen focus on direct experience of reality coupled with its staunch military-style discipline was the fullest expression of Japanese identity. At times these teachers even claimed that this purified form of Zen had potential to be nothing less than the spiritual regeneration of all humanity. One of the main proponents of New Buddhism, Shaku Soen, had been a speaker at the first World's Parliament of Religions held in Chicago in 1893. He was invited back to the United States in 1905 to teach Zen and brought with him three of his top students, including Suzuki. Suzuki had studied as a novice under Soen, earning the Zen name Daisetz (Great Simplicity) after having his own realization experience.

Suzuki served as translator for Shaku Soen during his tour of America, where he came under the influence of Paul Carus, one of the most prominent American figures to embrace Buddhism near the turn of the twentieth century and author of the still-influential work *The Gospel of Buddha* (1904). Suzuki and Carus became good friends, and they collaborated for many years translating and interpreting Asian religious and philosophical traditions for an American audience. Later, with his American wife, Suzuki founded the journal *The Eastern Buddhist,* which remains an important academic outlet for the study of Mahayana Buddhism. He studied and lectured at various American universities, most notably Columbia, and in 1956 the Zen Studies Society of New York was founded to support his efforts.

Over his lifetime Suzuki wrote many important books on Buddhism, including *The Training of a Zen Buddhist Monk* (1934), *Zen and Japanese Culture* (1959), *An Introduction to Zen Buddhism* (1969), and *The Zen Doctrine of No-Mind* (1969). Scholars note that Suzuki's works can be divided into two opposed categories: those maintaining that Zen arises within and can only be understood as part of the (Japanese) Buddhist context, and those arguing that the essences of Zen transcends all cultural and conceptual boundaries. In this latter sense, Zen is a transcendent spiritual and aesthetic realization of the Truth within a single moment.

Suzuki's more universalist works had a profound impact on how the American public understood Buddhism. For many Americans, Buddhism *was* Zen, a tradition geared toward cultivating a pure, mystical experience of reality outside of any specific religious doctrine. This idea of a universally accessible intuition of Truth and Beauty was seized upon in particular by members of the growing countercultural movement in the United States during the 1950s and 1960s, much of which was protesting the materialism and uniformity being promoted in American society. Beat writers such as Jack Kerouac and Allen Ginsburg were entranced by Suzuki's mystical presentation of Zen, viewing it as providing the answers to their own personal artistic and spiritual quests.[16] The late Philip Kapleau, author of the classic work *The Three Pillars of Zen* (1965), was introduced to Zen through Suzuki's lectures at Columbia. The lingering influence of Suzuki's popularized notions of sitting meditation *(zazen)* as a way to realize beauty in the midst of the everyday can still be felt in how Buddhist meditation in all forms is taught to Western audiences. Suzuki's own protege, Masao Abe, has established himself as his mentor's true heir, becoming a major international expert in Buddhist Studies and a key figure in Christian-Buddhist dialogue.

Zhengyan (1937 –)

It was in China that Buddhism began to see the formation of organizations devoted to charitable projects. This tradition lives on in Ciji (the Buddhist Compassionate Relief Love and Mercy Foundation), which was established in 1966 by a Taiwanese nun, Zhengyan. As a young woman, Zhengyan sought solace in religious teachings, resolving to become a *bodhisattva* to aid others. She ran away from home in 1962 to seek ordination, eventually making her way to a small monastery near the city of Hwalien. Her style of teaching others through simple explanations of complex Buddhist doctrines and her insistence on working to support herself rather than living off alms won her a small but loyal following. In 1966 she was struck by the sufferings of the poor in her area and vowed to establish a charitable institution to help them. Seeking advice from some Catholic nuns, she was told that Buddhism could not serve as the basis for such efforts because it promoted a passive attitude and ignored others' needs.

Taken aback by such pronouncements, she gathered her few disciples and some lay supporters and together they resolved to become Guanyin's eyes and hands in the world, compassionately working to insure that Buddhism was never accused of being passive again. From such humble beginnings the Ciji foundation has grown to become a major force in contemporary Taiwan.

Currently Ciji is the largest nongovernmental organization in Taiwan, with an annual budget of more than $300 million. Most of its funding comes from donations from wealthy members of the Chinese community living in various areas around the world. It is largely run by its five million lay volunteers, although it also includes some 100 monastics. Its volunteers are involved in medical and social welfare programs, providing major funding for building free hospitals (a novelty in Taiwan), a medical school, and a university. Their bone-marrow registry is currently the third largest in the entire world. The foundation has also expanded beyond Taiwan, running a medical mission in Shanghai and providing aid for poor residents in inner cities in the United States. Volunteers have also begun serving as companions in America's old-age homes.

Much of Ciji's success stems from the way in which it marries charitable work with spiritual cultivation. The foundation encourages its members to view giving aid to others as a way to cleanse one's heart. Ideally, they are trained to perform their work in a mindful fashion, recalling the various forms of suffering in the world so as to detach from their own pettiness and greed. Through such work the foundation's members cultivate gratitude toward those whom they help and greater appreciation for each other and their families. The idea is that this process will eventually lead to the creation of a more harmonious social realm, which is seen as a larger family that includes all sentient beings.

Dharma Master Zhengyan and her followers are often quite critical of many traditional Buddhist rituals, preferring good deeds to offerings of incense aimed at gaining merit. Although this disturbs some Taiwanese, who argue that Zhengyan is actually founding an entirely new school of Buddhism, her followers respond by claiming that they are only returning Buddhism to its original, simple form. This focus on simplicity is reflected in the architectural style favored by the foundation; rather than traditional ornate temple architecture, the foundation favors clean, unadorned lines in its buildings. By reason of its external charitable focus and internal simplicity, the Ciji association is pointing the way for a new style of Buddhism that is emerging in the twenty-first century.

Aung San Suu Kyi (1945–)

One of the most unlikely heroines of contemporary Buddhism is Aung San Suu Kyi, a Burmese lay Buddhist and activist who won the 1991 Nobel Peace Prize. Known among the Burmese people simply as "the Lady," she is the daughter of General Aung San, himself a devout Buddhist and leading figure in the movement to win Burma's independence in 1948. Aung San was educated in Rangoon, went to India, and then on to Britain, where she studied at Oxford. There she married Michael Aris, an Oxford professor. She only rose to public prominence after her return to Burma. In August of 1988, she became involved in the prodemocracy movement that was challenging Burma's ruling military junta. Her political party, the National League for Democracy, drew its inspiration from the work of Mahatma Gandhi and Rev. Martin Luther King Jr. It won 82 percent of the vote in the national election held in 1990, but the military government refused to relinquish power. Instead, government forces placed Aung San under house arrest, where she remained in strict isolation until July of 1995. Her release was predicated on certain restrictions that she violated by intentionally traveling to areas of her country deemed "off limits." In 2000 she was again arrested, but this time her international reputation made it impossible for her to be completely isolated. In May 2002 she was released unconditionally and has since returned to her activism.

Although not a Buddhist scholar in a strict sense, Aung San is a devout Buddhist, modest yet resolute, who publicly attests to the role her faith plays in her work. As her writings reveal, she has undergone deep Buddhist training and abides by a strict Buddhist code of ethics forbidding her to cause harm to others, or to respond out of hate or fear. During her confinement she would meditate for an hour a day and study Buddhist teachings. She has testified that meditation calms and strengthens her. Rather than succumb to complacency, she argues that Buddhist teachings such as *karma* (action and its resulting reaction) can motivate one to take an active role in transforming society.

Despite her years in confinement, Aung San has become a prominent spokeswoman for Buddhism, especially the contemporary movement of Engaged Buddhism. Like the 14th Dalai Lama and Thich Nhat Hanh, she has become an international celebrity because of media attention. One of the best examples of this is the Hollywood movie *Beyond Rangoon*, released in 1995 and based on true events. Although it was not a commercial or critical success, most reviewers agree that the movie's most riveting scene is one in which an actress playing Aung San confronts a group of armed soldiers and, through sheer moral authority, leads a crowd of her followers past them unharmed. In October 2004 a CD, *For the Lady*, was released in her honor. Featuring tracks by such rock and pop stars and groups as Paul McCartney, R.E.M., and Avril Lavigne, the proceeds went to fund relief for the people of Burma (Myanmar).

Through her various speeches and published works such as *Freedom from Fear and Other Writings* (1991), *Letters from Burma* (1997), and *The Voice of Hope* (1997) she continues to spread the idea that the Buddha Dharma can be a means for achieving positive changes in life. Rather than a spiritual tradition aimed at individual rewards and merit, Aung San presents Buddhism as a practical system of tools for social action. Aung San views Buddhist teachings and practice as integral to her political life. Although many conservative Buddhists decry her political radicalism, she is fully in line with Theravada tradition, which has long emphasized close relations between state and *sangha*. She has become an international symbol of peaceful resistance to oppression, often being compared with Nelson Mandela and Archbishop Desmond Tutu, both of whom were leaders in the movement to end the apartheid government of South Africa. Aung San is an inspiration for political and spiritual activists the world over, especially for women, who may be used to understanding Buddhism as a religious tradition relegating women to only secondary roles.

NOTES

1. Ashoka was one of the great builders of antiquity. Before his time most Indian structures were made of wood and tended to decay rather quickly. Ashoka instead used stone for his monuments, a startling innovation that has enabled many of them to survive to the present. In addition to his rock edicts and stone pillars (incised with inscriptions of his policies and often decorated with remarkable carvings of animal figures), Ashoka also saw to the construction of many relic mounds *(stupas)* and basic public works projects such as roads, wells, and rest houses.

2. In this regard he resembles the Roman Emperor Constantine (r. 306–37), who established Christianity as the official religion of the Roman Empire and presided over the Council of Nicea in 325, where many of the technicalities of Christian doctrine were hammered out.

3. To cite just one example, Ashoka's generosity inspired the legend of King Sirisanghabodhi, a Sri Lankan monarch from the fourth century C.E. According to Sri Lankan tradition, Sirishanghabodhi was so pious that he

abdicated the throne when confronted by a rebellious minister who threatened a civil war. Instead, the king retired to the forest to become a hermit. This step, however, only increased his reputation for holiness among his former subjects. The usurper, fearing the former king's popularity, branded him an outlaw and put a price on his head. Unperturbed, Sirisanghabodhi surrendered himself to a poor peasant who had shared some food with him. This action accomplished several things: it benefited the peasant by enabling him to claim the reward, it avoided further violence and civil unrest, and it established a powerful example of Buddhist piety that continues to be revered.

4. One story goes that the gods, wishing to test Buddhaghosha further, hid the text of The Path of Purity twice, yet each time the monk rewrote it without changing a single syllable.

5. Buddhaghosha's stress on "secret teachings" resembles Vedic ideas found in the Upanishads, texts often regarded as containing "secret knowledge" which could only be passed on at the feet of a teacher.

6. Other examples of such thaumaturges (wonder workers) include the prophets Elijah and Elisha from the Old Testament, Jesus Christ, and various Christian saints.

7. For details on the Madhyamika school see Chapter 3. Kumarajiva is often regarded as the founder of the Three Treatise school, the Chinese version of Madhyamika.

8. Chan, like other Chinese schools, is organized as a system of lineages in which the teachings are passed down from master (patriarch) to disciple, much like family heritage passes down from father to son. Each of the masters mentioned here (Mazu, Linji, Dongshan) is a prominent patriarch of a particular Chan lineage. This idea of lineage continued when Chan went to Japan (becoming Zen) and to this day, each Chan/Zen teacher traces his lineage back to one of the great masters. All followers of Chan, however, trace their lineages back through Huineng to Bodhidharma (fifth-sixth century?), who allegedly brought Chan teachings to China from India. Ultimately, Chan claims descent from the Dharma transmitted to Mahakashyapa by the Buddha during his famous Flower Sermon.

9. Philip B. Yampolsky, trans., *The Platform Sutra of the Sixth Patriarch* (New York: Columbia University Press, 1967), 138.

10. Ibid., 136.

11. Quoted in Wm. Theodore de Bary et al., ed., *Sources of Japanese Tradition, Volume One: From Earliest Times to 1600,* 2nd ed. (New York: Columbia University Press, 2001), 51 (material in brackets added by the author).

12. Both Saicho and Kukai received special imperial honors and titles; Saicho was dubbed "Dengyo Daishi," while Kukai was styled "Kobo Daishi" (*Daishi* is an honorific term meaning "Great Teacher").

13. A popular tradition in Japan holds that Kukai did not die but merely retired into a deep meditative trance, thus still serving a source of blessings for the devout.

14. Eisai actually made two trips to China, one in 1168 and another, longer one from 1187–97.

15. Some accounts have Honen arranging the marriage and conducting the wedding ceremony.

16. Kerouac met Suzuki in person the very day that his novel *The Dharma Bums* (1958), the most famous of his explicitly Buddhist books, was published. The story of their meeting is vintage Kerouac and a wonderful illustration of what Alan Watts, a great protege of Suzuki, called "Beat Zen." Kerouac eventually published the story in the *Berkeley Bussei,* the magazine of the Berkeley Young Buddhist Association, in 1960.

GLOSSARY

Most of the following terms are given in Sanskrit with Pali forms in parentheses preceded by a P. Terms from other languages are indicated as follows: Chinese (C), Japanese (J), and Tibetan (T).

Abhidharma (P, Abhidhamma): "higher teaching"; the third division ("basket") of the Buddhist scriptures comprising systematic elaboration on certain topics found in the discourses and sermons (*sutras*). Abhidharma teachings typically analyze "reality" into its basic components (momentary physical and mental events and factors that comprise our experience) without reference to a lasting or abiding "self."

Ahimsa: "nonharming"; one of the primary Buddhist virtues and a basic precept by which all Buddhists vow to live. Encourages a more mindful and peaceful way of life and as such, is an important foundation for spiritual advancement.

Alayavijnana: "Storehouse Consciousness"; the primordial base consciousness according to Yogachara teachings underlying the seven "higher" levels ("mind" plus the six sense-consciousnesses). Contains the "seeds" (traces) of past *karma* that keep one bound to the cycle of life and death *(samsara)* as well as "pure seeds" that will eventually lead to Awakening.

Amitabha Buddha (C, Omitofo; J, Amida butsu): the "Buddha of Infinite Light/Life"; the Celestial Buddha who established a western paradise or Pure Land where his faithful followers will be reborn. Worshipped in the Pure Land schools and often invoked in prayers and chants (C, *namo Omitofo*; J, *namu Amida Butsu*).

Anatman (P, *anatta*): "no self"; one of the Three Marks of Existence and a basic Buddhist teaching. An outgrowth of the teaching of impermanence as it applies to human life, *anatman* refers to the fact that nothing (no thing) lasts; there is no permanent or abiding "self" or "soul" underlying the continuous flux of existence.

Arhat (P, *arahat*): "worthy one"; person (usually a monk) who is free from defilements and who has attained the state beyond suffering *(nirvana)*. According to Theravada tradition, the *arhat* is the highest stage of spiritual and is the ideal to which devout followers should aspire.

Bardo (T): "intermediate state"; usually refers to a state of limbo between death and rebirth when the Tibetan Book of the Dead is read to the deceased. The *bardo* typically lasts 49 days during which the deceased experiences visions based upon past *karma.*

Bodhisattva: "wisdom being"; a Buddha-to-be, one who has experienced the "thought of Enlightenment" *(bodhichitta)* and aspires to the wisdom and freedom of a Buddha. The ideal in Mahayana tradition, a *bodhisattva* vows to attain Enlightenment for the sake of all beings and is reborn continually into *samsara* to assuage their sufferings.

Brahmins: "priests"; The highest caste in traditional Indian society and the custodians of the Vedas (sacred texts).

Buddha: "Awakened One"; one of the titles given to Siddhartha Gautama after his Enlightenment. Theravada Buddhism maintains that there can be only one Buddha at a time. According to Mahayana and Vajrayana traditions, however, there are innumerable worlds in the cosmos, each with its own Buddha.

Chakras: (lit. "wheels"); Centers of energy located within and around the body which, according to tradition, can be strengthened and tapped into by trained meditators.

Chan (C; J, Zen): "meditation"; derived from the Sanskrit term *dhyana,* which the Chinese translated as *chan-na,* Chan has come to designate the great meditation school that arose in China during the seventh century. It is especially associated with the practice of "just sitting" (C, *suochan;* J, *zazen*) and the use of *gongan* (J, *koans*) to provoke sudden insights into one's Buddha-nature.

Dazang (C): Chinese Buddhist canon (lit. "Great Storehouse/Library"); the Chinese translation of the Sanskrit Tripitaka (Three Baskets), which denotes the authoritative collection of sacred Buddhist texts. The

Chinese term probably comes from the official imperial libraries that housed the Chinese classics and their commentaries as well as other books deemed particularly valuable. The Chinese version of the Tripitaka is basically a Mahayana version and contains materials not found in the Pali canon.

Dharma (P, *dhamma*): ancient Hindu notion of "duty" or "righteousness." In Buddhism, usually refers to the "truth" or "teachings of the truth." Can also mean "true phenomena," that is, the momentary phenomenal elements that in Abhidharma analysis comprise everyday experience.

Dhyana (P, *jhana*): "meditative trance"; a level of deep concentration and absorption, often part of a numbered series (four or eight). It has also sometimes been used to refer to Buddhist meditation in general.

Dzogchen (T): "Great Perfection"; A Tibetan meditation practice in which the practitioner becomes aware of the innately pure and luminous nature of the mind.

Gongan (C, J *koan*): (lit. "public case") a short anecdote, saying, or riddle given by Chan/Zen masters to students to provoke insight. *Gongan* have no logical solution but are meant to subvert normal discursive thinking so that a student has a sudden realization of truth. Among the most famous *gongan* are "What is the sound of one hand clapping?" and "Show me your original face before you were born!"

Guru (T, *lama*): "teacher"; a spiritual and philosophical teacher-mentor who imparts wisdom and practices to his disciples. The idea has very ancient Indian roots. In classical India, a young boy would go to live with a guru for several years, serving him while learning the knowledge necessary for taking his place in society. Over time it came to have a religious connotation, with the guru serving as an intimate personal guide to the spiritual path. In Tantric circles a *guru* is someone who has mastered secret meditations and rituals, and is empowered to pass them on.

Hinayana: "small vehicle"; a pejorative label used by followers of Mahayana Buddhism to denigrate other, more conservative Buddhist schools that espouse the *arhat* as the highest spiritual ideal. The term probably refers especially to some of the more abstruse Abhidharma schools known for their painstaking analysis of everyday experience into its constituent elements *(dharmas)*. Hinayana does *not* refer to Theravada tradition.

Jatakas: "birth stories"; accounts of the Buddha's previous lives that illustrate his great wisdom and virtue. Jataka tales are among the most beloved of genres of Buddhist literature and are often used by monks in instructing the laity.

Karma (P, *kamma*): "deed" or "action"; an intentional action that will have definite future consequences for the actor. A basic Indian teaching in which the consequences of past actions largely determine a person's present life circumstances. More broadly, *karma* can refer to the cosmic/moral law of cause and effect.

Madhyamika: "adherent of the middle way"; major school of Mahayana Buddhism that emphasizes the "empty" nature of all things. Madhyamika has sometimes been mistaken for a form of nihilism because of its consistent denial that Ultimate Truth can ever be captured through words and concepts.

Mahayana: "Great Vehicle"; the major branch of Buddhism dominant in East Asia, in which devotees seek to become Buddhas themselves. The Mahayana ideal is the *bodhisattva* ("wisdom being;" a Buddha-to-be) rather than the *arhat*.

Mandala: "cosmic diagram"; a pictographic representation, usually circular in shape, of the sacred Buddhist universe. *Mandalas* typically depict Buddhas and other deities and are often used in visualizations and rituals, especially in Tantric tradition.

Mantra: "instrument"; a powerful word or phrase (e.g., *om mani padme hum*) used to evoke a deity or gain protection. *Mantras* are usually Sanskrit and can also serve as a focus for meditation.

Mudra: "seal"; a ritual gesture or hand position. Buddhist images depict Buddhas and *bodhisattvas* making certain *mudras* to symbolize their powers and activities. Tantric rituals often entail adepts practicing specific *mudras*.

Nembutsu (J): "remembering the Buddha"; *See* Nianfo

Nianfo (C): "remembering the Buddha"; Most common spiritual practice among followers or Pure Land. Involves focusing one's attention on Amitabha and reciting his name over and over.

Nirvana (P, *nibbana*): "extinguishing a fire"; the term commonly used to refer to the ultimate goal of the Buddhist path; the opposite of *samsara*, the cycle of life-death-rebirth. *Nirvana* connotes the cooling of the passions, serenity, and freedom from suffering.

Paritta (P): "safety runes"; chanted passages from the Pali scriptures typically used in Theravada rituals for protection. *Parittas* may help ward off demons, illness, and misfortune, and are also a means of conveying blessings or merit.

Prajna: (P, *panna*), "wisdom"; the ability to discern the true nature of reality. *Prajna* is not the same thing as (worldly) knowledge but instead has a specifically religious/spiritual connotation. It is essential for attaining Enlightenment.

Pratitya samutpada: (P, *paticca-sammupada*), "Dependent Origination"; a core teaching of Buddhism and most likely the "truth" that the Buddha realized under the *bodhi* tree. *Pratitya-samutpada* refers to the manner in which all phenomena of experience are produced through the combination of various causes and conditions; the basic interdependence of all existence.

Samadhi: "holding together completely"; a mindful, undistracted state in which awareness is focused on a specific object. *Samadhi* is a calm, stable meditative state; "one-pointed concentration."

Samatha-vipashyana (P, *samatha-vipassana*): "calm and insight"; the basic twofold form of meditation practice taught in all schools of Buddhism. *Samatha* practices seek to produce tranquility and stillness in the mind, while *vipashyana* practices uncover negative and unwholesome attitudes and dispositions that cause our mental and emotional afflictions. Both skills are needed to achieve Wisdom *(prajna)* and attain Enlightenment.

Samsara: "flowing together"; the wheel of birth and death in which all beings are trapped by ignorance. *Samsara* is ordinary existence, the world of suffering in which the Buddha appears to lead us to Enlightenment.

Sangha: "community"; the collective name for all Buddhists, both lay and monastic. The *sangha* is one of the Three Jewels (along with the Buddha and the Dharma) in which a Buddhist takes refuge.

Satori (J): "realization"; a sudden insight or awakening into the true nature of reality in Chan/Zen Buddhism. Traditionally, the experience of *satori* did *not* mark full and final Enlightenment but was merely the first stage of a series of ever deepening insights into the nature of existence.

Shamanism: Type of religious practice among tribal peoples around the world. Centers on a religious leader (shaman) who contacts gods and spirits, often in a state of trance.

Shogun (J): military dictators; Samurai lords who were the main political rulers of Japan during the Middle Ages.

Shramanas: Wandering ascetics seeking a holy life outside the traditional Indian caste system. The originators of several Indian religious movements such as Buddhism and Jainism.

Shunyata: "emptiness"; a reinterpretation of the Buddhist teaching of *pratitya-samutpada* emphasizing the basic *lack* of any permanent substance in our experience. According to Mahayana views, the fundamental nature of reality is *shunyata.*

Siddha: "accomplished one"; a practitioner of Vajrayana rituals and meditation. Many of the legendary siddhas were renowned for their occult powers.

Stupa: "memorial mound"; a shrine or reliquary housing relics of a Buddha or *bodhisattva. Stupas* are the focus of devotion and can be found all over the Buddhist world. In East Asia, they typically take the form of pagodas.

Sutra (P, *sutta*): "thread"; a discourse or sermon attributed to the Buddha.

Tantra: "loom"; an often secret (esoteric) ritual manual usually associated with the Vajrayana school of Buddhism. Tantras are typically written in a symbolic or veiled style ("twilight language") that requires interpretation by an accomplished guru.

Tantrism: Another name for Vajrayana, the secret ritual style of Buddhism that dominates the Himalayan region.

Tathagata-garbha: "womb/embryo of Buddhahood"; the innate potential to awaken possessed by all sentient beings. "Buddha-nature."

Theravada: "Teaching of the Elders"; the major branch of Buddhism that dominates in Southeast Asia. Theravada has the reputation of being the most conservative form of Buddhism and promotes the *arhat* (one who has attained *nirvana* but does not have omniscience) as its spiritual ideal.

Tripitaka (P, *tipitaka*): "Three Baskets"; the canon of sacred Buddhist texts. The three divisions of the Tripitaka are the Sutra (discourses, sermons), Vinaya (discipline), and Abhidharma (higher Dharma).

Tulku (T): a reincarnation of an advanced spiritual adept, usually a teacher *(lama),* who resumes the duties of his/her former life. A *tulku* is understood to be a particular manifestation of a *bodhisattva* who has voluntarily undergone rebirth to aid suffering beings.

Vajra: "diamond" or "thunderbolt"; the ritual wand used in Varjayana ceremonies. Said to represent the powerful weapon wielded by the great god Indra.

Vajrayana: "Diamond Vehicle"; the major branch of Buddhism that emphasizes secret Tantric practices. Vajrayana is the dominant form of Buddhism in the Tibetan region and is often acknowledged to be the most powerful and dangerous.

Vedas: (lit. "knowledge"); the most sacred of all Hindu scriptures. Written in Sanskrit, the Vedas were the centerpiece of ancient brahmanical society and are still chanted during many Hindu rituals.

Vinaya: "discipline"; the third "basket" of the Buddhist canon; it consists of texts outlining the basic precepts and rules governing Buddhist life. The Vinaya covers both monastic and lay discipline.

Yogachara: "the practice of yoga"; Mahayana school of philosophy based on analysis of mental states and experiences arising in yoga practice. Often mistakenly viewed as a form of metaphysical idealism, Yogachara teachings stress the way in which our own attitudes and predispositions help construct our experiences of reality.

Zazen (J; C, *suochan*): "seated meditation"; The key meditation practice in Chan/Zen Buddhism in which the practitioner sits cross-legged and focuses on the breath. Said to be an ideal practice of stilling the mind so that the "Buddha-nature" shows itself.

ANNOTATED SELECTED BIBLIOGRAPHY

BOOKS

Amore, Roy C. *Two Masters, One Message*. Nashville, TN: Abingdon Press, 1978. Intriguing comparison of Jesus Christ and Shakyamuni Buddha.

Badiner, Allan Hunt, ed. *Mindfulness in the Marketplace: Compassionate Responses to Consumerism*. Berkeley, CA: Parallax Press, 2002. Anthology of essays by various teachers associated with Engaged Buddhism presenting a critical Buddhist view of the ethic of endless consumption that dominates the developed world. Contributors include the Dalai Lama, Thich Nhat Hanh (an internationally known Vietnamese monk), and Sulak Sivaraksa (lay activist famous for his work on behalf of Thailand).

Batchelor, Stephen. *The Awakening of the West: The Encounter of Buddhism and Western Culture*. Berkeley, CA: Parallax Press, 1994. An interesting and very readable historical overview of the contacts between Buddhist culture and Western Civilization.

Batchelor, Stephen. *Buddhism without Beliefs: A Contemporary Guide to Awakening*. New York: Riverhead Books, 1997. A simple presentation of basic Buddhist teachings emphasizing their practical applications to everyday life.

Bhikku Nanamoli, trans. *The Path of Purification (Visuddhimagga) by Bhadantacariya Buddhaghosa*. 5th edition. Kandy, Sri Lanka: Buddhist Publication Society, 1991. English translation of the classic manual of Buddhist cultivation by the foremost Theravadin commentator.

Burtt, E. A., ed. *The Teachings of the Compassionate Buddha.* New York: Penguin Books, 1982. Nice collection of excerpts from various primary Buddhist texts covering early Buddhism, Theravada, Mahayana, and Chinese and Japanese devotional forms.

Cabezon, Jose Ignacio. *Buddhism and Language: A Study of Indo-Tibetan Scholasticism.* Albany: State University of New York Press, 1994. Scholarly study of philosophical developments in the Dharma within the Indian and Tibetan university contexts.

Ch'en, Kenneth K. S. *Buddhism in China: A Historical Survey.* Princeton, NJ: Princeton University Press, 1964. Extensive historical overview of the place of Buddhism in Chinese culture.

Cleary, Thomas, trans. *Shobogenzo: Zen Essays by Dogen.* Honolulu: University of Hawaii Press, 1986. Annotated English translation of Treasury of the Eye of True Teaching, one of Dogen's most remarkable collections of essays. Essential for understanding Zen thought.

Conze, Edward. *Buddhist Thought in India: Three Phases of Buddhist Philosophy.* Ann Arbor: University of Michigan Press, 1967. Excellent in-depth philosophical discussion of major developments in Buddhist thought by one of the foremost figures in Buddhist studies.

Conze, Edward, trans. *Buddhist Scriptures.* New York: Viking Penguin, 1959. Anthology of texts from all major Buddhist traditions, focusing on core teachings and how they have been elaborated in different cultural contexts.

Conze, Edward, trans. *The Large Sutra on Perfect Wisdom (with the divisions of the Abhisamayalankara).* Berkeley: University of California Press, 1975. English translation of another early Mahayana text that was particularly influential in the rise of the *bodhisattva* ideal.

Conze, Edward, trans. *The Perfection of Wisdom in Eight Thousand Lines and Its Verse Summary (Astasahasrikaprajnaparamita sutra).* Bolinas, CA: Four Seasons Foundation, 1973. English translation of one of the most important and influential early Mahayana scriptures.

Corless, Roger J. *The Vision of the Buddha: The Space under the Tree.* New York: Paragon House, 1989. Very creative introduction to Buddhist tradition presented "Buddhistically," that is, not historically but cued to key events in the life of the Buddha.

De Bary, William Theodore, ed. *The Buddhist Tradition in India, China and Japan.* New York: Vintage Books, 1972. Extensive anthology of Buddhist texts from three major areas showing both continuity and development across time and space.

Dumoulin, Heinrich. *Zen Buddhism: A History—Volume I, India and China.* Translated by James W. Heisig and Paul Knitter. New York: Macmillan, 1988. Detailed history of Chan (Zen) from its traditional beginnings in India through its development and eventual decline in China.

Dumoulin, Heinrich. *Zen Buddhism: A History—Volume 2, Japan.* Translated by James W. Heisig and Paul Knitter. New York: Macmillan, 1990. Companion volume to the above, tracing the history of Zen, from its transmission from China to Japan until the modern day.

Eppsteiner, Fred, ed. *The Path of Compassion: Writings on Socially Engaged Buddhism.* Berkeley, CA: Parallax Press, 1988. Collection of writings from Buddhist teachers, monastics, and other leaders that provides a sampling of various trends in Engaged Buddhism.

Fields, Rick. *How the Swans Came to the Lake: A Narrative History of Buddhism in America.* Boston: Shambhala, 1992. Very readable account of the spread of Buddhism in America by one of the founding editors of *Tricycle.*

Garfield, Jay L., trans. *Fundamental Wisdom of the Middle Way: Nagarjuna's Mulamadhyamakakarika.* New York: Oxford University Press, 1995. English translation of the signature treatise by the thinker whom many scholars regard as the greatest philosopher in Buddhist history.

Gernet, Jacques. *Buddhism in Chinese Society: An Economic History from the Fifth to the Tenth Centuries.* Translated by Franciscus Verellen. New York: Columbia University Press, 1995. Detailed critical analysis of the social and economic dimensions of Buddhism in China during the Middle Ages.

Gregory, Peter N. *Inquiry into the Origin of Humanity: An Annotated Translation of Tsung-mi's Yuan jen lun with a Modern Commentary.* Honolulu: Kuroda Institute, University of Hawaii Press, 1995. English translation of an important Chinese Buddhist treatise exemplifying the harmonizing tendencies so characteristic of East Asian Buddhism.

Gregory, Peter N. *Tsung-mi and the Sinification of Buddhism.* Princeton, NJ: Princeton University Press, 1991. Detailed historical discussion of a prominent Buddhist monk during the late Tang dynasty and his role in the formation and institutionalization of the Chan and Huayan schools of Buddhism.

Gross, Rita M. *Buddhism after Patriarchy: A Feminist History, Analysis, and Reconstruction of Buddhism.* Albany: State University of New York Press, 1993. Landmark work by one of the most prominent Buddhist feminists.

Hakeda, Yoshito S., trans. *The Awakening of Faith.* New York: Columbia University Press, 1967. English translation with extensive commentary of one of the most influential treatises in East Asian Buddhism.

Harvey, Peter. *An Introduction to Buddhism: Teachings, History and Practices.* Cambridge: Cambridge University Press, 1990. A comprehensive overview of Buddhist tradition in Asia and the West. Good for undergraduates as well as an educated lay reader interested in learning about the diversity of Buddhist practice worldwide.

Hirakawa Akira. *A History of Indian Buddhism: From Shakyamuni to Early Mahayana.* Translated and edited by Paul Groner. Honolulu: University of Hawaii Press, 1990. Comprehensive discussion of the first 500 years of Buddhism, covering history, doctrine, and practice.

Hurvitz, Leon, trans. *Scripture of the Lotus Blossom of the Fine Dharma: Translated from the Chinese of Kumarajiva.* New York: Columbia University Press, 1976. Annotated English translation of best-known Chinese version of the most influential Mahayana *sutra.* Includes preface and glossary.

Kalupahana, David J. *Buddhist Philosophy: A Historical Analysis.* Honolulu: University of Hawaii Press, 1976. Introductory survey of basic Buddhist philosophical teachings focusing on early views of *karma* and causality and tracing their various elaborations in later Buddhist schools.

Keown, Damien. *Buddhism and Bioethics.* New York: Palgrave, 2001. Thoughtful presentation of mainstream Buddhist positions on a number of contemporary biomedical issues by the co-editor of the *Journal of Buddhist Ethics.*

King, Sallie B. *Buddha Nature.* Albany: State University of New York Press, 1991. Study of the teaching of "Buddha-nature" as proclaimed in an early treatise translated into Chinese in the sixth century. Excellent discussion of major aspects of Buddhist philosophy that had a decisive impact on Chinese thought in particular.

Kitagawa, Joseph M., and Mark D. Cummings, eds. *Buddhism and Asian History.* New York: Macmillan, 1987. Excerpts from the multivolume *Encyclopedia of Religion,* the standard reference work in religious studies featuring essays by top scholars in the field.

Lester, Robert C. *Theravada Buddhism in Southeast Asia.* Ann Arbor: University of Michigan Press, 1973. Short overview of Theravada tradition, covering scriptural ideals and actual social practice.

Lhalunga, Lobsang P., trans. *The Life of Milarepa.* Boston: Shambhala, 1985. Illustrated English translation of the autobiography of Tibet's most beloved yogi and saint. Good example of traditional Tibetan folklore with its emphasis on magical and wondrous events.

Liebenthal, Walter. *Chao Lun: The Treatises of Seng-chao.* 2nd rev. edition. Hong Kong: Hong Kong University Press, 1968. Fully annotated translations of four essays by one of the chief disciples of Kumarajiva, the great fifth- to sixth-century translator of Buddhist texts into Chinese. These treatises are an excellent example of the use of Daoist and Confucian terminology to interpret Buddhist teachings. Liebenthal includes a detailed historical introduction with short commentaries on each treatise.

Lopez, Donald S., Jr., ed. *Buddhism in Practice.* Princeton, NJ: Princeton University Press, 1995. Anthology of almost 50 texts from India, China, Japan, Korea, Tibet, Nepal, Sri Lanka, Thailand, and Burma. Provides a broad overview or a large range of diverse Buddhist practices.

Lopez, Donald S., Jr., ed.. *Curators of the Buddha: The Study of Buddhism under Colonialism.* Chicago: University of Chicago Press, 1995. A critical history of the study of Buddhism, with essays by some of the foremost contemporary experts in Buddhist Studies.

Lopez, Donald S., Jr., ed. *The Heart Sutra Explained: Indian and Tibetan Commentaries.* Albany: State University of New York Press, 1988. Scholarly translation and analysis of one of the most important Mahayana texts.

Matsunage, Alicia and Daigan. *Foundation of Japanese Buddhism.* Volumes 1 and 2. Los Angeles: Buddhist Books International, 1974. Meticulously detailed overview of the history of Japanese Buddhism from its beginnings under Prince Shotoku through the Kamakura and Muromachi periods, when Buddhism became a truly mass movement. Includes charts outlining the development of major schools.

Mitchell, Donald W. *Buddhism: Introducing the Buddhist Experience.* New York: Oxford University Press, 2002. Excellent comprehensive survey of Buddhist traditions by one of the foremost figures in the Buddhist-Christian dialogue. Includes 22 personal narratives from prominent contemporary Buddhists such as the Dalai Lama, Sulak Sivaraksa, and prominent Buddhist feminist Rita Gross.

Murcott, Susan. *The First Buddhist Women: Translations and Commentary on the Therigatha.* Berkeley, CA: Parallax Press, 1991. Readable translation of sections from the earliest texts attributed to nuns, with commentary highlighting how the *sangha* challenged prevailing patriarchal practices and assumptions in ancient India.

Nakamura, Hajime. *Indian Buddhism: A Survey with Bibliographical Notes.* Reprint edition. Delhi, India: Motilal Banarsidass, 1989. Overview of history of Buddhism in India, drawing primarily on recent Japanese scholarship.

Nakasone, Ronald Y. *Ethics of Enlightenment: Essays and Sermons in Search of a Buddhist Ethic.* Fremont, CA: Dharma Cloud, 1990. Collection of essays, sermons, and reflections by a Pure Land Buddhist Priest applying Buddhist teachings to contemporary social and ethical issues.

Nhat Hanh, Thich. *Being Peace.* Edited by Arnold Kotler. Berkeley, CA: Parallax Press, 1987. Collection of Dharma talks the famous Buddhist activist gave to peace workers and meditation students during a 1985 tour of North America. Excellent introduction to his unique and simple teaching style.

Nhat Hanh, Thich. *Peace Is Every Step: The Path of Mindfulness in Everyday Life.* With a foreword by H. H. the Dalai Lama. Edited by Arnold Kotler. New York: Bantam Books, 1991. A guidebook for learning to live in a more meditative, mindful fashion based upon the author's lectures, writings, and personal conversations. Simple and very practical.

Nikam, N. A., and Richard McKeon, eds. and trans. *The Edicts of Asoka.* Chicago: University of Chicago Press, 1959. Translation and analysis of the major pillar, rock, and cave edicts erected by the great Indian Emperor throughout his realm.

Paul, Diana Y. *Women in Buddhism: Images of the Feminine in the Mahayana Tradition.* Berkeley: University of California Press, 1985. Annotated anthology of original texts presenting a wide array of Buddhist views of the place and role(s) of women.

Prebish, Charles S., and Kenneth K. Tanaka, eds. *The Faces of Buddhism in America.* Berkeley: University of California Press, 1998. Collection of essays on the increasingly diverse Buddhist community in America.

Rahula, Walpola. *What the Buddha Taught.* Revised and expanded edition. New York: Grove Press, 1974. Classic exposition of basic Buddhist teachings by a monk and scholar, primarily from a Theravada perspective. Includes selections from the Dhammapada and various *suttas.*

Raju, P. T. *The Philosophical Traditions of India.* Delhi, India: Motilal Banarsidass, 1992. Good survey of major schools of Indian thought. Useful for gaining a broader understanding of the context from which Buddhism arose.

Rhys-Davids, T. W., trans. *Buddhist Suttas.* New York: Dover, 1969. Reprinted translations of important selections from the Pali canon; originally published as Volume 11 in Max Muller's multivolume series *The Sacred Books of the East,* one of the first English translations of Asian religious texts. Selections include the Buddha's first and last sermons as well as discourses on morality, spiritual practice, and mysticism.

Robinson, Richard H. *Early Madhyamika in India and China.* Madison: University of Wisconsin Press, 1967. Classic study of the earliest phase of development of one of the most important schools of Mahayana thought. Includes annotated translations of many important Sanskrit and Chinese texts.

Robinson, Richard H., Willard L. Johnson, and Thanissaro Bhikku (Geoffrey DeGraff). *The Buddhist Religion: A Historical Introduction.* 5th edition. Belmont, CA: Wadsworth, 2005. Most recent edition of a truly comprehensive and lucid overview of Buddhism in its early, Indian, Tantric, Southeast Asian, East Asian, and Western forms. Long a standard textbook for university students in the United States.

Sadakata, Akira. *Buddhist Cosmology: Philosophy and Origins.* Translated by Gaynor Sekimori. Tokyo: Kosei, 1997. Extensively researched introduction to early Buddhist and Mahayana conceptions of the universe with concluding discussion of resemblances to modern scientific views.

Saddhatissa, Hammalawa. *Buddhist Ethics: The Path to Nirvana.* London: Wisdom, 1970. Clear overview of the central place of ethics in Buddhist tradition by a lifelong Theravada monk.

Shantideva. *The Way of the Bodhisattva.* Translated by the Padmakara Translation Group. Boston: Shambhala, 1997. One of the classic works of Mahayana spirituality by one of the tradition's greatest poets. Includes appendices on the life of Shantideva and Dharma talks by Tibetan Nyingma master Kunzang Pelden.

Sharma, Arvind. *The Philosophy of Religion: A Buddhist Perspective.* New York: Oxford University Press, 1995. Discussion of major themes in the philosophy of religion (e.g., the concept of God, the problem of evil) from a Buddhist perspective.

Shaw, Miranda. *Passionate Enlightenment: Women in Tantric Buddhism.* Princeton, NJ: Princeton University Press, 1994. Scholarly discussion of the history of Tantric tradition arguing that Tantric theory affirmed the spiritual capacity and power of women.

Sherill, Martha. *The Buddha from Brooklyn.* New York: Random House, 2000. Intriguing, often disturbing study of a Tibetan Buddhist community in the Maryland suburbs of Washington, D.C. Illustrates problems that can arise when traditional Buddhist teachings are transplanted wholesale into contemporary American settings and the dangers of blind obedience of charismatic teachers.

Snellgrove, David. *Indo-Tibetan Buddhism: Indian Buddhists and their Tibetan Successors.* 2 vols. Boston: Shambhala, 1987. Comprehensive survey of Indian Buddhism from its founding up to and including its establishment in Tibet, with special attention given to Tantric theory and practice. Written by one of the great scholars of Buddhist tradition, this two-volume work includes numerous illustrations and extensive quotes from various original sources.

Sole-Leris, Amadeo. *Tranquility and Insight: An Introduction to the Oldest Form of Buddhist Meditation.* Boston: Shambhala, 1986. Overview of the main methods of meditation in Theravada tradition.

Somers, Robert M., ed. *Arthur F. Wright: Studies in Chinese Buddhism.* New Haven, CT: Yale University Press, 1990. Anthology of essays by one of the great scholars of Chinese Buddhism.

Strong, John S. *The Experience of Buddhism: Sources and Interpretations.* Belmont, CA: Wadsworth, 1995. Comprehensive anthology tracing the development of Buddhism through Asia and the world. Ideal companion to *The Buddhist Religion* by Robinson et al.

Suzuki, Daisetz Teitaro. *An Introduction to Zen Buddhism.* With a foreword by C. G. Jung. New York: Grove Press, 1964. Basic presentation of Zen philosophy and practice by the foremost interpreter of Zen for a Western audience.

Suzuki, Daisetz Teitaro. *The Training of the Zen Buddhist Monk.* Illustrated by Zenchu Sato. New York: Globe Press, 1934.. Reprint, Rutland, VT: Charles E. Tuttle, 1994. Detailed overview of Zen monastic practice with forty-three illustrations depicting the artist's first-hand experiences of Zen life.

Suzuki, Daisetz Teitaro. *Zen and Japanese Culture.* New York: Pantheon, 1959. Collection of essays illustrating the remarkable influence Zen has exerted on Japanese Culture. Highly romanticized but still very perceptive.

Takakusu, Junjiro. *The Essentials of Buddhist Philosophy.* Edited by Wing-tsit Chan and Charles A. Moore. Westport, CT: Greenwood Press, 1976. Somewhat dated but still authoritative description of the basic teachings and scholars of the major schools of Buddhist philosophy. Presented in the traditional Japanese scholarly style.

Thurman, Robert A. F., trans. *The Holy Teaching of Vimalakirti: A Mahayana Scripture.* University Park: Pennsylvania State University Press, 1976. English translation of an important Buddhist text based on Tibetan versions. Includes an introduction and three glossaries of technical terms.

Trainor, Kevin, ed. *Buddhism: The Illustrated Guide.* New York: Oxford University Press, 2001. Up-to-date scholarly overview focusing on key Buddhist teachings, principles, and practices. Especially noteworthy for including more than 150 color photographs of important sites, artworks, and rituals.

Verdu, Alfonso. *Early Buddhist Philosophy in the Light of the Four Noble Truths.* Delhi, India: Motilal Banarsidass, 1985. In-depth philosophical discussion of "scholastic" Buddhism highlighting the sophistication of early systems of Buddhist thought.

Ward, Tim. *What the Buddha Never Taught.* Toronto, ON: Somerville House, 1998. Intriguing first-person account of a modern-day Westerner's time living in a Thai forest monastery. Humorous, revealing, and unsettling, it provides a unique window into contemporary Buddhist monasticism.

Warder, A. K. *Indian Buddhism.* Delhi, India: Motilal Banarsidass, 1970. Classic historical study of Buddhism's origins and development.

Williams, Paul. *Mahayana Buddhism: The Doctrinal Foundations.* New York: Routledge, 1989. Detailed and accurate overview of the major schools of Mahayana Buddhism, placing them within their historical and cultural context.

Wright, Arthur F. *Buddhism in Chinese History.* Stanford, CA: Stanford University Press, 1959. Short historical overview of Buddhism in China by one of the foremost scholars.

Yampolsky, Philip B., trans. *The Platform Sutra of the Sixth Patriarch: The Text of the Tun-Huang Manuscript.* New York: Columbia University Press, 1967. English translation of one of the seminal texts for Chan/Zen tradition. Includes an extensive historical introduction.

Zurcher, Erik. *The Buddhist Conquest of China: The Spread and Adaptation of Buddhism in Early Medieval China.* Leiden, The Netherlands: E. J. Brill, 1959. Meticulously detailed history of the earliest stage of Chinese Buddhism with extensive notes and translations.

JOURNALS AND MAGAZINES

There are a number of popular and scholarly periodicals devoted to Buddhism, many of which also have their own Web sites. This is a sample of some of the more prominent.

BuddhaZine. Official online magazine of Buddhanet, a major Buddhist Web site.

Buddhism Now. A quarterly Buddhist publication from the United Kingdom billing itself as being for "ordinary Buddhists."

The Eastern Buddhist. Scholarly English language journal founded by D. T. Suzuki and published by Otani University in Kyoto. *The Eastern Buddhist* focuses on Mahayana Buddhist tradition.

Electronic Journal of Korean Buddhist Studies. Scholarly online journal focusing on Korean Buddhism. Publishes articles in English, Chinese, Japanese and Korean. http://www2.gol.com.

Journal of Buddhist Ethics. One of the leading online Buddhist publications, *JBE* provides a worldwide forum for those interested in researching and investigating ethical issues from a Buddhist perspective. http:// www. jbe.gold.ac.uk.

Journal of Global Buddhism. Major online resource of scholarly articles on Buddhist history, teachings, and practice worldwide. http://www.global. buddhism.org.

Journal of the International Association of Buddhist Studies. A leading scholarly journal, *JIABS* is published twice yearly out of the Center for Chinese Studies and the Department of Asian Languages and Cultures of the University of Michigan. As the official organ of the International Association of Buddhist Studies, *JIABS* covers all facets of Buddhist studies.

The Middle Way. Official journal of the Buddhist Society of the United Kingdom, publishing scholarly and popular articles on the full range of Buddhist topics.

Pacific World: Journal of the Institute of Buddhist Studies. Annual journal covering all aspects of Buddhist tradition (historical, textual, critical, etc.) in general and Pure Land Buddhism in particular. *Pacific World* is published by the Institute of Buddhist Studies, a Pure Land Buddhist seminary in the United States.

Shambhala Sun. A popular publication founded by Buddhist practitioners that addresses contemporary issues from a contemplative perspective.

Tricycle: The Buddhist Review. The world's leading popular Buddhist publication dedicated to exploring all aspects of Buddhist tradition. *Tricycle* regularly includes interviews with noted Buddhist teachers and celebrities, movie and book reviews, and article from various Buddhist writer, scholars, and practitioners.

Turning Wheel: The Journal of Socially Engaged Buddhism. An official organ of the Buddhist Peace Fellowship, *Turning Wheel* is published quarterly and features articles from Buddhist activists on a number of peace- and justice-related issues.

Vajra Bodhi Sea: A Monthly Journal of Orthodox Buddhism. Published by the Dharma Realm Buddhist Association, *Vajra Bodhi Sea* is a bilingual (English and Chinese) journal presenting a traditional Chinese Buddhist perspective on a variety of topics related to Buddhist history, practice, and social/moral issues.

ELECTRONIC RESOURCES

CD-ROMS

This is only a small sample of the various CD-ROMS on Buddhism currently available. The explosive growth of electronic media in the past decade has made the production of CDs cheap and relatively easy. Not surprisingly, this has resulted in thousands of CDs on Buddhism coming on the market, many of which are of dubious technical and scholarly quality. Most CD-ROM versions of encyclopedias include detailed entries on Buddhism, as do various CD-ROMS on world religions in general.

Buddhist Basics and Kalachakra Animated CD. Gesellsharft zur Forderung. An interactive multimedia presentation of the Kalacharaka Tantra along with an explanation of basic Buddhist teachings.

Buddhist Studies for Primary and Secondary Schools. 3rd edition. BuddhaNet. com. Information from BuddhaNet.com's Web site packaged in CD form and designed for classroom use.

Diamond Sutra Dem CD. Institute for Advanced Studies of World Religions. Encyclopedic collection of various texts of this important *sutra* along with commentaries, glossary of technical terms. Includes an audio of Chinese recitation of the *sutra* along with pictures of rituals in which the *sutra* plays a large role.

Illustrated Dhammapada—Sayings of Buddha. An illustrated electronic version of the Dhammapada, one of the most famous Theravada texts, with audio by the Ven. Saroda Maha Thero. Includes versions of the text chanted in both English and Pali, as well as the epic poem *The Light of Asia,* a book-length work by Sir Edwin Arnold that did much to popularize the Buddha's life story among Westerners in the late nineteenth century.

Janaka, Saydau U. *Insight Meditation Talks.* A collection of 10 Dharma talks on insight meditation by a contemporary Burmese master.

Living Buddhism. I-Seek/Microbooks. Comprehensive multimedia guide to Buddhism, including an English translation of most of the Pali canon. Part of a series on world religions.

Rumble, Paul. *The Face of Buddhism in the New Millenium.* GAIA Educational Services. Educational CD surveying Buddhism in the early twenty-first century, primarily geared toward teachers.

A Thousand Books of Wisdom. Release 4. Asian Classics Input Project. A vast assortment of Tibetan Buddhist material including both the Kanjur and Tenjur. The recently published "Release V" contains more than 200 previously unreleased Tibetan texts.

Web Sites

There are thousands of Buddhist-related Web sites, and it seems that more are being created every week. Many of these sites have very short lives in cyberspace, but some flourish and are regularly updated. The following is a small selection.

http://www.acesstoinsight.org. Dedicated to Theravada tradition. Has links to various other sites, includes outline of the Pali canon, glossary, and answers to basic questions on Buddhism.

http://www.asianclassics.org. The Asian Classic Input Project, a worldwide effort to digitalize Eastern texts, especially Buddhist ones. Large resource for Tibetan materials.

http://www.bpf.org/html. Buddhist Peace Fellowship. Great source of information on current and future projects, upcoming events, news stories. Includes selections from *Turning Wheel* (BPF's quarterly journal), resources for social action, and allows user to make donations.

http://www.Buddhanet.org. One of the most extensive Buddhist Web sites with links to various resources covering the entire spectrum of Buddhist practice and belief.

http://www.ciolek.com/WWWVL-Buddhism.html. Largest internet guide to Buddhist studies. A veritable treasure trove that includes links to virtual libraries for Pure Land, Tibetan studies, Zen, Buddhist art, newsletters, and journals. Also includes directories of Buddhist centers all over the world, mailing lists, photographs, and so forth.

http://www.dharmanet.org. One of the oldest Buddhist Web sites, officially established in 1991 out of Petaluma, California. Links to various resources, bibliographies, directories, publishers, and bookstores.

http://www.drba.org. Dharma Realm Buddhist Associations, the orthodox Chan Buddhist organization founded in 1959 by Master Hsuan Hua. Major clearinghouse for information on Chinese forms of Buddhism, texts and other materials published by the Buddhist Text Translation Society (BTTS), and schedules at monasteries and Dharma centers affiliated with DRBA.

http://www.globalbuddhism.org. *Journal of Global Buddhism,* an online resource of scholarly articles on Buddhism worldwide.

http://www.hm.tyg.jp/~acmuller/ebti/htm. Electronic Buddhist Text Initiative, a worldwide group of scholars and clerical organizations dedicated to storing and preserving Buddhist texts in digitalized form. Begun in 1994.

http://www.hooked.net/~csangha. *CyberSangha: The Buddhist Alternative Journal.* Important resource for understanding aspects of contemporary Buddhism, especially in the United States.

http://www.shin-ibs.edu. Institute of Buddhist Studies (IBS), a Pure Land Buddhist Seminary granting masters' degrees in Buddhist Studies and professional degrees for ministerial candidates in the Buddhist Churches of America (BCA).

http://www.tipitaka.org. Vipassana Research Institute of Dhamma Giri, Igatpuri, India. Includes links to various publications and the entire Pali canon online.

http://www.Tricycle.com. *Tricycle: The Buddhist Review.* Includes archives of past issues, additional stories, interviews with Buddhist teachers, daily Dharma talks, merchandise, and so forth.

REFERENCE WORKS

Buswell, Robert E., Jr., editor-in-chief. *Encyclopedia of Buddhism.* Volumes 1 and 2. New York: Macmillan Reference USA, 2004. Includes photos, maps, diagrams, timelines. Very thorough, authoritative articles by many of today's leading experts in Buddhist studies.

Prebish, Charles S. *Historical Dictionary of Buddhism.* Metuchen, NJ & London: The Scarecrow Press, Inc., 1993. Volume 1 in *Historical Dictionaries of Religions, Philosophies , and Movements*, ed. Jon Woronoff. Comprehensive one volume dictionary of most major Buddhist terms from all canonical languages. Very accessible and useful.

Soothill, William Edward, and Lewis Hodous, eds. *A Dictionary of Chinese Buddhist Terms*. London: Kegan Paul, Trench, Trubner & Co. Ltd., 1937; Reprint, Delhi, India: Motilal Banarsidass, 1977. Classic reference work compiled by two early twentieth century scholars of Buddhism. Lists nearly all technical Buddhist terms in their Chinese forms with Sanskrit equivalents and varying English definitions. Includes indices of Sanskrit and Pali as well as Buddhist terms in other languages (Tibetan, etc.) cross-referenced to their corresponding Chinese entries. Invaluable tool for scholars of Buddhism.

INDEX

Boldface numbers refer to volume numbers: 1: Judaism; 2: Confucianism and Taoism; 3: Buddhism; 4: Christianity; 5: Islam; 6: Hinduism.

About the Authors

EMILY TAITZ is an independent scholar and author of *The Jews of Medieval France: The Community of Champagne* (Greenwood, 1994) and numerous essays on Judaism and the coauthor of *Remarkable Jewish Women: Rebels, Rabbis and Other Women from Biblical Times to the Present* (2002), among other works.

RANDALL L. NADEAU is Associate Professor of East Asian Religions at Trinity University, San Antonio, Texas.

JOHN M. THOMPSON teaches in the Department of Philosophy and Religious Studies, Christopher Newport University, Newport News, Virginia.

LEE W. BAILEY is Associate Professor of Philosophy and Religion at Ithaca College.

ZAYN R. KASSAM is Associate Professor of Religious Studies and Chair of the Religious Studies Department, Pomona College.

STEVEN J. ROSEN is an independent scholar and prolific writer on Hinduism.